CW00750164

GHOSTS

Of

Fife

Accounts, Stories and Legends
from over 80 places in the Kingdom of Fife

Incorporating
A Trail of 25 Haunted Castles

RICHARD FALCONER

1st Printed Edition
Written in 1990, updated 2013

ISBN 978-0-9927538-1-8

Cover design, many of the enclosed photos & content layout by Richard Falconer. Cover photo; *Winter at Balgonie Castle* taken by Stuart Morris of Balgonie Castle and reproduced with his kind permission.

www.obsidianpublishing.com
enquiries@obsidianpublishing.co.uk

Dedicated

To the Fifers of the Kingdom

*

To all who came forward in the 1980s to present day
from across the world with their own eyewitness accounts
and stories of supernatural encounters
in the Kingdom of Fife

*

And to Bob Miller who drove 800 miles in three days so I could take photos of
the locations for this book and my companion books
Ghosts of St. Andrews and *A St. Andrews Mystery*

Acknowledgements

I would like to thank many for their assistance in making this book a reality after an idea 27 years ago.

Tom Perrott, former President of the Ghost Club, London, for our early correspondence and exchange of accounts in 1989. Scottish script writer and author Lorn Macintyre. Tom Ruffles of the SPR. The librarian of the SPR when I visited in the late 80s. Katrina Dolan and the Paranormal Research Team at Paranormal Discovery in Dundee. The National Trust for Scotland, Historic Scotland and Visit Scotland. Bob Miller for accompanying me to take photos of over 100 haunted locations in the Fifeshire countryside and St. Andrews. All done in 3 days and without us running for the hills! Helen Wilson for her friendship and support. Howard Davies for entrusting me with his expensive digital camera, and Maddi his daughter for her upbeat enthusiasm, together with Ashley of the Doreen Valiente Trust, Sarah of NPN fame, Esme and David Knight and Alison of PP for the same. I would also like to thank the staff of the Hay Fleming Library and the University Library in St. Andrews for their assistance in the late 1980s. Allowing me to camp in their buildings buried knee deep in books for nine months whilst conducting the mainstay of research. Especially to the Hay Fleming for gradually bringing me the entire contents of the reference library to my table then clearing them away each evening without a grumble. To former hotelier Mr David Tong of the Lundin Links Hotel in 1988 for his enthusiastic welcome and his generous time all those years ago. A time when others thought the supernatural was relegated to a Dennis Wheatley novel! To Paul, Craig and Chris in Edinburgh. Dave and Isabelle in Crail and Colin Frame in Cambridge for his help in the early 90s. Alison Rowe in London for her patience at that time. John and Edith in St. Andrews who kept me alive whilst researching this book, by feeding me when starvation was afoot – I have never forgotten your hospitality. Lenny and Chris, JB, Laura, Geoff, Bez, Malcolm, Carol, Carl, Eamonn, Keith and Russell ST who have helped remind me that because the physical world is an optional extra, for the time we have immersed in it we should enjoy the company of those we meet to the full.

To Julia who was the first to see the manuscript after 20 years, for her words of encouragement, and for putting up with the motionless life of an author!

To those I have inadvertently missed from this page, I apologise. To any I have not been able to contact, I hope the acknowledgements to each of you in the appropriate places throughout this work will serve as my gratitude and appreciation in the absence of a more substantial and individual communication.

The haunted places of Fife covered in this book

A Brief Introduction

Here you will find a wealth of supernatural legends and tales of ghosts and poltergeists plus many previously unpublished firsthand accounts. The first part of this book is the Ghosts of Fife Castle Trail, p.11. The second is an A-Z Collection of Fife's Ghostly encounters, p.115.

The early researches for this book
I was brought up in St. Andrews and have lived in a number of locations throughout East Fife and the East Neuk. With growing up in this magical Kingdom, I have always had a deep-rooted interest in the paranormal. In 1987, I set about correlating what I could of the tales, the stories, the legends and the accounts initially into the form of a book encompassing both St. Andrews and Fife. During the course of research, I endeavoured to unearth as many sightings as possible through both firsthand accounts and published information. Beginning in the Hay Fleming Library and the University Library in St. Andrews in the autumn of 1987, I spent nine months pouring through books spanning some 6 centuries on all aspects of St. Andrews and Fife, as well as going through all the copies of the local newspaper *The St. Andrews Citizen* and a number of Victorian periodicals.

Firsthand accounts
With no internet in the 1980s, I placed letters in the *Readers Digest*, the *Scots Magazine, Dundee Courier* and the *St. Andrews Citizen* for any to come forward with experiences of a paranormal nature they may have had, either in St. Andrews or across Fife. A few weeks after their publication I began receiving postmarks from across the world: Europe, America, Africa, Australia and Scotland.

There were letters of experiences and stories from all walks of life, from retired ministers and those in business, to doctors, cleaners, teachers and even a retired general with each having spent time in St. Andrews and Fife. I also received accounts from residents of a number of towns and villages throughout Fife including a few from a local St. Andrews medium.

Early submissions
With computers still in their infancy, I originally wrote the book on an old word processor in 1990. Once finished I submitted it to a number of publishers but with interest in the paranormal at a general low it wasn't until around the

mid 1990s with the advent of programmes such as the X Files series taking hold that interest in the paranormal grew around this subject. Added to this the specialist location wasn't deemed commercial enough for the publishers I contacted to take on board. So one Christmas in the early 90s, I set it aside and gave a hard copy of the manuscript to a couple of dear friends I was staying with in Perth.

Life has many interesting twists and turns as ghostly tales began capturing many imaginations, and now new generations have become fascinated by this unusual phenomenon hovering on the edge of reality.

A *book rediscovered!*

It wasn't until early 2013 when I came across two floppy discs of the manuscript in a box. This renewed my interest for what I had completed over twenty years earlier. All was nearly lost however as the discs were so old nothing I could do would recover them, and I felt sure I had no other copy, but an impression came to mind which took me upstairs to a thick pile of papers stored on a shelf in the hallway. On looking through them, low and behold there it was – a copy of the manuscript I had previously submitted to one of the early publishers. So the manuscript and the valued eyewitness testimonies, accounts, stories and legends have been salvaged after so many years. After refreshing the contents to bring it all up to date, I realised the information for St. Andrews and Fife were too great to be incorporated into one book, so I have split it into two works; *Ghosts of Fife* and its companion *Ghosts of St. Andrews.*

Most of what is included here is not particularly gruesome or frightening until you realise they are for the most part true, having been witnessed by somebody at some point in history. A visit to some of these locations will breathe life into these accounts, as the setting gives further pause for reflection and plenty of opportunity for that unaccountable feeling of being watched by these ghostly encounters. So take a journey through the beautiful countryside of the Kingdom of Fife. With this book as your guide and a circular trail of Fife's *Haunted Castles*, maybe you will be one of the lucky ones to stir the breeze and awaken some of the past inhabitants to be found at every quarter. See if you can spot those ghosts who slip through the boundaries of time, and continue to shape the fabric of this ancient Kingdom with their colourful tapestry, weaving the past and the present together before your very eyes.

If you know any stories or legends, or have the privilege of witnessing any type of phenomenon, I will be most interested and grateful in hearing from you for inclusion in future editions of this book or my book *Ghosts of St. Andrews.*

Richard Falconer

The 'Green Jean' Ghosts of Fife

Whilst researching this book I received two letters about ghosts of Green Ladies known as 'Green Jean'. The stories were from two independent sources about two different locations; Kinglassie House and Pitcairlie House, yet there were striking similarities between the two reports. In addition, as I continued my researches I soon realised these locations were not the only ones to have a Green Jean haunting their premises. Out of the following rare collection of 11 locations in Fife to have the ghosts of Green Ladies (so called because they each wear green dresses) the first five are called 'Green Jean' or in the case of Balgonie she is called 'Green Jeanie' and was recorded as being a "well known phantom" as far back as 1842.

Other than speculation, the name Green Jean, far from revealing an identity, appears as part of an ancient folklore tradition in this quarter. Of these, the first 4 are in the south of Fife – only a few miles from each other, in fact, all 5 Green Jean's are within a 10 mile radius of Balgonie Castle, which again localises the folklore to this region. There is also another shared factor between 3 of the Green Ladies; they each have the same legend as to how they died:

Kinglassie House: Green Jean fell to her death from the balcony.
Pitcairlie House: Green Jean threw herself over the battlements.
Fernie Castle Hotel: A Green Lady threw herself out of a window of the castle.

---

[i] Refer to *Ghosts of St. Andrews* (2013) and *A St. Andrews Mystery* (2014) by the present author.

Scots mythology has a term 'Glaistig'. The word describes these ghostly figures in green, and connects them with the nature of fairies harbouring the potential for both benevolence and malevolence. They are also known as 'maighdean uaine', meaning Green Maiden. Here she is a beautiful woman wearing a long flowing green dress. She watches over dwellings, which seems also to be her purpose at some of these haunted locations, it certainly seems to be the case at Balgonie Castle where I saw her peering at us through the iron grate of a window. This in turn is connected with the Sacbaun and is where the name comes from. A sacbaun is a ghost or wraith known also as 'Green Jean'.

The name Green Jean is also associated with other castles across Scotland, although it is only the three in Fife (2 Green Jeans and a Green Lady) so far as I am aware who seem to share the story of falling to their deaths from buildings.

Needless to say, 'Green Jean' is the most prevalent name for unidentified ghosts independently haunting the historic buildings of Fife.

In Fife folklore at least, green is considered an unlucky colour to get married in, and brings disaster and even death to any who wear it. Mary Queen of Scots wore green when she married Lord Darnley which might contribute to these associations of misfortune. Only five months before her marriage Mary stayed at Balgonie Castle then went onto Wemyss Castle – the two most established locations for the reports of 'Green Jean'. It was while she was at Wemyss that she met her cousin Darnley and forged a relationship that was to become the catalyst for his eventual murder and her eventual execution.

With this it is possible – although not directly attributable for a number of The Green Jean's in Fife to also be of Mary. If this were the case it would certainly form a connection between some of the Green Jean's roaming this quarter. She loved to spend time in this part of the countryside hunting and visiting, and alongside staying at places such as Balgonie Castle and Wemyss Castle; she visited a number of the other locations listed above. Certainly, Balgonie Castle has another possible identity for the Green Jeanie but it is possible for the Green Jean of Wemyss Castle to be of her. As an omen or portent of death Mary features in a 1911 story in Fife called *The Fair Woman*. In the story, she is a ghost, also wearing a green dress she is called the 'woman of death'.[ii]

[ii] The story is included in my book *A St. Andrews Mystery* (2014)

Part One

Ghosts of Fife Castle Trail

Location Reference Map

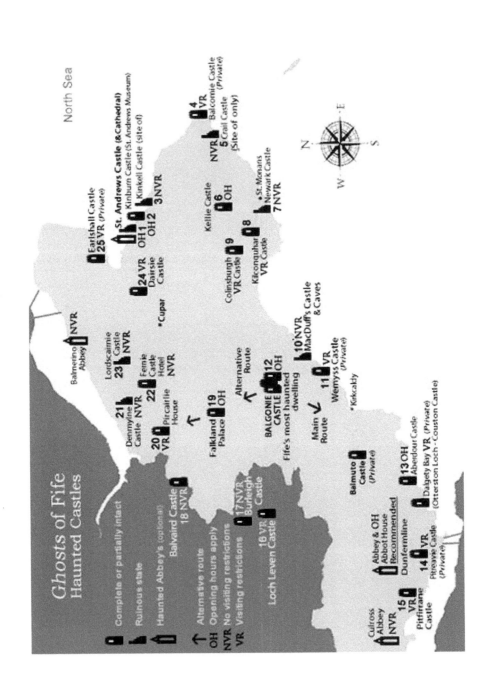

Ghosts of Fife
Haunted Castles

Complete or partially intact
Ruinous state
Haunted Abbey's (optional)

↑ Alternative route
OH Opening hours apply
NVR No visiting restrictions
VR Visiting restrictions

North Sea

25 VR (Private) Earlshall Castle

St. Andrews Castle (& Cathedral)
Kinburn Castle (St. Andrews Museum)
Kinkell Castle (site of)

OH 1
OH 2
3 NVR

4 VR

5 Crail Castle
(Site of only)

NVR

Balconie Castle (Private)

24 VR
Dairsie
Castle

*Cupar

Kellie Castle

6 OH

St. Monans
Newark Castle
7 NVR

Colinsburgh 9
VR Castle

8

Kilconquhar
VR Castle

Balmerino NVR
Abbey

Lordscairnie
23 NVR Castle

Fernie
22 Castle
Hotel
NVR

10 NVR
MacDuff's Castle
& Caves

Denmylne 21
Castle NVR

20 VR Pitcairlie
House

Falkland 19 OH
Palace

Alternative
Route

11 VR
Wemyss Castle
(Private)

*Kirkcaldy

12 OH
BALGONIE
CASTLE

Fife's most haunted
dwelling

Main ↘
Route

Balmuto
Castle
(Private)

13 OH
Aberdour Castle

Balvaird Castle
18 NVR

17 NVR
Burleigh
Castle

16 VR
Loch Leven Castle

Abbey & OH
Abbot House
Recommended

Dunfermline

14 VR

Dalgety Bay VR (Private)
(Otterston Loch – Couston Castle)

Pitreavie Castle
(Private)

Culross
Abbey

NVR 15 VR

Pitfirrane
Castle

N
E
S
W

A Trail of 25 Haunted Castles with 22
In The Kingdom of Fife

Legend

Private residence. View from the outside or at a distance only

* Open occasionally to the public, at certain times of the day or year.

** Historic Scotland

*** National Trust for Scotland

**** Hotel/self catering accommodation

For each castle article that requires it you will find before the main body of text: *On the GOF Castle Trail* (On the Ghosts of Fife Castle Trail). This gives directions from the previous castle to the next castle location on the trail.

The Ghosts of Fife Castle Trail

A book dealing with Fife ghosts wouldn't be complete without a tour of its numerous haunted castles. Like the A to Z collection of haunted places in Fife this is the most complete collection of haunted castles presented to date for Fife, though both are far from being definitive collections. There are a great many more haunted castles to be discovered in the Kingdom. This is because there is one assured characteristic about ghosts – they are everywhere, and each are lying in wait with their own stories to be told by those willing to spend a little time in contemplation of their company.

Within Fife, many castles are to be found spread throughout its rich and diverse landscape, in towns, villages, in fields and on cliff top promontories. They comprise a mix of traditional Castles, Palaces and Fortified Mansion Houses built by Royalty and Fife's great nobility. Some remain in good repair, while others have crumbled leaving no trace of their former stature. One unfortunate commonality with many is their failing through a lacking of funds, or having just out served their purpose such as St. Andrews Castle.

Some have been lovingly restored at no little time and expense to their owners and are open to the public by the families in residences, others are run by Historic Scotland or the National Trust for Scotland, with a few available to hire for holidays or for a shorter stay such as Kilconquhar Castle.

Care needs to be taken at some of these locations, especially if following an apparition up an old stone spiral stairway. The old stonework in the more ruinous of abandoned mansions can prove none too safe and lead the unwary to a perilous end.

Kinkell Castle and Crail Castle no longer remain. They have been included here because their ghosts still linger around these former sites as a sad reminder of tragedies past. Three castles have been included which are in Perth and Kinross but fringe the border with Fife. These are Loch Leven Castle, Burleigh Castle and Balvaird Castle, which sits only a few yards across the border. This castle was in Fife until 1891 when the council then changed the counties boundaries.

A few of the castles are private but I have included them as the castles or the grounds are open to the public at certain times of the year. Respect should be given for privacy at other times. The following information will be found at the start of each corresponding article and includes the degree of accessibility:

Ghostly associations in brief
Visiting restrictions/fees
Directions

St. Andrews Castle Ghosts
Ghosts of Fife Castle Trail Ref: 1

Drawing by the author 1983

Ghostly associations in brief
With such a bloody history you might suppose the grounds of St. Andrews Castle to be overrun with ghosts. Certainly a keen eye will pick up more flitting amongst the ruins than the mind can ignore. The possible ghosts here include James Hepburn, 4th Earl of Bothwell – the third husband of Mary Queen of Scots, George Wishart, Cardinal David Beaton, Marion Ogilvy, Archbishop John Hamilton and a number of unidentified apparitions.

Visiting restrictions/fees
The castle is run by Historic Scotland and opening times and fees apply. The Castle Sands are free.

Directions
The castle is situated on the north eastern side of St. Andrews overlooking the sea between the West Sands and the pier.

The following pages comprise of a potted history of the castle directly related to each of these apparitions as a background to those often complex events leading up to their deaths, or the tragedies to have befallen them whilst alive. It focuses primarily on one of its darker periods being 1546 leading up to the reformation of 1559, which is also the time period from which most apparitions seen in the castle today originate.

All is designed hopefully with effect to give a clearer picture of why they may still linger in these iconic grounds, as a little of the historical complexities surrounding them is unravelled.

Early History and the Ghost of James Hepburn
Known also as the Archbishops Palace the castle sits perched on a cliff top promontory overlooking the North Sea. The current remains of this building – in like manner to that of the Cathedral give little away of its former grandeur and importance.

The castle stronghold was built in the 13th century by Bishop Roger de Beaumont. It is difficult to believe today that at its height this ancient dwelling was thought to have been able to house around 1600 people within its walls, including servants, guards and guests alike, which lends an idea of the scale it must have once commanded.

The castle has been rebuilt at least four times because of attacks by the English and French, and incredibly it was rebuilt twice after the Scots demolished it in 1337 and 1447 to prevent its recapture, firstly by the English and latterly by the Protestants. The rebuilding of the 1337 episode was in the early 1400s by Bishop Walter Trail, who imprisoned Thomas Platter for the murder of Prior Robert De Montrose, the monk who now haunts the area of St. Rules Tower in St. Andrews.

The bloody past of the castle has included countless murders, executions and plots. In 1319, it was the seat of the Scottish Parliament under King Robert the Bruce. It has also been a prison, a garrison, and a residence of the Archbishops and Cardinals of Scotland including Archbishop James Beaton who died here in 1539 aged 66. James Beaton had Patrick Hamilton burnt at the stake outside St. Salvator's Chapel in St. Andrews. The castle was also home to James Beaton's nephew, Cardinal David Beaton on his inauguration after his uncle's death.

Within the Sea Tower, a deep bottle shaped pantry has been hollowed out of the rock forming the shape of a large upright rounded flask or bottle. The pantry was used for the storage of food and the preservation of meat. It has also been used for the storage of valuables but this has almost been forgotten by a reputation it acquired for another purpose. Patrick Hamilton, Henry Forrest, George Wishart and Walter Myln were each incarcerated in what became a most unusual and gruesome dungeon before being taken from this place and burnt at the stake for heresy. They are commemorated at the Martyrs Memorial erected on the Scores in 1842.

Once within it was impossible to escape. Its depths are only accessible by rope thrown down its 11 foot well like neck, reaching into the larger near rounded stone cavity. When any found themselves here they knew they were about to die a most abhorrent death. Some of those unfortunates to perish here died of starvation.

The Ghost of James Hepburn

Now known as the 'Bottle Dungeon' it still exists today and the depths of this cold stark place are now lit by electric light to highlight the confined extent to which those trapped within had to endure. One of the Victorian ghost writer W. T. Linskill's stories speaks of the ghostly figure of James Hepburn, 4th Earl of Bothwell – the third husband of Mary Queen of Scots being glimpsed by Captain Chester leaning against the door of the Sea Tower.[iii]

The Kitchen Tower
photo by the author

Another ghost in period costume is to be seen here momentarily looking across the bay near the Kitchen Tower of the castle, standing to the north-east. He has been witnessed by those who have been on the Castle Sands in summer evenings after the castle has been closed to the public. This might be the same apparition Linskill also refers to, but being in a slightly different location, it was either this location he was meaning or he may well have been seen in both.

[iii] W. T. Linskill's *St. Andrews Ghost Stories* with annotations is available as part of the companion book *Ghosts of St. Andrews* (2013) by the present author.

The Prophecy and the Ghost of George Wishart

George Wishart was in his time the most famous Protestant preacher in Scotland and the mentor of John Knox. Cardinal David Beaton believed Wishart was also a spy for Henry VIII and had him arrested. On his capture, he spent some time in the prison of Edinburgh Castle before being brought to the Archbishops Palace of St. Andrews. Following a token trial by David Beaton, he was condemned and imprisoned in the Bottle Dungeon to await his fate. He followed his uncle's example with regard to burning Patrick Hamilton and carried on the zeal the Roman Catholic Church had for the violent persecution of supposed heretics. He had already condemned another heretical reformer to the Bottle Dungeon – a Friar by the name of John Roger who was murdered in the castle. Officially, he seems to have 'died whilst trying to escape'. If he did try to escape, it certainly would not have been from the bottle dungeon, with no doors or windows it is probably the most secure of its kind.

On the 1st March 1546, George Wishart was taken from this living tomb to meet with his destiny.

George Wishart and a woodcut of his martyrdom
in front of the castle in 1546

'It is averred by some writers, that he prophesied in the midst of the flames, not only the approaching death of the cardinal, but the circumstances also, that should attend it. Buchanan's account is as follows: After relating the manner in which Mr. Wishart spent the morning of his execution, he proceeds thus: "A while after two executioners were sent to him by the cardinal; one of them put a black linen shirt upon him, and the other bound many bags of gun-powder to all the parts of his body. In this dress they brought him forth, and commanded him to stay in the governor's outer chamber, and at the same time they erected a wooden scaffold in the court before the castle, and made a pile of wood. The windows and balconies over against it were all hung with tapestry and silk hangings, with cushions for the cardinal and his train, to behold and take pleasure in the joyful sight, even the torture of an innocent man; thus courting the favour of the people as the author of so notable a deed. There was also a great guard of soldiers, not so much to secure the execution, as for a vain ostentation of power: and beside, brass guns were placed up and down in all convenient places of the castle. Thus, while the trumpets sounded, George was brought forth, mounted the scaffold, and was fastened with a cord to the stake, and having scarce leave to pray for the church of God, the executioners fired the wood, which immediately taking hold of the powder that was tied about him, blew it up into flame and smoke.

The governor of the castle, who stood so near that he was singed with the flame, exhorted him in a few words to be of good cheer, and ask pardon of God for his offences. To whom he replied, 'This flame occasions trouble to my body indeed, but it hath in no wise broken my spirit; but he, who now looks down so proudly upon me from yonder lofty place (pointing to the cardinal) shall ere long be as ignominiously thrown down, as now he proudly lolls in ease.' Having thus spoken, they straitened the rope which was tide about his neck, and so strangled him; his body in a few hours being consumed to ashes in the flame."'[1]

The potential for distortions in the detail of the history from this period is high. Much depended on the particular religious fever of the author of the time as to the viewpoint they would have on the incidents they were writing about. Perhaps nothing has changed in this respect. Wishart may or may not have made what would become a traditionally eloquent martyrs speech whilst in the process of being blown up – and just before being strangled, and in this instance the side you were on would influence or shadow whether Wishart's prophesy was actually stated or not. If indeed he did say those words, it would just as easily induce others to take the initiative from his idea as it would be to fulfil itself as a prophecy.

Certainly after a hearty meal and entertaining his guests, Beaton, like an emperor waiting for the games to begin in Rome's Coliseum had his way with the burning of Wishart. This was despite some reservation by the other prelates he had summoned to St. Andrews as to what to do with such a famous prisoner. The minds of these other prelates were more in line with limiting the potential repercussions back onto the clergy – or more the point back onto themselves than they were to any questioning of their own morality. A suggestion by a prelate from Glasgow was to appoint some nobleman to conduct the trial to deflect any repercussions. The cardinal however would have none of it despite a number of potential niggling legalities that may or may not have been taken care of by the time he went ahead with his trial by prosecution.

The Ghost of George Wishart

A ghost was seen in the early 1960s standing on the road looking towards the castle. A report believed it to be a young looking John Knox, but it is far more likely to be that of George Wishart. His horror highlighted the call for a major religious change in the climate of many Scottish minds that was mirrored in various parts of Europe at the time.

The initials of George Wishart marking where he was burnt to death

photo by the author

His extreme suffering at the hands of this catholic prelate had emblazoned his energy on the spot where he was tied to the stake, and like Patrick Hamilton, his initials are displayed on the ground where he so callously died.

Once Wishart was dead, 'the cardinal was pleased with himself, imagining he had given a fatal blow to heresy.'[2] How wrong he could be, the decision to burn him created exactly the kind of fervour the other prelates had been looking to avoid, especially as Beaton already had a reputation for both lavish excess and excessive cruelty. The following is an account from Perth in 1544, some two years earlier. It was included in a Historical Gazetteer of Scotland written in 1856. I have included it here, as the circumstances typify the mounting air the citizens of Scotland were developing for changes to be made in the religious and political system. Beaton had to be stopped from committing the persecutions and atrocities he was conducting across the country under the banner of his church. The following puts into perspective more of the reasons why he had to go, as well as retribution for Wishart's death it gives a contextual frame, one that would spur the common and decent folk into rebellion, and culminate in the eventual reformation:

'Perth, as to a considerable number of its citizens, early received the reformed doctrines; and suffered more severely than most places from the truculent wrath of the blood-drinking priests of Rome. That the Perthensians, and our readers, in general, may prize the respect now paid to the sacred rights of conscience, and see from how horrible a thraldom the Reformation was the means of delivering the "fair city" and Scotland at large, we must quote in full, from the historian of the town, the narrative to the leading incident of one year – the year 1544. "This was a busy year. Cardinal Bethune, in the last convention, having obtained an act in favour of the bishops and clergy, to persecute and punish heretics to death, came in January this year to Perth, with the Regent Hamilton, Earl of Arran, who was a weak man. Friar Spence accused Robert Lamb and his wife Helen Stark, William Anderson, James Ronald, James Hunter, and James Finlayson. Lamb and his wife were accused of interrupting Spence in a sermon, in which he taught that there was no salvation without intercession and prayers to the saints. They confessed the charge, declaring that it was the duty of everyone who knows the truth to bear testimony to it, and not suffer people to be abused with false doctrine, as that was. Anderson, Finlayson, and Ronald, were indicted for nailing two ram's horns to St. Francis' head, putting a cow's rump to his tail, and eating a goose on All-Hallow even. Hunter, a butcher, simple and unlearned, was charged with haunting the company of the heretics. Helen Stark was further charged with refusing to pray to the Virgin Mary when in child birth and saying that she would only pray to God in the name of Jesus Christ. They were all imprisoned in the Spey tower, being found guilty and condemned. Great intercession was made to the regent for them, who promised that they should not be hurt. The citizens, who were in a tumult, relying on a promise of Arran, dispersed and went peaceably home. The cardinal, who had the regent in his power, had taken his measures. Determined to make an example of these heretics, he brought them forth next day to the gibbet, January 25th, being St. Paul's day, and feasted his eyes from the windows of the Spey tower with their execution.[iv] The men were hanged, and Helen Stark was drowned. Robert Lamb, at the foot of the ladder, made a pathetic exhortation to the people, beseeching them to fear God, and forsake the leaven of popish abominations. Helen Stark earnestly desired to die with her husband, but her request was refused; however, they permitted her to accompany him to the place of execution. On the way, she exhorted him to constancy in the cause of Christ,

---

[iv] This is exactly as has been described when Beaton then watched the death of George Wishart at the Castle some two years later.

and, as she parted with him, said, 'Husband, be glad, we have lived together many joyful days, and this day of our death we ought to esteem the most joyful of them all, for we shall have joy for ever; therefore I will not bid you goodnight, for we shall shortly meet in the kingdom of heaven.' As soon as the men were executed, the woman was taken to a pool of water hard by, where having recommended her children to the charity of her neighbours, her sucking child being taken from her breast, and given to a nurse. She was drowned, and died with great courage and comfort." This atrocious murder of excellent persons, under the pretext of serving the cause of religion, exerted a powerful influence, along with the kindred martyrdom of George Wishart and Walter Mylne at St. Andrews, to render the character and superstitions of the popish priests an object of public execration, to fan the ignited elements of ecclesiastical, doctrinal, and moral reform, and to push up to a crisis the silent but powerful process of antagonism which was at work between a large portion of the people and their cowled and ghostly oppressors.'[3]

Retribution!

Fuelled by anger at the barbaric murder of George Wishart and amid growing tensions 'over the Cardinal's property transactions rather than by politics or religion,'[4] the Protestant reformers on the 29th May 1546 did something that would change history. Everything came to a head on this particular day. In fact the whole future of how religion was to play its course in Scotland came to a head on this day in May. Norman Leslie, Master of Rothes with four separate parties of men comprising Fifeshire Lairds went to the castle at dawn. In order to gain entry a few posed as stonemasons, others that an appointment with the Cardinal had been arranged.

After killing the Porter on the gate, and dealing with the guards, eight others gained entry, allowing the servants and some workmen to leave the castle. According to John Knox, Beaton's mistress or wife Marion Ogilvy also left the castle by the privy postern (a private backdoor or gate).

Leslie and his men having secured the castle and by all accounts having done so expediently and in relative silence, went straight to Beaton's quarters and found the Cardinal was still asleep in his chamber. Hammering on his door they forced entry and despite his imploring they repeatedly stabbed and mutilated him in his bedchamber. The whole process from start to finish was swift and efficient.

Word spread quickly of what was happening, probably by the workmen and servants having been banished from the castle. Before long it was said 400 of the town's people led by Provost James Learmonth of Dairsie, a supporter of

Beaton had gathered outside the castle demanding to know what had happened to their Cardinal. Having dealt with the Catholic garrison in the castle, and to stop any attempts at a rescue, they hung his naked body by an arm and a leg from the window he had been gloating from for all to see. Like a rag doll Beaton's body bloodied by his wounds now hung in the form of a human St. Andrews Cross, and with this the castle was now in the hands of the reformers.

As can be imagined, the Protestants now in charge of the castle were in no hurry to see Cardinal Beaton buried. So as some small retribution his body is believed to have been incarcerated within the Bottle Dungeon for a few months where he had himself imprisoned George Wishart and numerous others. Beaton's body was either pickled in a barrel of brine or as John Knox had stated; 'they covered his body in salt, wrapped it in lead and buried it in the Sea Tower'[5] until arrangements were eventually made for his burial. These arrangements were carried out in strict secrecy by John Beaton of Kilrenny and Silverdykes, lest the mob found him and desecrated it. He was taken to Kilrenny near Cellardyke and was buried at Kilrenny Kirk yard in the tomb of the Beaton's of Balfour. The tomb still exists but is now a ruin. Being such a cold place, among all its uses, the bottle dungeon had been used a number of times to preserve bodies having met their end within its walls before burial.

An ancient local folk saying from East Fife in 1546 is associated with the body of Beaton whilst interred in the Bottle Dungeon and runs as follows:

> "'Marry now, maidens,
> Maidens, marry now;
> For stickit is your Cardinal,
> And sautit like a sow."

Robert Chalmers writing an article in 1829 relating to this piece states: 'I am informed that the boys of St. Andrews, and also of other towns in the east of Fife, are in the habit of singing this stanza to an air, as they perambulate the streets in bands at night. It is evident, in my opinion, that it must have been composed in 1546, immediately after the assassination of the Cardinal, while he was still lying pickled in the dungeons of the castle.'[6]

The Reverend James Kirkton in 1817 records another version from the 17th century:

> "'Maids be merry now,
> maids be merry now,
> For stickit is our Cardinal,
> and saltit like ane sow.'"[7]

The Ghosts of Cardinal David Beaton

There are various ghostly appearances of Cardinal David Beaton, looking out of the window at the front of the castle from where he watched the execution of Wishart, and from where his body was subsequently hung. He has also been observed walking or standing in various parts of the grounds wearing his red robe and biretta.

The following is one such account of the ghost of Cardinal David Beaton published in a longer article by the National Observer dated January 7th 1893, entitled *St. Andrews Ghosts*:

Cardinal David Beaton – Murdered 1546

'Long ago on the evening of Midsummer's day three masons were sitting relaxing by the drawbridge within the castle ruins, they were waiting for a friend to arrive, after a while they heard footsteps approaching – but deliberately. 'Jocks takin his time the nicht,' said one. The steps came slowly nearer, passed the ford of the ruined stairs, and began climbing them one by one, 'I'll go and meet him,' said one, he started forward but his feet recoiled, and he stood with the rest. And turning to greet their friend, now on the last step of the staircase, they saw it was not he but a woman; for who but a woman would wear that trailing gown, that big red hat?

She approached them and they realised it was a man. He said no word and went straight by them seeming to be unconscious of their presence 'he aye looked out to sea,' said one of them afterwards. 'The face was ghastly – one set in a look of dreadful sadness. One man started sobbing.' It was now on the opposite staircase, slowly it went down. They then ran to the steps but it had gone.' [8]

The Ghost of a Woman – Marion Ogilvy?

The ghost of a woman has been seen here which might be Beaton's wife or mistress – Marion Ogilvy, as she also haunts Claypotts Castle across the Tay in Angus. This would fit with the following account recounted by James Wilkie in 1931. He makes no suggestion as to who she might be, but it would be of interest to note that Marion Ogilvy was 80 when she died.

'A sojourner sat within the courtyard watching to the eastward the great breakers roll in and dash in spray upon the cliffs. The tide was nearing the fall and the nor easter [wind] blew strong and salt. It was the hour between one and two in the afternoon when the castle and cathedral alike are left to a stray visitor. No footfall sounded on turf or gravel, but the mortal became aware he was not alone. Over the grass in a diagonal line from the gatehouse and past the draw-well came a lady of old years "gazing straight on with calm eternal eyes. "She pressed steadily forward to the boundary rail where there is no exit. "The unspoken question formed itself "whither?" and the unspoken answer was flashed back, "it matters not to you." She passed on through the rail to where the sea broke in foam below, and turning to her left where no foot can now tread disappeared beyond the masonry.'[9]

Her exit was into the Great Hall that once stood by the Castle Sands and had finally collapsed into the sea in 1811.

Claypotts Castle Anniversary Ghost

Situated across the Tay to the east of Dundee, there was a ferry-landing site here in 1546 before the castle was built. The ghostly figure which appears on this site is the ghost of Marion Ogilvy. She makes her appearance here every 29th of May, on the anniversary of Beaton's death. Dressed all in white she is seen waving in the direction of St. Andrews Castle.

Although Claypotts Castle wasn't built at the time she is also attributed as being seen peering out of one of its windows.

The dress of the female ghost at St. Andrews Castle isn't stated but Linskill makes reference to a white lady being seen at the castle which could be another connection with Marion.

The Siege of 1546-47 and the Ghost of Archbishop John Hamilton

Following Beaton's death amid panic amongst the Catholic Church in Scotland they immediately succeeded him with John Hamilton, appointing him as the new Archbishop in the same year. With this he took over all of Beaton's legacies – both good and bad. It was Archbishop John Hamilton who granted the right for the people of St. Andrews to play the game of golf on the links of St. Andrews in 1552.

With the reformers including Leslie and Knox now occupying the castle, it became a centre for the Protestant cause, forming the first Protestant congregation in Scotland with John Knox preaching from within its walls. In the winter of 1546-47 the Governor of Scotland laid an unsuccessful siege to the castle for three months, during which a siege mine had been dug out of the rock to gain entry into the castle. The reformers on finding out about this, dug a successful counter mine to meet them. The work involved in this task on both sides must have been incredible. The mines were big enough for ponies to enter and fetch out the rubble. They were successful in meeting with the incoming mine and thwarted plans that would have otherwise blown up part of the castle.

The mine was rediscovered in 1879 and mistakenly in this instance; it bolstered Linskill's conviction that St. Andrews was festooned with subterranean passageways. He didn't know at that time what the reason and purpose of these mines were. He met with his premature enthusiasm on another occasion also, when a tunnel was found under the Pends Walk leading into the Cathedral grounds, only to find some years later it was a medieval latrine! He mentions this location at the end of the chapter *The Beckoning Monk* in his book *St. Andrews Ghost Stories*[v]:

'Next time I came to myself and opened my eyes I was out of the accursed passage. I saw the sky and the stars, and I felt a fresh breeze blowing. Oh! Joy, I was back on the earth again, that I knew. I staggered feebly to my feet, and where on earth do you think I found I had been lying?"

"I cannot guess," I said.

"Just inside the archway of the Pends gateway at St. Andrews," said Ashton.

"How on earth did you get there?"

"Heaven knows," said Ashton. "I expect the White Lady helped me somehow.'[vi]

By implying that this is the spot of the exit of the subterranean passageways, he might not have known its original purpose until after he wrote his book in 1911. Mines such as that of the castle are rare to see, the techniques used in its

---

[v] For a complete copy of W. T. Linskill's *St. Andrews Ghost Stories* refer to *Ghosts of St. Andrews*, (2013) by the present author.

[vi] Refer to Linskill *The Beckoning Monk*, p.270, *St. Andrews Ghost Stories* within *Ghosts of St. Andrews*

creation was the same as that adopted by the British soldiers in the Somme when they dug tunnels under the German defence lines to blow them up. These castle mines are open to the public and are well worth a visit. In fact many who come here are pleasantly surprised they are actually allowed in them. The mine and countermine certainly adds to the dramatic nature of the siege at the castle, the lengths the Catholics were going to in order to claim back their residence, and the lengths the protestants were going to retain it! It also gives an impression of what an underground passageway system in St. Andrews might be like.

With a number of the protagonists of the Protestant reformation being contained in this building and with it symbolising the increasing rise of the reformation stronghold in Scotland, in 1547, at the behest of King Francis II of France, in assistance to the government of Scotland, he sent a French fleet of 21 galleys headed by Leon Strozius - a priest and warrior to recapture the castle. They arrived in the Bay of St. Andrews to put pay to the Protestants and their reformation and immediately began bombarding the castle from the sea. The mêlée lasted for 20 days and although impressive, it had little impact on the castle itself. So on the 30th July 1547 they conducted a land assault. They brought 14 French canons onto the land. The artillery of the Scots Catholics also included two uncommonly large Scottish cannons nicknamed Crook-mow and Deaf-Meg, which they trundled through the old cobbled and earthen streets of St. Andrews to the castle. They also placed cannon on top of both the Cathedral roof and St. Salvator's Tower to cover a better vantage. The constant bombardment of the castle that was to ensue lasted for six hours, it only stopped when heavy rain began to fall. Of the lairds occupying the castle and the other reformers, a few were now struck by the 'plague' as it was put – meaning an illness. It is fair to say they had all had enough and duly surrendered. The French apprehended John Knox and the Protestant garrison at the castle. They took Knox and others as galley slaves, while others were sent to languish in French prisons.

After the eventual near ruin of the castle to the French, in the beginning of August 1547 Lyon writing in 1838 says; 'the governor, by the advice of the council, [took it a stage further and] demolished the castle, lest it should be a receptacle of rebels.'[10] Shortly after its near demolition, Archbishop John Hamilton who was building St. Mary's College at the time just off South Street, then set about rebuilding and strengthening it as a defence against any future attacks!

Despite all efforts, the Protestants some twelve years later in 1559 would again have their way, but this time not only in taking the castle once more, every catholic building in Scotland would feel the unrest of the people.

So to recap slightly; the Protestants seize the Bishops Palace, they then retake it and after destroying it further so the rebels wouldn't recapture it again, they decide to rebuild it the following year. Only to find the Protestants retaking it again anyway – and who says history is dull!

This time they left the building relatively intact, but the money for its upkeep wouldn't last much longer. Following the reformation, it became the residency of the Protestant Archbishops, and at one point, the constables in charge of the town's security occupied it. One of its last residents was Archbishop Patrick Adamson who suffered like a number of his time after being accused of consorting with a witch by his enemies.

The Ghost of Archbishop John Hamilton

The purported ghost of Archbishop John Hamilton has been seen in the castle grounds. For all his accomplishments with building and renovating many of the town buildings, he met his end by hanging in 1571 beside the Mercat Cross in Stirling. He was executed through association. His nephew had assassinated James Stewart, 1st Earl of Moray – an illegitimate son of James V of Scotland and half brother to Mary Queen of Scots. The Earl of Moray among his darker dealings had hung his archenemy William Stewart – a former Lord Lyon King of Arms in 1569 for crimes of necromancy. With one against the other, there was no end to the rumours and reasons for handing down judgement. No one was safe when all had enemies. The hanging of Archbishop John Hamilton was also retribution for his 'severe misjudgement' in the burning of Walter Myln outside Deans Court a number of years earlier.

Linskill in his book only gives a reference to the ghost of a Cardinal [Beaton], but it is the ghost of Archbishop John Hamilton he relates the story of, within its now near derelict walls as related by the butler of his fictitious Lausdree Castle: 'I was in the castle one evening, and I was sitting on the parapet of the old wall when I saw a head appearing up the old broken steps on the east side of the castle that once led down to the great dining hall. I knew no one could now come up that way without a ladder from the sea beach, and when the figure got to the level ground, it came right through the iron railing just as if no obstruction were there. I stared hard and watched the advancing figure. It looked like a woman. I had heard of the Cardinal's ghost, and wondered if it could be his Eminence himself. Nearer and nearer it came, and although it was a gusty evening, I noticed the flowing garments of the approaching figure were quite still and unruffled by the wind. It was like a moving statue. As it passed me slowly a few yards away, I saw they were not the robes of a Cardinal, but those of an Archbishop. I am a Churchman, and know the garments quite well. I saw all his vestments clearly, and I shall never forget the pale, ashen set face, and the thin determined mouth. Then I noticed one very very strange thing – the statuesque tall figure had a thick rope round the neck, and the end of the rope was trailing along the grass behind it, but there was no sound whatever. On it went and began to climb the stairs to the upper apartments.'

There are two main notes of interest or observations in this report. Firstly, the apparition appears on the same broken piece of stairway once leading to the Great Hall as the ghost of the woman. Secondly the description of the ghost being statuesque is a very unusual but precise way of describing what they saw, kind of reminiscent of Dr Who and the Weeping Angels. The Lairds wife at Balgonie Castle in the heart of Fife near Markinch who saw the ghost of Alexander Leslie in the Great Hall there described him in the same way "grey like a statue". Generally, ghosts appear real in every way. They are often mistaken for physical beings. With this, the only way of knowing they are a ghost is if they do something that defies the laws of physics.

End of Days for the Fortified Palace of St. Andrews

Moving back to the castles history: By the early 1600s Hamilton's reconstruction of the castle was showing major signs of decay. In 1635, the Protestant Archbishops switched from the castle to the Novum Hospitium – the 'New Inn' in the Pends. The decay of the castle this time was not through war, but through the ravages of long-term neglect. This coupled with Hamilton's reconstruction, which was proving to be an 'inferior structure'[11] led the castle to suffer from the same deterioration that was also taking place at the cathedral and the monasteries of the town after being abandoned following the reformation. The castle fell this time with no bloodshed or any such attempts to repair or rebuild it. It had simply out-served its purpose. How easily these buildings can fall without the aid of canon when they no longer provide a haven of importance. Some of what remains today is Hamilton's reconstruction work. His coat of arms can be seen above the castles south gate entrance, which was one of the areas he reconstructed.

Although in a fairly ruinous state the castle was still substantial. The ruinous state we see today is partly the result of the council in 1656 decreeing that the stones of the castle be taken and used in the building of the pier and a few of the nearby buildings. A great storm had completely destroyed the original pier the year before. With a rebuilding of the pier commencing in 1656, using the stonework from the castle the new pier we see today was finished in 1668. The decree of the council came seven years after they authorised the use of the cathedrals stones for the construction of the town's buildings.

Because of the castle's position, the sea also had a big part to play in its final destruction. Grierson in 1807 writes 'Martine [Archbishop Sharpe's secretary] says that in his time (1683) there were people living in St. Andrews who remembered to have seen bowls being played on the flat ground to the east and north of the castle, and that…cattle were driven between the castle and the sea.'[12] This report gives an idea of the area the castle once commanded in the seaward flanking directions and how it could house 1600 people within its walls at its height.

The rocks lying beneath are forever a reminder of how even a fortress is at the complete mercy of the tremendous North Sea tides; so much so that the cliff face has been gradually eroded by the powerful waves receding the land around the castle estate, crumbling away whole sections of the castle. The Great Hall that once entertained Kings, Queens and Great Nobles stood in that section where the sea now breaks and swirls between the Castle Sands and the Kitchen Tower. It finally crashed into the sea in 1801. The only remains today of its existence are those few haunted steps off the existing edge, leading the unwary to an early grave.

The Great Hall until that moment was a substantial building, and its collapse was another loss to the town. So much so the Reverend James Playfair, Principle of the University of St. Andrews, and the Historiographer Royal for Scotland, in recognising the potential for a lot more to fall into the sea 'obtained on a representation to the barons of the Exchequer in 1803, a grant of 211 pounds to be laid out in pointing and repairing those places of the castle most likely to give way. This was accordingly done under his direction, and will doubtless be the means of prolonging very considerably the existence of the ruin.'[13] So at least some of the historical value of the castle was preserved thanks to his early foresight and efforts. James Playfair was the father of Hugh Lyon Playfair who was to continue his father's work in the town and turned the fortunes of the town around from one of neglect and destruction to one of preservation and eventual prosperity.

Around this period a clearing amid the ruins of the castle was even being used by a tenant for the planting of tatties (potatoes). Such was the extent of its transformation, one where a residential symbol of pre-reformation decadence that many had lost their lives in fighting for or against, should now have no other purpose or position than to be a simple allotment for vegetables!

Unidentified Ghosts

The castle houses the ghosts of a number of unidentified figures. Whilst bringing this book up to date and conducting further research into the details of Mary Queen of Scots first visit to St. Andrews, I found a post on a blog by 'Geri, the History Lady' from May 2012. As interesting is it was, I didn't find what I was looking for, but with the nature of research taking some interesting turns, at the end of her post was an account by Chris, a former student at the university about ghosts he and a few others saw in the castle ruins around 1982. The post which is about these unidentified ghosts was dated October 2012'.

'When I saw your reply this morning I added up the years since I saw this phenomenon and I couldn't believe thirty years have passed since then. I was newly matriculated at the university. I was recently turned twenty and studying ancient history for a year abroad. My newly met mates from the residence hall, all of dubious quality, and I were returning home from an evening gaudy, an impromptu pier walk, and for one of our party, a dip into the sea. He scurried back to the hall immediately claiming hypothermia since none of us would give the coat off our backs for him. Needless to say we were young and we were very merry. As you know the castle ruins are not far from the old pier, at least that is what I remember, and in passing them at midnightish we thought it a great idea to explore the environs of our new college town. Back then the only hurdle separating us from our goal of viewing the castle green was a simple spiked iron fence. In true first year reasoning, if we were sober enough to climb over the fence we were qualified to view the grounds. I remember walking out onto the green space and seeing the ruined walls all around. One of my group initially spotted something and called our attention to it. What I saw were two figures suspended in space about a foot above the ruined walls and moving towards each other. They were wearing what I would now describe as clothes possibly from the Restoration [period of Charles II, 1660 to 1685]. They met and embraced. At which time, my friends and I came to the end of our courage. We bolted from the grounds, raced back to the RH sobered and somewhat relieved to be there. We all knew and confirmed we had seen something, but being guys, we found it very hard to verbalize what we had seen. This is how and what I remember seeing, as silly as it sounds.
Chris.'[14]

By the time of the restoration period much of the castle had virtually been reduced to a quarry but enough would have remained to walk on levels not now in existence. Lovers or long lost friends? The former sounds more appealing and ruins have always been a favourite trysting place for lovers.

The Castle Sands Entity

The Castle Sands with the open sea bathing pool
photo by the author

The Castle Sands lies at the foot of the castles eastern side. This is a picturesque area with its golden sands and impressive rock strata coving round the castle and shoreline. Along with the golden beach, it has an old open sea tidal swimming pool within an enclosed wall, which disappears with the high tide. This was a bathing pool for ladies in the 1800s so long as they could pay a sum for the privilege.

On a good day when the tide is low, it is possible to walk around the coastline from the castle to the nearby haunted 'Pipers Cave' then onto the beach near the St. Andrews Aquarium.

The harsh weather beating upon this area has been realised at times when the heavy rain and driving sea causes landslides of the cliff face along the entire sea front. This has caused the council to close the Castle Sands on a number of occasions over the years until repairs have been carried out to make the area safe again.

Along with being a vantage point for catching sightings of Hepburn at the castle above, a strange oppressing presence has been felt on these sands by the old bathing pond. Sometimes there is a feeling of fear, especially when swimming in the pool itself, as if a great danger is about to befall those swimming around. Perhaps it is the presence of one who drowned here many years ago and they are alerting those who swim here of the dangers.

Along with the East Sands, legend has it a Phantom Coach containing David Beaton careers down to the Castle Sands and into the sea.

The Kinburn House Ghost
Ghosts of Fife Castle Trail Ref: 2

Ghostly associations in brief
The ghost of a woman, footsteps, a fearful presence and a tape recording.

Visiting restrictions/fees
Kinburn House is now the St. Andrews Museum, owned and operated by Fife Council. Opening times apply for the museum, but the grounds and gardens have no opening restrictions. Entry to the castle, museum and the grounds are free.

Directions
Kinburn is signposted as 'St. Andrews Museum' from the mini roundabout of the A915 City Road west of Market Street and is only a short distance from the centre of town.

The following about the museum is from their website:
'The Museum explores St Andrews' heritage from early times to the 20th century, covering both the medieval period when the Cathedral was one of the great religious centres of Europe and the growth of tourism starting in the Victorian era. In the Arrival Gallery, imaginative displays combine with interesting artefacts to tell the town's story through the ages. The Kaleidoscope Gallery features a changing programme of temporary exhibitions on a wide variety of topics. The Activity Centre hosts lectures

and activities for children throughout the year. The Museum café serves light meals, teas, coffees and home baking. Kinburn Park offers tennis courts as well as bowling and putting greens.'[15]

Kinburn House was built in 1855/6 by David Buddo as a mansion in the style of an ornate castle with lawns, landscaped gardens and tennis courts covering its grounds. It was named after the victory of Kinburn during the Crimean War in which Buddo had been a medical officer in the Indian Army. Florence Nightingale served alongside Buddo in this war and like Buddo attended to the sick and dying. It was through her efforts of this war that she is known for her groundbreaking achievements in developing nursing.

In 1872 the mansion was bought by an ironmonger by the name of John Peterson and was later inhabited by the Provost of the Burgh from 1887-93. In 1920, the town council bought the premises and while workmen were redeveloping the building they discovered a large number of stone coffins or cists that were found to contain human remains. The building once housed the library of Hay Fleming and since 1991 has become the home for the St. Andrews Museum.

In the late 1980s whilst conducting initial researches that would lead to the publication of this and *Ghosts of St. Andrews* I had the pleasure of meeting a local St. Andrews woman by the name of Greta Boyd. Her natural mediumistic abilities have drawn occurrences to her from an early age. The conviction behind her firsthand accounts as she relived her paranormal experiences through the retelling of them to me was both spontaneous and detailed, and a testimony to how strange reality can really be.

In 1975 whilst working in Kinburn House, she heard heavy footsteps in the corridors at times when nobody else was in the building. Occasionally this was accompanied by the feeling of a presence standing behind her. It got so bad that on one occasion she rapidly left the building because of the feeling she had of a 'fearful presence.'

Her daughter saw the ghostly figure of a woman one evening in one of the upper stories. They had just finished work and were the last to leave the building. After locking the door of Kinburn, they began to make their way along one of the gravel paths spreading its way around the grounds, when her daughter turned and saw a woman staring down at them from a window in the building.

Around the same time these disturbances were presenting themselves to Greta and her daughter at Kinburn, Greta held a party at her home for a group of children in her company for the evening. After a few party games, they all decided to sing a few songs, so Greta brought out her tape recorder to record the event for them. Afterwards Greta rewound the tape as everyone earnestly gathered round with big grins of eager anticipation at the novelty of hearing their own voices. On playing it back however, instead of there being the merry sing-along that had been anticipated, there was only a menacing voice. Greta didn't know what to make of it at all; she had pressed the buttons to record so whatever noise it should have picked up was silenced by this singular very intrusive, very menacing and very strange voice. She didn't know if it were of a male or female but it kept repeating a message, the same message over and over again in a slow staggered voice thus:

"A---g---n---e---s.....H-e-l-p....m-e.....B-a-b-y....
A---g---n---e---s.....H-e-l-p....m-e.....B-a-b-y....
A---g---n---e---s.....H-e-l-p....m-e.....B-a-b-y....."

There was a short pause between each word and the word 'AGNES' sounded longer and more drawn out than the other words. It was almost the voice of someone in distress, someone dying and very weak with it. Upon hearing this, the silence of anticipation turned to a silence of confusion, disappointment and a few became scared. Those gathered knew it was impossible for whatever it was to be on the recording. They all soon became quite alarmed and frightened, as there was no rational explanation at all for this being on the tape. Shortly after, the children left the house leaving Greta to ponder on the tape and its eerie message.

She tried a number of times to record over the voice, but every time she played it back - there it was:
"A---g---n---e---s .....H-e-l-p ....m-e .....B-a-b-y...." repeated over and over again.

A few days after the message appeared on the tape she went out for a stroll and found herself in the Eastern Cemetery of the Cathedral ruins. Strolling around the many tombstones, her curiosity was roused by a leaf dropping down in front of her onto a grave. Leaning forward she looked at the inscription of the stone it had fallen by. To her astonishment, the grave was of a relation of a Provost who had lived in Kinburn House in the late nineteenth century. The woman's name on the grave was Agnes!

Now the correlation of all this isn't known other than there may be a connection between the plea for help on the tape and Kinburn House; perhaps the mother calling for help from her daughter Agnes who may have lived in Kinburn House? If so it could have been the mother who Greta's daughter saw at the window of Kinburn House, and could well be the same woman whose presence Greta had felt on a number of occasions whilst working in the building.

Greta kept the tape in a drawer at the house but it played heavily on her mind. Eventually after around 8 or 9 months, it finally got the better of her. Feeling it too spooky to keep any more she threw it out. Immediately it was like a weight had lifted from her shoulders. Although it had been her only real evidence of the strange occurrence, she was glad she had got rid of it.

In September 1975 at the Cross Keys in Peebles, there was a similar occurrence to the one above. Room 3 was subjected to ghostly phenomenon and a radio interviewer came hoping to make a recording of a ghostly human voice, in this he got an intriguing result – although not the kind he was expecting. The voice was of Donald Duck recorded at high speed![16]

Refer also to *the A915 St. Andrews – Leven Road just past Lathones Inn*, p.184

Kinkell Castle
& the Castle Golf Course
Ghosts of Fife Castle Trail Ref: 3

Kinkell Castle

Ghostly associations in brief
The ghost of a woman and a cavalier

Visiting restrictions/fees
The castle has long since gone, but although no traces now remains, the ghosts linger on. The site has recently been redeveloped as the Castle Golf Course with the Club House being built in the vicinity of where the castle – or at least its

grounds once stood. Commanding breathtaking views, it is well worth visiting. The Club House Restaurant, which is the prime location to spot one of the ghosts, is open to the general public and serves refreshments and food. Opening hours apply, but the entrance is free and no membership is required.

Directions
The entrance to the golf course is situated a couple of miles east of St. Andrews on the A917 Crail Road. The golf course is signposted on the left and the relatively new tarmac road eventually leads to the cliffs by the shore and the picturesque setting of the restaurant.

It is hard to believe now that in the 17th century, high on these cliffs overlooking St. Andrews Bay stood Kinkell Castle. This was a fortified mansion and stood a little inland of the cliff top roughly where the clubhouse is now situated. Although it isn't apparent from the vantage point on the cliffs high above the North Sea, the location is above Kinkell Cave and the Rock and Spindle, or Spindle Rock - a large volcanic plug, set between the cliffs and the sea and so named because of its shape.

The castle had a long gallery, a courtyard and a private chapel. A few illustrious families of Fife have been resident here over the years; amongst them were the Moubrays, then by marriage the Hepburns, the Monipennies of Pitmilly (of Pitmilly House fame)[vii], the Hamiltons and John Ramsay esq.[17]

No trace is to be found of this castle today, which drew large numbers to its illegal Presbyterian meetings in the 17th century. When Archbishop Sharpe of St. Andrews asked the provost to send the militia to break up the meetings, the provost said he could not, since the militia had also gone to hear the preaching!

Kinkell takes its name from the chapel of St. Anna built here by Kellach, Bishop of St. Andrews around AD 875 and means ceann coille or head of the wood. This area including Kinkell was once called Muckross from muic; meaning boar and ross being a promontory. From the 12th century the land was called Cursus Apri meaning Boar's Chase and was the hunting ground for wild boars by the early Scottish Kings and nobility.

The following has been taken from a brief article written by W. T. Linskill, which included Kinkell Castle and appeared in the St. Andrews Citizen dated 5th January 1929. This was part of his last entry to this local newspaper before his death:

[vii] Refer to *Pitmilly House* and its famous poltergeist activity, p.208

'It was believed to be haunted by the apparition of Lady Kinkell who silently roamed the area of the chapel. The original coastal road to Crail ran by the cliffs edge past this old castle, but the constant bombardment on the coastline from the elements has resulted in many landslides along these cliffs, ensuring that no trace may now be found of the castle, nor indeed most of the original coastal route baring on old maps of the area marking its original position.'[18]

Impressionistic Ghosts

There are a number of categories for ghostly phenomenon pending their particular displayed attributions. *Impressionistic Ghosts* is a term I use for an image impressed upon a locality as a snapshot in time. These are repetitive recorded images and are not generally disturbed by changes taking place to either the physical landscape or architecture. This is why ghosts appear to walk through walls where doors once stood or appear above ground when the level has since dropped, or appear with only the upper half showing when the level of ground has been raised. They are not spirits of the deceased so there can be no interaction.

In June 2008 a new 18 Hole Golf Course was opened at Kinkell on what was much of Kinkell and neighbouring Brownhills Farm land that extended to the Kinkell Braes – or steep rocky slopes leading down to the sea. The northern edge of the course runs along by this cliff top and its accompanying public footpath, which lead in places down to the shoreline.

Becoming the newest in the portfolio of St. Andrews courses, (this being number 7) it is appropriately called the Castle Course. The castle stood in the proximity of the new Castle Club House, amid grounds which the local farmers when it was a field called Castle Park.

Until now, there has never been a regular occupancy on this spot since the time of the castle itself. So with staff and visitors now being here from sunrise to sunset, it is far more likely for sightings of Lady of Kinkell to be seen once again either in the Castle Club House building, or wandering across the grassland when looking out of the restaurant window. The view from the window commands as it does, unrivalled panoramic views of St. Andrews Bay.

The Phantom Cavalier and the Ghostly Steed

This area is also haunted by something else. With this area once being known as the Boar's Chase, it now gives its name to the 12th hole of the golf course, and as mentioned just now the castle was the illegal meeting place for the Presbytery.

The location of the following story isn't stated, but these historical associations correlate to the story at hand. Without knowing them the location would never have been so obvious or perhaps known – that is, other than by encountering the following fearful apparition firsthand. The story is recounted by James Wilkie in 1931 in his Bygone Fife, where he says 'There hung till recently in the house of Lingo,[viii] which once belonged to the Priory of Pittenweem, a portrait of General Dalzell, "with his bald head and his beard to his girdle," although these lands only came in the family a few years before the '45. Beneath it were suspended the great riding-boots of him who, with Grierson of Lagg (Scott's Sir Robert Redgauntlet) and wild Bonshaw, Sir James Turner and Claverhouse, peopled the inferno of the Whigs. Legends yet linger concerning these boots. On nights when the moon shone in fitful gleams, as the clouds scudded over the sky, or when the stars of winter alone burned in the heavens, they would disappear from their accustomed place. Out on the moors that of old comprised the Boar's Chase flew a ghostly steed, the boots striking spurred heels into its flanks, and the feet of a bearded phantom filling them. It was the shade of the fierce old cavalier in wild pursuit of invisible Whigs, as in the days when word was brought in of an unlawful gathering in some remote hollow,[ix] and the general buckled on the broadsword, ever by his chair, and leaped on his ready bridled horse, calling on his men to follow.'[19]

Refer also to *Lingo House*, p.187

Balcomie Castle
Ghosts of Fife Castle Trail Ref: 4

Ghostly associations in brief
The sound of a whistle being blown, the apparition of a boy, a soldier and the moving of furniture within the castle.

Visiting restrictions/fees
The castle set in the East Neuk is a private residence with a 3 bedroomed 18th century farmhouse adjoining the castle available for holiday hire. The castle is not open to the public but it is possible to view from the grounds. Being a private residence, the privacy of the occupants should be respected.

[viii] Lingo House is a large white country mansion just off the B940 north east of West Lingo.
[ix] This is referring to 'illegal' meetings held at the Castle.

Directions

Head from the eastern edge of Crail out along Balcomie Road towards Balcomie Golf Course and Fife Ness. The turn off to Balcomie is halfway along this road on the left. The castle amid a cluster of trees will be seen way before the entrance plaque at the castle road entrance is found pointing it out.

Now used for such pursuits as go-cart racing Crail airfield sited half a mile to the east of Crail by the road heading out to the castle was an active airfield during the first and second world wars, serving the East Neuk – the name given to this quarter of Fife. Being an RAF base, it was never shown on the old maps of the area. Some of the buildings connected with the airfield are still standing – including the control tower, but having been disused for so long those left are now in a state of great dereliction with some of the stone work having been put to better use in the building of various houses.

Wandering around these old buildings the imagination is easily stirred into feeling the presence of the old airmen and personnel going about their business at this temporary and once secret place.

photo by the author

The road from Crail to the castle once formed part of the bases runway network. The road continues out to Fife Ness, the most easterly and barren point of Fife's coastline.

The only portion remaining today of the castle is the Peel Tower, a large dark stone structure possibly dating back to the 16th century. It was from this edifice the castle originally grew and took shape. At one time, it was said to be the largest in Fife with enough bedchambers for an entire troop of Dragoons and a stable for each of their horses. In the early 19th century most of the building was taken down by Thomas Earl of Kellie who bought the property after the death of Sir John Scot of Scotstarvit and Barns, a man who in his time was a great student and patron of letters. The remaining section is still very substantial and unlike many adorning the countryside is still inhabited which gives at least some indication of its former size.

The actual haunting of Balcomie Castle is probably the most famous within Fifes strongholds. It is related to us that around the time of Flodden a servant boy with a great love of music lived within the castle. Spending many an hour playing a kind of penny whistle he was known to wander through the corridors of the castle playing tunes as he went.

Early one cold wintry morning however he awoke his master with his playing. Furious at being disturbed at such an early hour the laird grabbed the boy and threw him in the dungeons for a few hours as punishment. He then retired once more to bed and thought nothing more of the incident. When he awoke for the second time the last thought on his mind was for the poor boy locked away under the keep in the cells, and with more pressing engagements at hand, he hurriedly left the castle on business.

A week later, the laird returned from his journey to be greeted with the news of the young musician's inexplicable disappearance. With great horror he then remembered what he had done the previous week and in a state of grave remorse ran down to the dungeon.

Unlocking the door with trembling hands his fears were recalled when on gazing upon the damp cold floor of the chamber he beheld the poor creature with terror stricken eyes lying quite still.

The ghost of the ill-fated boy has been seen on a number of occasions wandering around the grounds of the Peel Tower. His shadowy form has also been glimpsed at the top of the tower, sitting playing the whistle he loved so much.

Journeying on dark still nights to this place his distant haunting tunes may be heard, carried by the wind to the ears of those willing to hear.

'The story runs that through the passages and up and down the stairs he trod so long ago, a boyish form has been seen to flit by those who through the centuries have had eye to see, and that on winter nights when the stars burn sharp and clear and the moon is on the wane he wanders beyond the confines of the castle.'

'It has been said that the chairs in the castle are sometimes moved about by some invisible power, that the candles in the castle often burn blue, and that wild, unearthly whistling comes from the darkness of the Castle Keep. But perhaps the strangest story in connection with the castle was that told lately by an old Crail fisherman, who declared that he one night saw the minstrel's ghost sitting on the top of the castle flag-staff in full possession of a rusty tin-whistle.'[20]

The courtyard of the castle is also the haunt of a soldier seen with his musket in hand.[21]

Crail Castle
Ghosts of Fife Castle Trail Ref: 5

Site of Crail Castle
photo by the author

Ghostly associations in brief
A ghostly figure

Visiting restrictions/fees
Nothing remains of the castle. A Victorian folly stands overlooking the harbour where it once stood. The location is accessible all year round with no restrictions or entrance fee.

Directions
The site of the castle overlooks the harbour on its eastern side, between the sea and Castle Street. The site is now an open garden on the rocks sloping down to the seashore.

This was a royal residence in its day and quite possibly the earliest residence in this area. King David I who granted St. Andrews as a Royal Borough in 1140 often resided here, as did many other early Kings and nobles. A chapel within was dedicated to St. Rufus, this was St Maelrubha of Applecross.

The site records of Canmore state 'there seems little reason for doubting that it was once a royal residence and it is indisputable that it became the manor house associated with the office of the Constable of Crail. In 1310, Robert I confirmed the constabulary to Lawrence de Weirmerstoun, the charter declaring that his ancestors had held the office from ancient times. By 1563 a charter speaks of the castle becoming ruinous, with nothing remaining but the moat.'[22]

The last visible remnants of the castle were cleared away by the council of the time in 1706.

The picturesque area where the castle once stood is haunted by a ghostly figure who walks along part of the wall which no longer exists.

This part of the world is well worth a visit. The harbour alone is breathtaking and has the accolade of being the most painted and photographed harbour in Scotland.

Kellie Castle
Ghosts of Fife Castle Trail Ref: 6

Ghostly associations in brief
The feelings of oppression and intense fear, a presence, a haunted chamber and cold spots, footsteps, phantom slippers, at least one female ghost, and the ghost of James Lorimer.

Visiting restrictions/fees
The property is run by the National Trust for Scotland.
Opening times and entrance fees apply.

Directions
Inland: Take the A917 towards St. Andrews, then the B940. Following the sign for Colinsburgh turn left along the B9171. After around 8 miles the sign for the castle and gardens will come into view with a right turn along the long entrance road.

Coastal route: Drive along the A917 into Pittenweem and take the right turn along Charles Street signed for Grangemuir Chalet and Caravan Park, continue to the B9171 and turn left towards Largo and Leven. Follow this road and a sign for the castle will mark the long entrance road on the right.

Set amid its own woodland and park grounds the castle has undergone various stages of building over the centuries. The earliest part dates from the fourteenth century with its first occupants being the Oliphant family. The main part of the castle building was constructed between the late 16th and early 17th centuries.

It fell for a time to the elements, lying empty apart from the bats and rooks, and the grounds being used as farmland until 1878 when it was leased to James Lorimer. His ghost has been seen seated in one of the corridors of the castle.

Restoration of the castle began in the 1880s by the Earl of Mar and Kellie and was continued by Sir Robert Lorimer and the Lorimer family who eventually bought the castle in the 1957. Sir Robert also restored Earlshall Castle just after completing Kellie, as they were impressed with the work he had done here. The castle then passed to the National Trust for Scotland in 1970.

It is said the banqueting hall is hung with a tapestry, which may have adorned the palace of Mary of Guise. This palace was the haunted New Inn, a former Royal Palace and an Archbishops Palace situated down the Pends road in St. Andrews.[x]

The castle stands in the shape of a T. A tower forms each of its points and on its north and eastern side is a most attractive walled garden. A great many people have visited this place, with most taking time to enjoy the ancient splendour that has been carefully restored and maintained.

Kellie Castle

photo by the author

A few who have visited the castle however have not been so relaxed. These are the ones who have been affrighted by something they believed to be either lurking inside, or from something terrible they sense happened within this ancient home many years ago.

I have spoken to quite a number who have visited this castle and have had experiences of this nature here. A consistently high proportion without prompting, have described their visits here as being a "chilling encounter". One woman felt quite distressed on setting foot through the doorway and took the opportunity to leave as rapidly as she had entered. Another got as far as the crypt on the ground floor before considering the air to be too asphyxiating in which to continue and withdrew. Others have had similar feelings of oppression within its walls, and the feelings can become so bad and intense, it can become a test for some to actually enter the building – and not all do! The foreboding experiences typified by the exasperating sense of dread not only within the castle but whilst making the initial approach is reinforced by this next account, once again from James Wilkie:

'Some of those who have dwelt in such an abode felt it an eerie house, of which the eeriest part was a room high up from which a far-flung prospect of land and sea is got. Their apartment was described as "quite a bright little room, with three small windows, reached by one or two stairs from the bedroom corridor; not at all a gloomy place." '[23]

---

[x] Refer to *Ghosts of St. Andrews* (2013) by the present author

Elsewhere in his pages he states: 'Kellie has, of course, its haunted chamber, a small room on the second storey of the keep entered from the wheel stair that climbs steeply to the top of the ancient tower. From this apartment access is had to one of those small and eerie recesses in the thickness of the wall, lit by a long and narrow window, which figure in so many ghost stories. In bygone days this was the Earl's room. Once a guest who had not before visited the castle and who knew nothing of the haunted chamber was given that apartment for the night, in the hope, it was said, that she might have some experience to relate.

Though aware that houses so historic have not infrequent visitants from the unseen, she fell asleep without fear or expectation of such an intruder.

In the "dim unhappy midnight," or in the ghostly hours that follows, she suddenly awoke with the sense of a presence felt but invisible. The moon was shining in an unclouded sky, and its dim radiance penetrated the room. All was silent but for the night wind stirring in the leaves. A feeling of terrible oppression, as when in a dream the dreamer strives to cry aloud and cannot succeed. It was accompanied by an abnormal chill in the atmosphere, which grew more intense as the unseen presence approached. It seemed to pass beside the chamber and to make its exit from the chamber through the door into what, in the days of good Queen Ann, may have been the powdering room.

Next morning the answer of the guest to her hostess's greeting was, after the Scots manner, a question as to whether there was a haunted chamber in the castle. In response to which came the avowal that there were stories as to the Earl's room. A visitant from another world was supposed to enter by the door from the stair and pass out by that in the thickness of the wall.

It was further believed that in the topmost storey of the keep a cradle might be heard rocking under certain circumstances; but why the phantom nurse or mother still watches over the phantom child is unexplained.

The house dog was want to stand at the foot of the stairs and howl, showing terror if carried up. In the room itself, this terror was accentuated the hair was seen to bristle all along the spine, and frantic efforts to escape testified to an environment, which, to the canine perception contained an element of the abnormal.

A pair of dainty red slippers have been seen running up and down the turret stairs.'[24]

The castle and grounds are also haunted by the ghost of Anne Erskine, a lady who fell from a castle window to her death and the sound of footsteps in the castle have been attributed to her. It is also believed a duchess who came from Balcaskie was murdered here. Others have it that a certain "Lady Mary" committed suicide within its walls.'[25]

With the castle having an atmosphere many find hard to endure for very long, the violent impact of a murder and the deep sorrow of a suicide have left these very tangible and uncontrollable impressions of oppression and fear on many who visit. Whatever the truth of the hauntings at Kellie Castle, it is undoubtedly a castle of secrets. When visiting maybe you will sense something of the past yet to be discovered in the present. Something yet to be recorded for the annals of history.

Newark Castle
(St. Monans)
Ghosts of Fife Castle Trail Ref: 7

Ghostly associations in brief
Castle: Ghostly screams

Visiting restrictions/fees
None. Care should be taken as some of the stones are precariously balanced.

Directions
The castle ruins sit on the cliff tops of the coast around half a mile to the west of the village of St. Monans. They are accessible either by walking along the Fife coastal path towards Elie, or by driving along the A917 in the direction of Elie. About half a mile out of the town turn left just past the first cottage you see, and continue along this single-track farm road to the castle ruins.

On the GOF Castle Trail from Kellie Castle turn right along the B9171, left onto the B942 then right at the turn off for Abercrombie and St. Monans, right at the A917, then left in around half a mile just past a cottage onto the farm road to the castle ruins by the sea.

The Castle
A castle has stood on this site since the 13th century. 'After the defeat of the Marquis of Montrose at the battle of Philiphaugh in 1645 many of his men and camp followers, some of them Irish women, were taken to Newark where they were slaughtered in an orgy of killing. The place where the killing occurred is said to be haunted by the ghostly screams of those so brutally butchered.'[26]

Lieutenant General David Leslie bought the site of the castle in 1649. The ruins of today are believed to be the remains of what he built.

Photo taken of Newark Castle by John Patrick of Kirkcaldy in 1867

A fairly substantial part of the ground floor still remains of this castle, but most of what was seen in 1867 on the left side of the castle has now crumbled and collapsed.

photo by the author

Refer also to *St. Monans Historic Kirk*, p.233

Kilconquhar Castle
Estate and Country Club, Village and Loch
Ghosts of Fife Castle Trail Ref: 8

Ghostly associations in brief
A ghost in one of the castles apartments
Ghost of a girl in the Lindsay room
Ghost by the main gates
Presence in the main building
Feelings of fear
Electrical problems
Shadows and ghosts at the nearby loch

Visiting restrictions/fees
The Castle and Estate is now a family holiday resort. It is possible to visit or stay here as they specialise in self-catering or bed and breakfast breaks. They cater also for weddings, corporate events and functions. Unless you are a resident or taking part in one of the functions, the castle may only be viewed from the outside.

Directions
Off the B941 just north of Kilconquhar village.

On the GOF Castle Trail from Newark Castle continue another half mile along the A917 from St. Monans toward Elie, turning first right along a narrow unsignposted country road called Balbuthie Road. Continue along this road into Kilconquhar turning right at the T junction onto the B941. Just a short distance out of the village the estate entrance and gates will be found on the right. It is signposted Kilconquhar Estate and Country Club.

Fleming in 1886 about Kilconquhar says 'This is the Name of a parish, a village, a loch, and a mansion, and is said to mean "the cell, the burying-place, or place of worship, at the head or extremity of the fresh water lake.' [27]

Kilconquhar Castle Estate
Situated about half-a-mile to the northeast of the loch, just north of Kilconquhar village, the castle is set in 120 acres of land and dates from around the 12th or 13th century. In the 16th century, a tower house was added, and numerous extensions have been added since.

photo by the author

This was once the family seat of Adam of Kilconquhar. Following his death during the crusades in 1271, his wife Marjorie Countess of Carrick married Robert de Brus, 6th Lord of Annandale in the same year. Their son was the famous Robert the Bruce. However he wasn't born here as some reports suggest, he was born at Turnberry Castle in Ayrshire, but this was his ancestral home. Now a family country club with a large indoor swimming pool and an equestrian centre, recent reports say that a three apartment suit on the top floor of the castle is haunted by a ghost. The staff I spoke with said they have had a strange feeling, which seems to overwhelm them with a sense of fear. The consensus was that it is a creepy place – especially at night when no one else is about.

For a long time the Lindsay Room on the ground floor has had a reputation for being haunted. The walls of the room are covered with ornately carved wooden Jacobean panelling, and a very beautiful large fireplace comes from a mansion in Edinburgh. The room is host to many events and wedding receptions and is also a restaurant at certain times of the week for the guests staying on the grounds.

The staff here are more than aware that this room is also haunted and often won't step inside unless there are two of them. Some say the room is haunted by the ghost of a woman, perhaps a green or grey lady. This is certainly what seems to have been reported, but the main ghost here is that of a little girl.

The beautiful Lindsay Room with its Jacobean panelling
photo by the author

Many years ago, she was a family member of the occupants. She was disabled or had learning difficulties and in those harsh times, this was looked upon as being a curse, and any who displayed such were kept well hidden. Especially from any guests they might have had. Even to the extent of not acknowledging they had a disabled son or daughter. This is reminiscent of Glamis Castle where the son of one of the Earls was kept hidden and secret from visitors. He was only let out of his room high in the castle when visitors were not around. On occasion he 'escaped' and was seen roaming the grounds or the walkway around the top of the castle. This gave rise to reports and rumours of the 'Monster of Glamis' being seen.

It was Bill, one of the staff members at Kilconquhar I spoke with whilst I was staying here who kindly told me about her. "She was kept in the turret of the castle," he said, "and was only let out occasionally. With a great deal of spent up energy she would run around the rooms and especially the Lindsay room."

Her energy would have been very chaotic, sporadic and oppressive and this is what seems to hit each who experience it. Bill described an 'odd' feeling he has sometimes. He has also had the same feeling between this room and the toilets along the basement. On more than one occasion, he has also felt a presence with him, someone standing next to him when no one else has been around.

The Lindsay Room, trapdoor to the left of the window
photo by the author

The Lindsay Room has a trap door to the left of the large window. Former occupants may have used this as an access door into the room for the little girl so she wouldn't have been seen wandering through the building. One day a staff member hid under it with a white tablecloth over him and waited for a female member of staff to enter the room. Not that any needed any additional prompting to be frightened in this room, but for the sake of a prank, he then sprang up through the trap door and she ran out screaming.

On par with many places, the electrical equipment is often prone to playing up with lights turning themselves on and vacuum cleaners doing the same.

A couple of years ago, at the main entrance gates to the estate an elderly couple were leaving to go home after I imagine a very enjoyable stay at Kilconquhar. When nearing the entrance they saw a woman to the left of the track walking towards the gatehouse, and as they drove closer, she promptly disappeared through a wall. They posted their experience online and have never been back since!

The Village

A Culdee missionary in the 5th or 6th century called Conquhar founded a cell or church on the site of the present church of Kilconquhar. The site had been used for burials over a long period and in 1821 when the present church was being built they found a great many human bones.

David Hay Fleming writing in 1886 says 'The Burying-Ground contains some curious old tomb-stones, but the most remarkable is an effigy in armour, known as "Jock o' Bucklevie." At the best, this effigy has been a piece of rude work, and it has suffered much from the ravages of time, and the selfishness of the heritor's who cast it out of the old church. It has been conjectured that Bucklevie, or Balclevie, was at one time an independent estate, and that the effigy represents one of the lairds.'[28]

The village is steeped full of history with the Kinneuchar Inn dating to 1750. The spelling of the Inn is how the name Kilconquhar is pronounced.

Kilconquhar Loch with the village to the right
photo by the author

Fleming says 'The Loch, which is a beautiful sheet of water, lying close to the village and church, covers fully 96 acres. It abounds with water-plants of many kinds, and is said to swarm with pike and eel. It has long been a favourite haunt of swans, and its glassy surface is generally dotted with these majestic sailors. In Vedder's ballad on the Witch o' Pittenweem, is said;

> "They tied her arms behind her back,
> An' twisted them with a pin;
> And they dragged her to Kinnoquhar Loch
> An' coupit the limmer in -
> An' the swans flew screamin' to the hills,
> Scared with the unhaly din."'

William Ballantine, a former "laird of Kilconquhar," is said to have been drowned while skating on the loch on the 28th of February 1593.'[29] This was also the time of the witch trials in the area.

Skating and curling still takes place when the loch is frozen in the winter months by the intrepid Balcaskie Curling Club. The Kilconquhar website says 'Intemperate curlers have even been known to fall through the ice, the heat generated by the whisky causing it to melt!'[30]

Not surprisingly the loch is said to have its shadows and shades (ghosts) flitting about the tree line on the shore.

Colinsburgh Castle (Balcarres House)
& the Alchemists Tragedy
Ghosts of Fife Castle Trail Ref: 9

Ghostly associations in brief
The Omen, Crisis Ghost

Visiting restrictions/fees
Since 1986 the house has been leased by the family to the charity Balcarres Heritage Trust who run the agricultural estate from these premises. They maintain the property and the gardens and administer the estates farming land and properties. The house is only open during the month of April each year, opening times and entrance fees apply. It is possible to visit at other times by written permission only. The park, woodland and garden with designed landscapes are open during the summer months, opening times and fees also apply.

Directions
Off the B942 north of Colinsburgh. Take the private road east of Colinsburgh ('Private road' off to the right before entering Colinsburgh from the east)

On the GOF Castle Trail from Kilconquhar House travel north on the B941 turning left onto the B942. 200 metres along this road a turning to the right flanked by two stone pillars and a small sign with 'Private Road Balcarres' will take you to the Castle Estate.

This is an unusual old building, with an unusual atmosphere all to its own. It once had something very special within its walls, something rare, something written by the hand of a very talented and unusual man – an alchemist.

David Hay Fleming writing in 1886 says, 'Balcarres House is situated fully a mile and a half north west of the loch [Kilconquhar Loch], and has been a seat of the Lindsay's for three centuries, having been acquired, in 1587 [1586], by John Lindsay, who six years before had assumed the title of Lord Menmuir on being appointed a Lord of Session. This John Lindsay, who was the second son of the ninth Earl of Crawford, died in [September] 1598, in his mansion of Balcarres, which he had only built in 1595. His death is said to have been one of the "notable effects" of

Original	Translation
"that maist conspicuus eclipse of the sunne," which six months before "strak all creatours with sic estonishment and feir, as tho the day of Judgment haid bein com."	"that most conspicuous eclipse of the sun," which six months before [March 1598] "struck all creatures with such astonishment and fear, as though the day of Judgement had come."

His second wife was "a termagant," and was imprisoned for her violence.

Following the death of John Lindsay, his 'eldest son died three years after himself; but his second son, David, who is said to have had the best library of his time in Scotland, [partly inherited from his father] was created Lord Lindsay of Balcarres, by Charles the First, in 1633.'[31]

Solar eclipses have always marked human conflict and tragedy, typified especially by war but always by death. A fascinating and original book was published May 2013 entitled *The Wheals of God*. Researched and written by Esoteric Historian Keith Magnay of London. He uses as a reference solar eclipse paths from 1801, forecasting them to 2027. For many centuries solar eclipses have been considered an ill omen. Magnay says the book contains 'startling new revelations about the correlations between solar eclipse paths and human geopolitical conflict.' Maybe I am a little biased here because I had a hand in its production for publication, but I recommended it for any with an interest in solar eclipses for its revealing effects on the darker side of our human condition.

Leighton in 1840 says of David: 'He was a laborious alchemist and there were 10 volumes in the library at Balcarres, written in his own hand, upon the Philosopher's Stone.'[32]

Being an alchemist he would have been well aware of the destructive associations of a solar eclipse, believing it to have caused his father's death the incident would have had quite an impact on him and the nature of his alchemical research. Thoughts of John's son David inheriting an existing library are born out as follows: 'The second son, David, who after his brother's death inherited the estate of Balcarres, may be termed the second founder of the library. The father's love of books and learning seems to have in a very large measure descended to the son. He added to the library until it became one of the best in the kingdom.'[33]

'The library of Sir David Lindsay, Lord Balcarres, continued at the family seat on the shores of the Firth of Forth until comparatively recent times. Sibbald in 1710 mentions the 'great bibliothek' at Balcarres. In Sibbald's time the owner, Colin, third Earl of Balcarres, had added many books to the library, and spent the evening of his days in the pursuit of letters.'[34]

Entrance to the Chapel

David collected alchemical and Rosicrucian manuscripts. He was also a Rosicrucian of the Rosy Cross and a mason. 'David died at Balcarres in 1641, and was buried in the little Gothic chapel which he had built [in 1635], and which now stands roofless near the road-side.'[35]

Was it possible for his father John Lindsay to also have been an alchemist and that David had inherited his work and carried on in that direction? John died at the age of 50 after being conferred with many honours and a fairly rapid build up of his status in Fife and Scotland. All this was in-keeping and in character with one who had attained to the proficiency of his involvement.

Fletcher writing in 1902 says: 'During his short though eventful life he took a leading part in State affairs, being much trusted by his Sovereign, King James

VI. He was a man of varied talents—lawyer, statesman, man of business, scholar, man of letters, and a poet. He seems to have been familiar with Greek, and to have corresponded in the Latin language. Besides these he acquired knowledge of French, Italian and Spanish. He accumulated many State papers and letters from distinguished persons both at home and abroad.'[36]

Leighton in 1840 says 'in 1592, [aged 44] he was appointed master of all the metals and minerals within the kingdom. He was also Chancellor of the University of St. Andrews [1597-1598].'[37] With a rapid rise to great power and riches – had John Lindsay found the Philosophers Stone? Not so much to the elixir of eternal life but the physical 'side effects' I call it of riches and power that can occasionally accompany the good deeds of men in tandem with the real riches – the blossoming of their spirit. John Lindsay was buried in the nearby parish Kirk of Kilconquhar.

The Large Book Stamp of Alchemist David Lindsay

The Tragedy

Fletcher in 1902 also says 'When Lady Balcarres, great-grandmother of the present Earl of Crawford, left Fife and removed to Edinburgh, whilst her son was in the West Indies, the greater portion of the library was literally thrown away and dispersed – torn up for grocers as useless trash, by her permission. Of the library collected by generations of Lindsay's, all that now remains is a handful of little over fifty volumes.

The books of David Lindsay, first Lord Balcarres, who died in 1641, are recognisable from his signature, and on many of them his arms are impressed in gold on the sides.'[38] The library David and his father had amassed, the 10 handwritten alchemical volumes mentioned by Leighton in 1840 had gone.

In the grounds of Balcarres is a 17th century sundial which once stood in the grounds of the former Leuchars Castle.[xi] Also of interest on the estate is Balcarrres Crag. I have no details of any haunting at the crag itself but mention it here as a point of interest, because it is one of the most prominent features of the area. Atop this crag is a Gothic ruined tower. It is in fact a folly built in

---

xi Leuchars Castle was re-build in the 16th century from its 13th century origins. It was finally demolished in the 20th century and a doocot in a field is all that now remains.

1813 by Robert Lindsay when such edifices were a popular feature of country estates.

Colin, third Earl of Balcarres who Sibbald spoke of as continuing what had now become a family tradition by expanding the library until it was for the most part wantonly destroyed, is also known in the area for creating the village of Colinsburgh. After the Jacobite rising of 1715 he built the village to house soldiers from his regiment. Colin is now the focus of our attention in the two following accounts as we move on from alchemy to omens and apparitions.

Colin, Third Earl of Balcarres[xii]

The Wedding and the Omen of Death
'Colin....third Earl of Balcarres.....was engaged to be married to Muaritia de Nassau, daughter of the Count of Beverwaert and Anverquerque, in Holland. The marriage day arrived, "the noble party were assembled in the church, and the bride was at the altar; but, to the dismay of the company, no bridegroom appeared! The volatile Colin had forgotten the day of his marriage, and was discovered in his night-gown and slippers quietly eating breakfast!....Colin hurried to the church, but in his haste left the ring in his writing case. A friend in the company gave him one; the ceremony went on, and without looking at it, he placed it on the finger of his fair young bride – it was a mourning ring, with the mort head and cross bones. On perceiving this at the close of the ceremony she fainted away, and the evil omen had made such an impression on her mind, that on recovering she declared she should die within the year; and her presentiment was too truly fulfilled.'[39]

Like David Lindsay, Colin was no doubt a mason, and a number of his friends at the wedding would also have been masons, which makes sense of the ring. The mort head and cross bones is a Masonic ring which is why one would have been readily available. It does denote death but esoterically speaking it is also symbolic of an initiatory transition, unfortunately his bride would not have been aware of this.

[xii] The painting is by John Riley and in the care of the Traquair Charitable Trust

Fleming in 1886 writes; 'His life was a very eventful and suffering one, for he had another three wives, and was an incorrigible Jacobite. He lay in a common jail; was confined in Edinburgh Castle, of which his father had been made hereditary governor; endured ten years' exile; and was confined to Balcarres, with a dragoon to attend him. When imprisoned, the ghost of his friend Claverhouse is said to have visited him the morning he was slain at Killiecrankie. This Colin was a lover of paintings and of books, and he it was who built the village of Colinsburgh. He died in 1722.'[40]

The Crisis Apparition of 'Bonnie Dundee'
More details of the above story of the Ghost of Claverhouse appearing to Colin runs as follows: 'John Graham of Claverhouse, Viscount Dundee, known as 'Bonnie' Dundee was a Royalist General who raised the clans to fight against covenanter's at the battle of Killiecrankie on the 27th July 1689. The Royalists won this battle but 'Bonnie' Dundee was struck down as his victory was declared. Early the next morning his apparition appeared to Lord Balcarres in his bedroom, who had himself been unable to fight with his friend. 'Balcarres, waking, saw the curtains of his bed drawn back. There by his side stood Claverhouse, with his long dark curled locks and glittering breastplate, his face calm and pale. Surprise paralysed the faculties of the Earl, and for a while he was unable to move or utter a word of greeting.

John Graham of Claverhouse
'Bonnie Dundee'

Then he saw his visitant turn towards the fireplace, lawn for a space upon the chimney-piece and, with a last look at him, pass out by the door without speech on either side. Earl Colin, like others who have had a similar experience, had at the time no suspicion that there was anything abnormal in what he had witnessed.

His only emotion was amazement at his friends presence and then at his behaviour.

Leaping from his bed, he called repeatedly on him to return, but no answer reached his ears. He had vanished as if he had been a blink of the sun, or a whip of the whirlwind, and could no more be seen....

In that moment, as he learned later, the viscount had succumbed to the silver bullet that pierced his right spule-blade.'[41]

I have not heard of any other reports about any hauntings at the house or in the grounds of Balcarres, so it may well be that the apparition seen by Colin was a one off occurrence. I contacted Balcarres House and received a kind reply from Lord Balniel, Chairman of the Balcarres Heritage Trust, who said of the ghosts: "I fear I am going to disappoint you in that there have been no family stories of ghosts passed down the generations or indeed activity of a paranormal nature that I know of."

This confirms my thoughts that the crisis apparition was indeed a one off occurrence. Lord Balniel continues "you rightly say that Sir David Lindsay did collect books relating to alchemy but the bulk of the collection was either destroyed or sold. We do however have some manuscript volumes on deposit in the National Library of Scotland. These are copies of well-known alchemy books and not the original writings of Sir David Lindsay. Presumably, he could not afford to buy the printed books so had them copied, or perhaps they were not available in Scotland at the time. They are very fragile and written in old Scots. In fact they have recently been consulted by two professors who specialise in the field."

Crisis Apparitions
Seen, heard or felt by somebody known to the apparition. The appearances are triggered by very powerful emotions generating intense energy and projected as memories of association to the recipient in a time of extreme crisis. They occur some twelve hours before or after death or a near death through a severe illness, but they can appear sometimes up to four days after. The recipient is unaware they have died or have suffered.

Accounts are on record that during the First World War, soldiers would appear to family or friends when they were many hundreds of miles away suffering the barbaric carnage of the battlefields. Often knocking on the house door they would typically disappear once inside. The timing of their appearances being around the same time they either died or were seriously wounded in action. These are different to *Post-Mortem Ghosts* where the recipient is aware they have died.

MacDuff's Castle and Caves

Ghosts of Fife Castle Trail Ref: 10

Ghostly associations in brief
Castle and Caves – The
ghost of Mary Sibbald

Visiting restrictions/fees
None

Directions
The Castle is situated by the
shore overlooking the North
Sea. When coming into East
Wemyss from the east along
the A955 High Road, park
up at the Macduff Cemetery.

MacDuff's Castle
photo by the author

The path to the castle and caves runs parallel along the outside of the cemeteries
eastern wall to the shore.

On the GOF Castle Trail from Kilconquhar or Colinsburgh take the A9127 west
to Upper Largo then the A915 to the B930 turn off on the left signed for
Buckhaven and East Wemyss. Follow this to the A955 turning right towards
East Wemyss and MacDuff Cemetery is on the left. Follow the footpath along
the left of the cemetery down to the castle.

The Grey Lady
On the south coast of Fife, a couple of miles south-west of Leven are the ruins
of MacDuff's Castle on the coastal edge of the village of East Wemyss. The land
was once the residency of the MacDuff Earls – the most powerful family in Fife
in the middle ages who originally owned Falkland Palace. The present castle
was built by their descendants and successors the Wemyss family around the
14th century. Below the ruins of MacDuff's Castle lies a network of 11 caves
stretching back into the cliffs, the largest number in Northern Europe. Some of
which have Pictish carvings. Like those of St. Andrews most of these caves are
now too dangerous to explore, being formed out of red sandstone they have
suffered badly from erosion and many landslides. One cave in particular is very
unusual. In the 17th century, it housed a workshop for the making of glass.
Unlike the others it is still in a good state of repair, the roof is about twenty feet

in height and it stretches into the cliffs for about forty feet, the walls of the cave are covered in shelves about one foot square carved out of the sandstone to a depth of about the same. It is believed to have housed craftsman's tools and glass products all those years ago.

One of the caves is named the Court Cave, after the Medieval Baillie Courts at which Landowners dispensed their own justice and summoned people to attend meetings inside the cave by ringing a bell suspended from its roof.

It also received its name from James IV who often came here incognito in his role of the Guardian of Ballangeich. Once he stumbled upon a band of gypsies inhabiting the cave and was nearly killed when a quarrel broke out among the Romanies. One of the gypsies had been in love with Mary Sibbald, daughter of a local landowner. She had left home to live with him and was falsely accused of stealing by a jealous gypsy woman. Sentenced to be flogged the shock was too much for Mary who was believed to have died in the castle of a broken heart.

On one occasion of a visit by James IV, several of the tribe were accusing one Jean Lindsay in the Court Cave, who it would transpire was the real thief. With these accusations, her kinfolk drew swords to protect her. A fearful fight was about to break out when the ghostly figure of a woman – believed to have been that of Mary Sibbald made its appearance, she glided through the cave and all fled the cave in terror. James made his way to the nearby castle and told the Baron Baillie what had happened. The Baron confessed that he too had been haunted since the morning of Mary Sibbald's trial.

The ghost continued to haunt the cave until the real thief confessed her guilt, and even yet, it makes occasional appearances in the grounds of MacDuff's Castle and this cave. An old woman who died in 1909 maintained that as a child she had seen the apparition of a fully dressed woman looking out of the east tower of MacDuff's Castle, to which there is no longer any access.

'In recent years [1970s] a visitor took a flashlight photograph of the interior of the cave which appeared to be completely empty, but when the film was developed it showed the figure of a seated woman.'[42]

The ghost of Mary Sibbald, who still haunts the castle and caves, is known as the 'Grey Lady', although reports have her wearing white.

The family of Wemyss moved from this castle to another dwelling, which is the feature of these next accounts.

Wemyss Castle
Ghosts of Fife Castle Trail Ref: 11

Wemyss Castle
photo by the author

Ghostly associations in brief
The Ghost of 'Green Jean' and a Grey Lady

Visiting restrictions/fees
The castle is a private family residence and is *not* open to the public. The beautiful gardens are open by prior appointment during the summer months, entry fee applies.

Directions
With it being a private residence the best vantage point for this castle is from the sands along the shore, just to the east of West Wemyss, accessed from the eastern terminus of the village's Main Street.

On the GOF Castle Trail from MacDuff's Castle, follow the A955 west, turning off to the left at the sign for West Wemyss. This is the Main Street that runs down and through the village. Follow this to its conclusion on the eastern side of the village by the shore then walk a short distance eastwards along the shore to view the castle.

The Ghost of 'Green Jean'
Sir John Wemyss built the fortified castle in 1421. This is a large dwelling with extensive landscaped gardens restored in the 1950s. The castle still belongs to the Wemyss family as a private residence.

It is most famously known as the residence where Mary Queen of Scots stayed in 1565 and was joined by her cousin Henry, Lord Darnley on the 17th February. She then married Darnley five months later in Edinburgh at Holyrood Palace on the 29th July 1565. They had a son James the following year, who would become James VI of Scotland and James I of England following the death of Elizabeth I.

Almost two years to the day after their meeting at Wemyss Castle, Darnley would be murdered at Kirk o' Field in Edinburgh on the 9th February 1567, not far from where they were married.

In the dead of night, a band seized his house at the Kirk o' Field[xiii] in Edinburgh and blew it up. Narrowly missing death Darnley fled into the grounds in his night attire just as his house by all accounts completely collapsed. In the ensuing chaos, he was captured and duly strangled by his unknown assailants. His ghost appears in a number of locations across Scotland and his murder to this day remains one of the most famous unsolved historical cases. Both the Earl of Bothwell who Mary married only 3 months after Darnley's death and Mary herself, have always been suspected as being two of the co-conspirators. Her innocence wasn't favoured by appearing to have no grief for Darnley's death. She was seen playing golf in Musselburgh only a few days after. The whole episode was to spell the end of Mary with her forced abdication soon after her marriage to Bothwell and her imprisonment in Loch Leven Castle.

An account of the ghost at Wemyss Castle by James Wilkie says: 'The restless spirit that wanders through certain of its (the castle of Wemyss) rooms and corridors is familiarly known as Green Jean, a beautiful lady of the olden time, tall and slim, clad in a trailing gown of green, that "swishes" as she glides. Her history may still be known to the family but, like the secret of Glamis, it is confined to a few.'[43] [xiv]

The following is the last chapter of 'My Memories and Miscellanies' by the Countess of Munster, London 1904. The chapter is entitled *"A true ghost story"* and concerns this apparition of Green Jean at Wemyss Castle as follows:

---

xiii The site is now Chambers Street in Edinburgh, in front of the National Museum of Scotland.

xiv Wilkie also describes the story of Countess Munster which I have taken from source.

A True Ghost Story
1904

'My last reminiscence will be of a ghost story, for which I can vouch the truth.

My sister Millicent (who married Mr. Hay Erskine Wemyss, of Wemyss Castle) herself told me the story.

There was a large party staying at Wemyss Castle for Christmas, and my sister had arranged some theatricals for Christmas evening for the amusement of her guests. She had driven out to Kirkcaldy, the nearest town in those days, to purchase several requisites for the evening's amusement, and had not returned when what I am about to relate took place.

I ought to have begun by stating that "the ghost of Wemyss Castle was always styled "Green Jean," and was supposed to appear in the form of a beautiful, tall, slim lady, clad in a long gown of green that "swished" very much as she walked, or rather *glided*, by. No one seemed to know her history, or, at all events, it was a subject which was avoided.

But to the story.

Everything had been prepared for the theatricals, which were to take place in a large room, which was then used as the dining-room. A stage had already been placed at the further end, and a curtain was hung in readiness. It must be noted that there was a small room which led from the stage, its door being in front of the curtain and within view of everybody. This door was *kept shut*, the room being generally used by the butler to keep glasses, &c., in. At the time it was perfectly empty.

On the afternoon in question, two girls, my sister's eldest daughter and a girl friend, were sitting over the fire. It was a cold, wet afternoon, and though it was late, except for the fire, which was a roaring one in an enormous fireplace, there was no light; the room was shut up and candles were not lit yet.

My niece and her friend were talking over the coming theatricals. Nothing could be heard but their two voices, and the violent rain which was pouring against the window. Suddenly, a rustling sound smote their ears, as if coming from the stage. They looked up; the curtain, however, remained down. But presently it was gently pushed aside to make room for the entry of a tall, pale looking lady dressed in green, who held a sort of Egyptian lamp (lit).

The lady took no notice of either of the girls, but, holding the lamp well in front of her, she walked calmly (her long gown "swishing" after her as she went) up to the door, before mentioned, in front of the curtain. She opened it, passed into the room, and closed it noiselessly. My niece was much excited. She sprang to the door, and taking the handle in her hand called out to her companion,

"Get a candle quickly; there is no way out of the room into which she has gone, and it is quite dark." The other girl hurriedly brought a light and ran to the door. They opened it. It was pitch dark – no sign of the Green Lady. To their amazement she had disappeared into space.

Not long after my sister's carriage was heard driving up to the door. The two girls rushed out to meet her, and told her. "We have seen 'Green Jean!'" My sister knew the effect such a report might have upon the visitors and the servants, and that it might alarm the latter so much as to spoil the arrangements and the pleasures of the evening. She was not the person herself to be alarmed at a ghost, but she feared the effects of such a report upon the others, so the story was hushed up.

Not long after my sister, herself, saw the Green Lady. But to relate this, I must state that my sister's sitting room, in which she always sat and wrote her private letters, overlooked the sea, into which you could easily throw a stone from the window. The door of this room was at the end of a long gallery, upon which the doors of several rooms opened. The next room to my sister's sitting-room was her son's sitting-room, in which he transacted all business, and that room led into his bedroom. All the doors of these rooms opened on a gallery, which looked out (or used to do so – for I have not been at Wemyss Castle for many years) onto a court-yard with a plot of grass in the middle.

On the evening of the event I am about to relate, it was, as often is the case in bonnie Scotland, a pouring wet night. My sister's son had been out riding most of the day, and he being at that time rather delicate-chested, his mother was anxious that he should come home.

Suddenly she heard the door-bell ring, and then her son's hasty footsteps into his sitting-room, and thence to his bedroom. Feeling much relieved, and knowing a young man's dislike to espionage, even as regards his health, she waited quietly in her sitting-room. In about half an hour's time, hearing no more, she put her head into his sitting-room, and walked through into his bedroom, which was lit by gas. Seeing that his wet clothes were all lying on the ground she was satisfied, and made good her way out on to the gallery, when, to her surprise, she saw, about twenty yards off, coming towards her along the gallery, a tall lady in green! Although the house was full of guests, my sister could not conceive for a moment who this lady could be, for it was someone she had never seen before.

The lady walked in a slow, dignified fashion, and seemed in no way put out at seeing another person on the gallery. For a moment my sister stared in astonishment, but in a flash she *felt who it was!*

"It is 'Green Jean.'" she said to herself, "and I shall wait till she comes up to me, and then I shall walk by her side, and see what she will say," She waited. "Green Jean" joined her, *but turned her head away!* My sister moved on by her side, but, as she afterwards told me, she felt *tongue-tied.* The figure accompanied her to the end of the gallery, and then – was gone!

My sister felt, I think, annoyed with herself for not have *done* or *said* something. But when afterwards someone rebuked her for her faintheartedness, she said truly, "I walked by her the whole length of the gallery, and I don't think there are *many* who would have done *that* – but speak, *I could not.*"

That is the end of the story.' [44]

Another account of the ghost of Wemyss is as follows:

'The Duke of Argyll, in his "Real Ghost Stories" in the London Magazine for November, 1901, tells of three other apparitions of apparently the same Green Lady, as often described to him by "the late Miss W [emyss] who lived in a castle in Fife." She had not seen anything supernatural for the first seventeen years of her life in the place, which, although altered for modern use, is throughout a large portion of the building of ancient date. One winter eve, a joiner was working in a little room which could only be reached by traversing the billiard-room, in which there was a fire, but no other light. The joiner had a lamp and Miss W. stayed with him a little time and then left him. As she re-entered the billiard-room, she felt there was somebody or something there, which craved her attention. She had a curious, indefinite feeling such as some have when another's eyes are resting on them. She looked up and saw at the other end of the billiard-room a misty, but defined figure advancing towards her. "The Green Lady" she at once thought, and stood still.

The figure coming towards her was moving slowly. While passing the firelight, rather curiously, Miss W. remarked that it was not reddened by it or made more distinct. The grey indefiniteness of the moving person kept the same neutral colour and was still advancing, though not now, more than ten feet away. Then it turned a corner of the billiard-table and without pause or change of pace or attitude went on through the wall! The same week this identical figure was seen twice by other inmates of the castle once in a passage upstairs and once in a room. Since this triple appearance the Green Lady, who seems to have of late appeared in grey, has not been seen.' [45]

A Family Omen of Death

The Countess of Munster in 1904 also wrote 'One other small circumstance I recall, also of Castle Wemyss. That, however, happened years before the appearance of the Green Lady.

My sister was going to have a baby. She had been suffering a good deal from many causes, and *one* was that her husband, Hay Wemyss, was in a very bad state of health. His sister, Fanny Balfour (since dead), told me the story. Poor Millicent had gone to bed, and Hay and his sister were talking about going to London, which they were about to do in a day or two. They were looking out of one of the windows which had a lovely view, and some terraces had lately been built going down towards the sea.

Wemyss Castle and terraces
photo by the author

The moon was shining brightly, and Hay said to his sister that he felt very *ill*. As they spoke together there was a crash, and part of one of the terraces smashed and fell. He turned to Fanny and said, "I am a dead man! For as a warning to the owner of Wemyss Castle of his early approaching death a piece of masonry always falls!"

Fanny tried to laugh him out of the idea, but he would say and hear no more. In a few days they went to London, and Hay Wemyss of Wemyss Castle died a fortnight before his youngest son was born!' [46]

Balgonie Castle

Fife's Most Actively Haunted Castle
Featured on the front cover of this book

Ghosts of Fife Castle Trail Ref: 12

photo courtesy of Stuart Morris of Balgonie Castle

If you are looking for a traditional Scottish Castle with a friendly laird; a castle full of Ghosts, complete with 14th century barrel-vaulted candle lit charm, open to the public 7 days a week and child friendly, then you have just found one!

Ghostly associations in brief
There are at least 10 ghostly apparitions to be discovered in this fine old Scottish Castle located in the heart of Fife.

Visiting restrictions/fees
The castle and grounds are open to the public 7 days a week from 11am to 5pm unless a wedding or function is taking place. A nominal fee is charged. As part of the family here are Deer Hounds, so dogs are not permitted in the grounds.

Travelling from the east
A915 turn right along the A911 heading for Markinch. Turn left at the sign for Milton and Coaltown of Balgonie. As the road veers to the left continue straight ahead and the castle will come into view on the right after 100 yards.

Travelling from the west
A911 east from Glenrothes signed Leven/Buckhaven. Ignore the first sign to the right signed Milton and Coaltown of Balgonie – take the second turn to the right signed Milton of Balgonie and Coaltown of Balgonie. As the road veers to the left continue straight ahead, the castle will come into view on the right after 100 yards.

On the GOF Castle Trail from Wemyss Castle return to the A955, turn right then first left just before Coaltown of Wemyss. At the end of this road turn right onto the A915. Follow to the roundabout and turn left along the A911 heading for Markinch. Turn left just past the sign for Milton and Coaltown of Balgonie. As the road veers to the left continue straight ahead, the castle will come into view on the right after 100 yards.

The 14th century tower and courtyard.

photo by the author

Balgonie means settlement of the Smiths. Built by Sir Thomas Sibbald of Balgonie in 1360, this is a substantial castle and ruins, with a number of additions and alterations having been made over the centuries. The castle is set in 3 acres of plush green countryside, richly furnished with foxes, kingfishers and birds of prey.

The 14th century tower of the castle is the oldest intact tower in Fife and one of the finest examples of its type in Scotland.

King James IV visited this castle in August 1496 and Mary Queen of Scots stayed here in February 1565. She then ventured to Wemyss Castle and her meeting with her first cousin Lord Darnley on the 17th of that month. This resulted in their marriage at Holyrood in Edinburgh five months later.

In January 1716 Rob Roy MacGregor stayed at Balgonie for a day or two with some 200 clansmen and 20 Hanoverian prisoners he captured in a skirmish at nearby Markinch.

The Balgonie castle website says: 'Other famous visitors to Balgonie Castle have included Daniel Defoe, Dr Benjamin Rush (signatory of the American Declaration of Independence), James Boswell and Dr Johnson.

The 8th Earl of Leven sold Balgonie in 1824 to Sir James Balfour of Whittinghame (grandfather of A. J. Balfour, 1st Earl Balfour, Prime Minister 1902-05) who gave the estate to his second son Charles.

By the 1840s letters were appearing in the Edinburgh press concerning the appalling state of Balgonie. The roofs were later taken off to avoid paying Roof Tax.

Following heavy vandalism of the 1960s [primarily by local kids pulling down ruinous parts of the buildings], the Castle was sold to David Maxwell of Edinburgh in 1971. He carried out restoration to the Tower before selling to the present Laird, Raymond Morris of Balgonie & Eddergoll, in 1985.'[47] The present Laird and Lady Balgonie together with their son are the first occupants of the castle since the 8th Earl of Leven sold the castle in 1824, and over the years they have all experienced some of the apparitions and phenomenon to be found here.

With a history now into its 8th century it isn't surprising the castle is haunted, what is surprising is the sheer number of ghosts reputed to haunt it. The castle is believed to have at least 10 ghostly presences plus many further aspects of what is termed the 'classic haunting'. Visitors and residents over the years have experienced many varied and unexplainable phenomenon here: Noises, smells, sudden temperature changes, fleeting shadows, darting lights, whispering, inaudible conversations, laughter of a woman and the feeling of being touched in a number of its rooms! You would think with all this the castle would be a cold and fearful place, but it appears to be the opposite on both counts. Wood stove heating and benign spirits give the castle a good air and atmosphere all year round. I can't imagine any would say of Balgonie that it has an 'oppressive' atmosphere. With this, an interesting observation is to be found. A few of the neighbouring castles in Fife are the complete opposite. Kellie Castle for example, which you may have read about earlier, is quite the reverse, with it having a number of people unable to enter the building because of the foreboding feelings of dread.

The Ghost of Green Jeanie
In the 15th century the castle was owned by Sir Robert Lundie, son-in-law of John Sibbald. A member of the Lundie family is said to be the ghost of a Green Lady known as 'Green Jeanie'. She haunts the roofless building in the courtyard and is recorded as being a "well known phantom" as far back as 1842. I visited the castle the last Friday in September 2013, the Laird told me she has been seen on the ground floor of the roofless building, and always walks from left to right and is only seen in the building, never in the courtyard.

Green Jeanie has also been seen by Lady Balgonie who describes her as a hooded figure wearing green – the green being a pea green colour. When we were in the courtyard not long after arriving that Saturday and the Laird was talking about the history of the building I saw someone briefly look out of the right hand ground floor window of the roofless building that has an iron grate across it.

The barred window of the roofless building
photo by the author

I didn't see the body, just a face briefly as someone moved right up to one of the square spaces between the iron bars and looked out at us. This is just down from the top of the window and slightly to the right, which on the photo I took on the left shortly after, places it 2 squares down and 2 in from the upper left hand corner. Volunteer workmen are helping with the continual process of refurbishing the castle, and a few were milling around this particular afternoon. With not having long arrived and being near closing time, I thought this was a workman looking to see who the Laird was talking to.

I didn't mention this at the time, knowing how easy it is to be suggestive of such things, but the impression of the face has played on my mind. I knew the workmen were working on the tower and not this section of the castle. It would still have played

The roofless building – location of the sightings of Green Jeanie. The barred window is on its right.
photo by the author

on my mind if I hadn't read Norman Adams book "Haunted Scotland" when I got back home where the Laird gives a few details I had been unable to gather given the short time I had there. Once I read this piece, it made sense of what I had seen. He says "'The Laird believes her favourite walk is between two rooms linked by a doorway. She walks in a left to right direction behind two barred windows, stopping to peer into the walled courtyard from the second window.'"

This second window if she is walking from left to right is the right hand window and the one I had seen the face peer momentarily out of before it went back into the blackness behind. It was only for a brief second – if that, but it was definitely someone peering out.

For Lady Balgonie's account, I never had the privilege of seeing her on my trip to the castle, but when she spoke with Norman, she said "'she saw the ghost when she let out the family's deer-hounds around 2:00 am.'"

The Laird mentioned to me that two painters have also seen Green Jeanie and some of the other ghosts have also been seen with this left to right "circular motion" he called it, meaning they appear to be on a loop, always moving from left to right – never the other way round. It would be easy to think Green Jeanie peering out onto the courtyard gives her an inquisitive air, but with her always repeating the same pattern this is confirmation that she and some of the other ghosts here are impressionistic ghosts, meaning they are recorded images, observable by those who have the sight to 'trigger' the appearance of an apparition into a specific action or sequence. On speaking with the laird subsequently about what I had seen, he told me "she passes the first barred window then peers out of the second. Her face has not been seen as she is wearing a hood." Maybe I am the first to see her face peering out at us. She had dull matt grey skin and wide eyes, looking quite deadpan. The face of the moon! The impression is in my mind even now. Her face was round and filled the square space between the bars. Like a silent anomaly, she was there then she was gone, all very brief, silent, unusual and very rare.

On relating to me his own encounters, the Laird said, "they are always fleeting. Only seen for a few seconds and gone before the mind has time to register what they might be." This is one of the familiar characteristics. As the Laird says "it takes longer for the mind to work out what it has seen than it does for the length of time they appear".

I have always found this to also be the case. They can be so quick. In one respect it is as if they have always been there, then in one blink they are literally gone, leaving you wondering what it was you really saw, but the impression on the mind is always lasting. Having witnessed phenomenon on numerous occasions I can attest to how the mind will do everything it can to make sense of what it is observing – even if we are looking out for them it will still try to give some kind of logic to these experiences. If we look for a simple explanation such as thinking as I did that it was a workman I had seen, we don't then enquire within ourselves any further – until later. It is only when we allow time to ponder the experience, we then realise it wasn't possible for it to have been what we thought it was at the time, with this the nature of what we have experienced then becomes more apparent.

Cover photo, winter at Balgonie Castle.
photo taken by Stuart Morris
of Balgonie Castle

I wasn't there to look for proof or to 'investigate', meaning I wasn't expecting or looking to find anything myself. I was there simply to record the experiences and the phenomenon that had taken place. To find out a little more about the many appearances, and to verify if the information I already had was correct or spurious. There was actually more concentration on my mind to record what the Laird was telling me of the experiences that he, his family and others have had. It was all coupled with concern that I was taking up too much of the dear Lairds valuable time. With it being late afternoon I was sure he must have been looking forward to his tea and a wee dram.

Up until a number of years ago, ghostly vigils were held here. They each 'appear' to have yielded successful results in one form or another, although it is rare for this to be the case. Ghosts are anything but 'perform on demand' entities. The paranormal is such a timidly shy creature when it comes to its observance. Green Jeanie like so many other apparitions is more an incidental encounter, and if you go looking for her, I doubt if you will ever see her. Such is the subtle nature of ghosts.

The following weekend I attended a dinner in Nottingham, which included a number of people from Markinch. I spoke briefly that I had been to Balgonie Castle the previous weekend and had spoken with the laird about Green Jeanie and other phenomenon at the castle. I told them of my experience and it turned out a couple sitting at the same table also saw Green Jeanie, in the same place I saw her when they attended a wedding at the castle 14 years ago.

The proud Laird of Balgonie Castle with one of his family Deer Hounds.
photo by the author

The courtyard. A figure walks from the left to behind the well, another walks by the well towards the wall.
photo by the author

The mix of the many and varied occurrences here, coupled with the frequency of the manifestations and the diversity of independent testimony over the years, is why this castle is the most paranormally active in Fife – if not one of the most actively haunted dwellings to be found anywhere. Certainly for its size this appears to be the case. One of the reasons for this being the castle is lived in 24 hours a day all year round, unlike many dwellings in the care of the NTS or HS where they are only open during the day.

The Laird hasn't seen Green Jeanie himself but he has seen other ghosts here. He was in the courtyard one day when he saw the figure of a 17th century soldier walking by the well towards the opposite wall from the tower.

He appeared to extend his hand out as if opening a door and promptly vanished.

At the same location, his son saw the figure of a man walking from the roofless ruin and disappearing between the well and the back wall. With two different apparitions disappearing at the same spot, it's as if a portal exists between realms at that location.

A 17th century soldier has been seen in the courtyard with a musket, and has also been seen walking through the castle gateway. The figure might be that of David Leslie, or at least a soldier wearing attire not too dissimilar to the portrait on the right. He was the '3rd Earl of Leven and raised a regiment in Edinburgh in 1689 (today they are The King's Own Scottish Borderers)'[48] He fought at the battle of Killiecrankie and became Governor of the Bank of Scotland until his death in 1728.

David, 3rd Earl of Leven[xv]

The Grand Hall Ghosts

The Grand Hall
photo by the author

The barrel-vaulted Grand Hall is full of classic Scottish character and charm. It is also 'the oldest and finest preserved hall in Fife.'[49] Lit by candles and being the most haunted part of the castle, the atmosphere alone here can't fail to transport any who enter back to the 14th century. I have to ask at this point, is there a more fitting location for a banquet? This grand hall hosts many lively weddings and functions and I have to say with such an old intimate space, probably not. Throughout the castle are

---

[xv] Painted by Sir John Baptiste de Medina, National Galleries of Scotland, Edinburgh

many murals the Laird has painted depicting historical scenes in the castles history. Around the Grand Hall are draped many heraldic coats of arms of the families having resided in the castle, which have also been made by the Laird over the years. His work is certainly a labour of love and his artwork is beautifully done.

The Grand Hall

photo courtesy of the Balgonie Castle website

Another ghost inhabiting the castle may be that of the Covenanter Alexander Leslie, Lord of Balgonie and 1st Earl of Leven.

Alexander Leslie (b.1582, d.1661)

He has been seen in the Grand Hall by Lady Balgonie. She had drifted to sleep in an armchair in the hall and awoke to see him looking at her. Dressed in 17th century costume and complete with his goatee beard, she described him as being "grey like a statue". He has also been seen in the Grand Hall by their son.

Alexander Leslie was the Laird of the castle in the 17th century. He was Lord General of the Scottish Army of the Covenanters during the English Civil War and died here in 1661 aged 79. There is a very famous nursery rhyme attributed to him:

There was a crooked man and he walked a crooked mile.
He found a crooked sixpence upon a crooked stile.
He bought a crooked cat, which caught a crooked mouse.
And they all lived together in a little crooked house.

The chair of the Blue Woman
photo by the author

An unassuming chair sits in the far left corner of the Grand Hall. It is difficult to see in this picture, but when you are there and you know the significance of this chair, it becomes the focal of the room. This is because the chair has the ghost of a blue woman sitting on it. She is seated in a long blue dress quietly doing her needlework.

Along the middle of the left hand wall is the ghost of a man, who stands motionless, possibly a servant from the 17th century.

The head of a woman has been seen floating out of the Hall and along the passage into the kitchen next door. She is wearing a large 17th century ruff, but contrary to some reports she has not been decapitated. On the contrary, it appears her body is also present but only her head and her ruff materialise.

In 1900, the *Dundee Courier* reported that a skeleton had been found under the floor of the Grand Hall at Balgonie but no further details of this are known at this time.

When we were in the hall, the Laird spoke of an incident. Two waitresses were laying the tables for a banquet when something touched them when no others were in the room.

Whispering, low level chattering and the laughter of a woman have also been heard in the Grand Hall.

Other phenomenon at the castle includes:
A White Lady in the kitchen
The hooded figure of a man
A man dressed in medieval garb
The smell of pipe tobacco and perfume

The ghost of one of the present Laird and Lady's former family members – a deer hound, has also been seen in the courtyard and on the stairs in the tower.

While Balgonie castle has many apparitions and while there are unseen activities of being touched, voices being heard etc., there doesn't seem to be the archetypal display of poltergeist activity often associated with 'classic hauntings'.

Its absence can only point in one direction – the energies here as I mentioned earlier are benevolent. There is no anger or malice associated with them, which is why there is rarely a feeling of negativity in either the tower or the grounds.

The Present Laird and his Family
The castle is a family residence and is described on their website as being run as "a working living castle." Earlier in the afternoon, before I arrived on the 28th of September 2013 they had just had their 1155th wedding at the castle. Over the years they have had wedding parties from 30 countries.

This is a very hospitable and welcoming family and the enthusiasm of the Laird can be seen in his kind and sincere eyes. Since the Laird and his family came to the castle in 1985, they have passionately committed themselves to its restoration, and have just completed the restoration of the vaulted 14th century kitchen known as Lundie Hall as a ground floor reception area. This is an ongoing process, a lifetime's work, and what they have thus far achieved with a small dedicated troop of volunteers is a credit to them, to Fife and to Scotland. They also have school parties visiting and they take the time and trouble to educate the children in the castles history and no doubt its ghosts!

When you first arrive at Balgonie Castle the first greeting is a Euro sign crossed out, straight away you know this is not an NTS or HS museum piece with plaques, cordoned off areas and overpriced sticky buns. This is a lived in family home that all are invited to explore – within reason of course. From being greeted at the entrance the family here will take good care of you, and when they extend the welcome I received, you will find it difficult to leave both their home, and this ancient seat of ghostly visitations.

My thanks to the Laird for his time in imparting to me some of the experiences they have had here over the years. My thanks also to Green Jeanie and her allowing me to see her face – possibly for the first time.

This is Fife's most haunted residence, it is also one of the most hospitable any will find. I cannot recommend this castle highly enough, and it is well worth a few visits to see how they are progressing with the restoration of this beautiful ancestral seat in the heart of Fife's green landscape.

Refer also to *Green Jean* as part of the introduction to this book, p.8

Balmuto Castle
(Private)

Ghostly associations in brief
The family ghost of Sir Alexander Boswell

Visiting restrictions/fees
This is a private residence in private grounds and I have recorded it here for its ghost, but it is not part of the *GOF Castle Trail.*

Directions
Situated just south of Auchtertool, midway between the B925 and the B9157.

Balmuto Castle is the private residence of the Boswell family and was initially a tower house, built by Sir John Boswell of Balgregie in the 15th century. Mary Queen of Scots stayed here on occasion when she was on one of her tours across Fife.

As with so many castles, Balmuto has undergone many alterations over the centuries. It was almost left to decay and ruin in the first half of the 20th century with the family no longer living there. In the 1970s the castle was rescued by the American arm of the Boswell family. Following substantial renovation, the castle of today has been restored to its heyday.

The castle has a family ghost in residence, namely one Sir Alexander Boswell, who fought in a duel near the castle on the 26th March 1822. He had been writing against a politician named James Stuart of Dunearn who found out about the words against him and challenged their author to a duel. He had aimed to miss but his opponent aimed to kill, and the bullet from the gun shattered his collarbone. Boswell was carried on a door to the castle and died of his injuries the following day. His ghost may still be seen roaming the precincts of the castle.

Aberdour Castle
Ghosts of Fife Castle Trail Ref: 13

Ghostly associations in brief
Poltergeist type activity, a presence and the ghost of a white lady

Visiting restrictions/fees
Run by Historic Scotland the castle is open to the public. Opening times and entrance fees apply.

Directions
Signposted and situated just off the A921 in Aberdour

The new and the old
photo by the author

Aberdour Castle is a 12th century fortified hall-house, standing amid a 16th to 17th century walled garden. This is possibly the oldest standing castle in Scotland.

The castle has had many additions over the centuries with the main family residents being the Mortimers, the Randolphs and the Douglases.

Stonemasons conducting work on the castle a number of years ago arrived one morning to hear the sounds of furniture being moved around in the hall above – there was no one in the castle at the time. When they investigated the room with the custodian all the heavy furniture had been moved to the centre of the room! No explanation has ever been found for this unusual disturbance.

Many years ago a presence was felt where the original entrance gates to the castle were positioned. Animals are sensitive to the unseen and they would shy away from this entrance.

A white lady has also been seen roaming the area.

Pitreavie Castle
Ghosts of Fife Castle Trail Ref: 14

Ghostly associations in brief
The Green Lady, Grey Lady, Headless Highlander

Visiting restrictions/fees
Set in its own grounds this building comprises of private residences and can only be viewed from the outside.

Directions
Located between Dunfermline and Rosyth off the A823 along the eastern end of Castle Drive.

Situated on the southern edge of Dunfermline, the estate land was once owned by Lady Christina Bruce, the sister of Robert the Bruce. The castle itself was built on the land in 1615 by Sir Henry Wardlaw, 1st Baronet of Pitreavie and Chamberlain to King James VI wife Queen Ann.

It has now been converted into a number of private residences and the grounds developed into private housing and a business park.

It has undergone many alterations over the years with the north and west walls being encompassed into the present dwelling. The castle was sold in 1922 to the RAF as a base to coordinate coastal operations between the RAF and the Navy. Known as *RAF Pitreavie Castle* it remained active all the way up until 1996 when the base was closed and the castle was sold to a private firm.

In the following account from David Beveridge's *Between the Ochils and Forth* 1888 he says 'the old house of Pitreavie seems to have been . . . honoured by the attendance of a ghost, whose special habitat was a small weird-looking chamber in the uppermost storey on the north side of the house. I never could learn what appearance the spirit was supposed to assume; but so fixed and persistent was the belief in it, that not many years ago, when the house was empty, and a number of harvest labourers were bivouacked there, nothing could induce them to do otherwise than congregate together in one large room.'[50]

The following article concerning Pitreavie was placed in the BBC's Doomsday project in 1986. It is a short anonymous piece speaking of Pitreavie Castle and the Dunfermline area and clarifies what Beveridge was unable to ascertain about the haunting:

'The Supernatural in Pitreavie
There are quite a few ghosts in our local history. The most famous being the Green Lady who is supposed to haunt Pitreavie Castle. The story grew that her husband was killed in battle in 1651. She died of a broken heart and is still in search of him. The Grey Lady's story is very much the same. Another ghost is the Headless Highlander who haunts Pitreavie Castle. He is supposed to go round looking for his comrades and groaning when he finds them dead.'[51]

Another version of the above at Pitreavie ties in both this headless highlander and the battle of 1651: 'Tradition says that this site is haunted by the ghost of a headless highlander who was killed at the nearby battle of Pitreavie in 1651.'[52]

The Battle of Pitreavie took place on the 20th July 1651. It was more a massacre than a battle. Staged between Cromwell's troops and Highlanders from the Maclean Clan, it is believed between 1600 and 2000 highlanders were massacred in the battle, with nearly the same again being taken prisoner and few casualties on Cromwell's side. A band of highlanders went to Pitreavie Castle for sanctuary, but Wardlaw did more than to just refuse them entry. An old account of this dark episode which leads up to what he did to the highlanders states: 'Before sounding the attack, the brave Sir John Brown ordered his men to kneel and pray for success to their arms; immediately after which the battle commenced, and continued for about six hours, when the Scots retreated to Pitreavie, but only to renew the conflict, which now raged with terrific violence for another two hours, when the Scots, after a most gallant resistance, were subdued. Mr. Coventry says – "When the battle was lost, the Highlanders fled to the Castle of Pitreavie for an asylum, invoking the Virgin Mary for protection, and aid, and in their native dialect, cried aloud, 'Oigh,

oigh!' They put their backs to the wall of the Castle (or house), and continued to protect themselves with their drawn swords, when those within threw down stones from the roof and bartizan upon the poor fellows and killed them." It was often remarked, after this "inhuman treatment," that, from that day, the Wardlaws of Pitreavie "fell awa' like snaw off a dyke."[53] ["fell away like snow off a dyke"]. The Wardlaw's from that day were cursed by the Maclean's for what they had done and were haunted by the highlanders they killed.

Pitfirrane Castle
Ghosts of Fife Castle Trail Ref: 15
Dunfermline Golf Club
(Private – members only)

photo by the author

Ghostly associations in brief
General paranormal activity

Visiting restrictions/fees
This is a busy private golf club. I have included it in the castle tour as it is open to visitors at certain times of the day, generally in the mornings, but tends to be more for golf enquiries and guests of members than general members of the public. Dress code restrictions also apply. No jeans, football colours, tracksuits, collarless shirts and mobiles must be on silent etc.

Directions
Situated two miles west of Dunfermline, left off the A994.

The castle dates back at least to the 14th century. Throughout its history it was the home of the Halkett family until the death of Miss Madeline Halkett in 1951. The estate was then sold to the Carnegie Dunfermline Trust and became the clubhouse for the Dunfermline Golf Club overlooking an 18 Hole Golf Course which opened in 1953. Up until that time it is said to have been the oldest inhabited house in Fife.

The Peoples Journal in 1970 reported that doors were left open and rooms were lit up which had neither gas nor electricity. The phenomenon was witnessed by several people in 1970.[54]

The castle has also been subject to more recent poltergeist type activity in the bar and a number of its rooms, and has been the subject of at least one vigil by paranormal researchers.

Loch Leven Castle
Ghosts of Fife Castle Trail Ref: 16

On the GOF Castle Trail we step out of Fife briefly into Perth and Kinross whilst heading north round Loch Leven with a few castles en-route to Falkland Palace. This is loosely following the 1891 border boundary between Fife and Perth and Kinross. By doing so the opportunity is afforded to take a look at the ruins of 3 haunted castles. They are so closely bordered to the Kingdom that to exclude them would be an injustice to any interested in haunted castles. They are each run by Historic Scotland and span the route in a relatively short proximity to each other.

Ghostly associations in brief
The Ghost of Mary Queen of Scots

Visiting restrictions/fees
The castle is viewable from the shore and accessible by boat. Run by Historic Scotland opening times and fees apply. The castle is open during the summer months and the modest entrance fee includes the ferry to the island. The following is from the Historic Scotland website for the castle:

'The castle is located on an island in Loch Leven and can be reached by passenger boat. The passenger boat is not equipped to carry passengers in wheelchairs. Water levels and weather conditions may make access difficult for visitors with limited mobility.

Once on the island, access is over grass, which can be muddy depending on the water levels in the surrounding loch. The castle towers are not suitable for visitors with limited mobility as they accessed by narrow stairs.'[55]

Directions
'The pier [for the boat] is signed from nearby Kinross. Parking is available 90 metres from the boat departure point.'[56]

Built around 1300 it was here that Mary Queen of Scots was forced to sign her abdication of the throne in favour of her 13 month old son James I in 1567. She was imprisoned here from June 1567 to May 1568 when she was helped to escape by the family who owned the castle by dressing as a servant and fleeing to Niddry Castle in Lothian.

The castle which was in ruins by the 18th century is believed to be haunted by her, her presence is especially felt in the round Glassin Tower – on the south-east corner of the castle, which still remains and is where she spent most of her time in captivity.

The castle on the island can be seen from many areas and can also be seen whilst travelling north on the M90 – should you find yourself passing in the winter months when the ferry is closed.

Burleigh Castle
Ghosts of Fife Castle Trail Ref: 17

Ghostly associations in brief
Haunted by the Ghost of Grey Maggie

Visiting restrictions/fees
Maintained by Historic Scotland, the castle grounds are open to the public with no restrictions or entrance fees. A nearby house has keys to the castle upon request – given acceptable time parameters.

Directions
The castle is just outside the east side of Milnathort on the left beside the A911.

On the GOF Castle Trail take the A922 through Kinross to Milnathort and follow the signs towards Glenrothes along the A911. The castle is just outside the east side of Milnathort on the left beside the road.

The fine ruins of this Jacobean Tower House were built in 1500 on an older timber site incorporating a mote. It was occupied by the Balfour's of Burleigh for hundreds of years. Robert Balfour, the 5th Lord of Burleigh was involved in the Jacobite uprising of 1715.

The roof of this castle has long gone, but apart from that this unusual structure still appears relatively intact.

For the haunting of this castle there is little to say, other than she is an elusive apparition by the name of 'Grey Maggie.' From this we can assume she is either dressed in grey or her pallid features have given rise to her name. No other details seem to be available at this time about who she is or why she haunts this location. Visiting is the only way to see her so the castle is well worth coming to for this reason alone.

Balvaird Castle
Ghosts of Fife Castle Trail Ref: 18

photo by the author

Ghostly associations in brief
A haunted room and a ghostly male figure

Visiting restrictions/fees
Maintained by Historic Scotland, the castle grounds are open to the public with no restrictions or entrance fees. The tower house is restricted to only being open

at certain times of the year such as when the *Fife Doors Open Day* event takes place.

Directions
The castle is two miles east of Glenfarg off the A912 Perth to Gateside road.

On the GOF Castle Trail from Burleigh take the A911 a short distance back into Milnathort, turning right onto the B996 which turns into the A91 St. Andrews road. Just after the Gateside Inn turn left onto the A912 signed for Perth. The castle is around two miles along this road off to the right opposite the road to Newton of Balcanquhal.

Like Loch Leven Castle and Burleigh, this castle is also in Perth and Kinross – literally only a few yards from the Fife border. Unlike these other two, until 1891 Balvaird was actually in Fife. In that year, the boundary commissioners of the newly formed Fife County Council (1889) changed the goal posts of Fife. They moved some of the counties boundaries, and areas of Fife's heritage such as Balvaird were lost to Perth and Kinross. However, Fife also gained in the deal, with places such as Culross now becoming part of the Kingdom.

Balvaird Castle is a red and grey stone structure built around 1500 on the site of an older structure for its first occupants Sir Andrew Murray and his wife Margaret Barclay. The structure comprises an L shaped Tower House which is still intact, while the courtyards surrounding its inner angle are now in ruins. Around the 17th century it became the family home of the Earls of Mansfield who still hold the property. It commands panoramic views of the surrounding landscape including the Lomond Hills to the south-east.

The tower is believed to have a haunted room where some mortals have been affrighted once inside. The ghost that haunts this place may be one of the former Lord Murray's before the Earls of Mansfield took up residence.

Falkland Palace
Ghosts of Fife Castle Trail Ref: 19

Ghostly associations in brief
The Grey Lady and an ominous feeling in certain rooms

Visiting restrictions/fees
Run by the National Trust for Scotland opening times and fees apply.

Directions
The Palace is in the heart of Falkland, signposted off the A912.

On the GOF Castle Trail from Balvaird Castle go back to the A91, turning left. Following this road the signs for Falkland Palace will come into view with a right turn onto the A912 for Falkland.

Falkland Palace is a very unique property. Its imposing fortress style structure has one of the most sold and chunky feels of any castle, and in many ways its location is quite unexpected being situated in the centre of the village.

photo by the author

The Palace grew in the first four decades of the 16th century into what we see today out of a former castle and home of the MacDuff's. Built by James IV and James V as a Royal Palace, James V died here of wounds sustained in the battle of Solway Moss only 6 days after the birth of Mary Stuart at Linlithgow Palace. It is said he died after he received the news of her birth. This made Mary the new Queen and she stayed here on numerous visits to Fife, hawking and hunting the nearby woods for wild boar. The Palace was set on fire by Oliver Cromwell in the 17th century and remained a ruin until 1887 when the Marquess of Bute began its restoration. The property is still owned by the Bute's and run by the NTS.

Photo taken by John Patrick in 1867

For such an impressive structure there is surprisingly very little reported paranormal activity here. The following is from the NTS Website:[57] 'The National Trust for Scotland's Falkland Palace near Cupar is a property with a long history. As Hallowe'en draws near, the conservation charity has unveiled stories of its ghosts. The palace, which has strong connections with the Stuarts, has reported a number of ghostly sightings over the years. The Tapestry Gallery is said to be haunted by a white or grey lady. One account has the ghost moving along the length of the gallery before disappearing through a wall, where there had formerly been a door. She is also described as emitting a 'greyish' light. The lady is said to have waited in vain for her lover, who never returned from battle.

And staff members have had some strange experiences there too.

Sonia Ferrás-Mañá Head Gardener at Falkland takes up the tale. She explains:

"I am a great believer that old houses have 'energy residues' or ghosts. I have had two experiences at the palace. One day I was coming up the drive at dusk after a bike ride when I saw a thick, very real shadow moving on the East Range. I'm told a ghost called the "Grey Lady" walks in that area.

"The other experience was different. I was looking around a bedroom in Lord Bute's flat, a lovely one, with fantastic ceiling decorations. I was there with a companion and we felt very unwanted in the room, as if we were intruders. We had a very bad feeling, like some energy was surrounding us. We left quickly!'"

Recently another NTS staff member at Falkland Palace described by one of her friends as a sober, matter of fact woman, and not one for making up stories, saw the Grey Lady gliding along the central isle of the chapel.

In the early 1800s Sir Walter Scott and a companion saw a ghost in the ruins of Falkland Palace which strengthened his belief at the time in their existence. So it would seem the ghost of the Grey Lady spans at least 200 years.

Refer also to *Falkland, Covenanter Hotel*, p.156

Pitcairlie House
Ghosts of Fife Castle Trail Ref: 20

photo by the author

Ghostly associations in brief
The Ghost of Green Jean

Visiting restrictions/fees
Part of the house is hired out for self-catering holidays so the ideal way to visit this old castle is to stay here. It is possible to view the property briefly from the outside, but privacy should be respected and maintained.

Directions

Situated off to the left, halfway between Auchtermuchty and Newburgh on the B936 road.

Pitcairlie House is a 16th century castle with alterations through each successive century to the present, with the main structure being developed at the turn of the 19th century. In the 16th century the estate formed part of the land Mary Queen of Scots toured whilst hunting and stalking. In the late 19th to the early 20th century Pitcairlie was home to Mrs Agnes Cathcart. She was interested in magical pursuits, and was one of the early members of a Victorian Magical Organisation known as the Society of the Golden Dawn in 1894. She was a member of the Edinburgh temple, known as Amen-Ra. She remained a member until the schism of 1901 when the Order then foundered. The house remained with the Cathcart's until the 1990s when it was sold and turned into a hotel. It has also been a venue for weddings and corporate events together with facilities for holidays with self-catering cottages in the grounds. Today part of the house can be hired out for self-catering holidays.

The 16th century tower and battlements
photo by the author

After placing a short advertisement in one of the local newspapers requesting information for this book, I received among the replies a letter concerning an apparition known as 'Green Jean'. Written in 1989 by a lady living in Arbroath it reads as follows:

Dear Sir,

This story of a haunting is about a ghost called 'Green Jean' and is said to haunt a gateway (a trysting place of this lady) on the Newburgh to Auchtermuchty road at an old mansion house called Pitcairlie.

I don't know how long ago this happened but the story goes that 'Jean' the daughter of the laird of Pitcairlie fell in love with a young footman and they had their trysting place near this gate. When her father discovered about this, in his rage he slew the young man – in the house and 'Jean' in her distress threw herself over the battlements.

This story was often told to me when I was young and stayed at a neighbouring farm called Easter Lumbernie. Any time we went down that way in late evening we always ran past in case we should see the ghost.

The housekeeper there in my time once said she would show me the bloodstains on the upper floor – when the master was away – but sadly the opportunity never came!

I often wonder if that story is still known.

Yours Sincerely,
Mrs Agnes Henderson

As I mentioned in the introduction I received another letter around about the same time also relating to a 'Green Jean' it had a very similar story attached to it, but her appearance is in a different house, this time at Kinglassie House.

Refer to Kinglassie House for the second letter, p.172

Through researching this book I have found 'Green Jean' to be the most popular name for a ghost in Fife. She is even more popular than the ghost of Mary Queen of Scots who hunted here and is reputed to haunt numerous buildings in the Kingdom and at least 14 altogether across Scotland. Could some of the reports of 'Green Jean' be Mary herself?

Denmylne Castle
Ghosts of Fife Castle Trail Ref: 21

Ghostly associations in brief
A female apparition

Visiting restrictions/fees
The water mill can be observed with no restrictions. Being by the roadside the ruins of the castle can easily be viewed, but it sits on private grounds and permission should be sought to observe any closer.

Directions
The castle is located just opposite a quarry, on the left of the A913, a mile past Newburgh when heading towards Cupar.

An engraving of the castle from 1791

Denmylne Castle is a 16th century dovecot tower house. The castle was residence to the Balfour family for over 200 years when it was sold to one Major General John Scott of Balcomie in 1772.

Perhaps he only bought it on a whim after his wife left him for another man the year before as the Major General never lived there, and it started falling into disrepair shortly after.

As the engraving above attests, in less than 20 years it had lost its roof, so it must already have been in a fair state of disrepair by the time he acquired it – which is also a good enough reason why he never lived in it. It now stands in a very ruinous condition on the private grounds of another house. The following excerpt about the castle is from John Leighton writing in 1840: 'Denmiln Castle for a generation was a centre of learning and refinement, the resort of the most

Denmylne Castle 2013
photo by the author

eminent in literature at the time, and the meeting-place of all who had the promotion of learning and the intellectual advancement of Scotland at heart. The great merits of Sir Andrew Balfour[xvi] as a naturalist, physician, and scholar, are commemorated, not only by Sir Robert Sibbald, in the *Memoria Balfouriana*, and elsewhere; but also by Professor John Walker, in his Essays on Natural History.'[58]

Nearby are the ruins of an old water mill, which is where the castle gets its name. It means Kings Mill from when the lands were granted to the Balfour's. The lintel above the doorway at the top of the stairs shown in the photo on the right has MB & ID

The ruined Water Mill with castle in background
photo by the author

with the date 1625. The mill also relates to the castles ghost, as told here by Alexander Laing in 1876:

'It was implicitly believed that the ghost of "the Lady of Denmiln" wandered, or, to use the expression invariably applied to ghosts, "gaed"[xvii] at nights around her old residence, restless because of her cheatrie[xviii] in selling the meal ground at the mill, and muttering to herself:

"The little lippie[xix] and the licht stane[xx]
Gars[xxi] me wander here my lane.[xxii]"[59]

Unless you know your Scots, at first sight this doesn't make much sense. But with a little deciphering (referring to my translated footnotes) we have: A little

---

[xvi] Sir Andrew Balfour (d.1694). Founder of the Botanical Gardens in Edinburgh.

[xvii] Old Scots word meaning 'go'

[xviii] Cheatrie is cheatery or cheated – fraud; a deliberate deception

[xix] A lippie is an old Scots dry measure. 1 lippie = .49 gallons or 2.26 litres.

[xx] Old Scots; licht is light, and stane is stone, meaning a measure – a weight. A Scots stone was standardised in 1661 to equal 16 Scots pounds. She was using a measure that was lighter. So a 'light stone' is a short measure.

[xxi] Gars is old Scots for compel or compels

[xxii] Old Scots for own

water in the ground meal to make it heavier, together with a false weight in her favour, compels her to wander here on her own. So the upshot here is that she sold the meal in short measure and for cheating she now wanders the grounds wrestling with her conscience.

Fernie Castle Hotel
Ghosts of Fife Castle Trail Ref: 22

photo by the author

Ghostly associations in brief
The ghost of a Green Lady

Visiting restrictions/fees
This hotel is open to both residents and non-residents all year round.

Directions
The castle is midway along the A92 Dundee to Glenrothes road by Letham.

On the GOF Castle Trail from Denmylne continue along the A913 toward Cupar, turn right onto the A92 and Fernie Castle Hotel is signposted on the left after two miles.

Built around 1353 its first inhabitant was the Earl of Fife, Duncan 13th. In 1680 it became the residence of the Balfours of Burleigh who took part in the massacre of Archbishop Sharpe on Magus Moor one year earlier. Refer to p.195

The castle has now been transformed into a charming hotel set in 17 acres of secluded woodland, with walks and its own loch to the rear adding to its Scottish charm. The Keep Bar dating back to 1530 is an ideal location to sample a malt and ponder the ghost that haunts this castle – which is believed to be a green lady. During the Protestant persecutions by the Catholics Prelates, in retribution for Sharpe's death the young Laird of Fernie was murdered and his wife threw herself out of a window. Falling to her death her ghost wanders the hotel wearing a long green dress as she looks for her lost husband.

The Scotland Magazine ran a story about Fernie Castle Hotel written by Roddy Martine in May 2004, entitled: *Visiting those old Haunts* and read as follows:

'FERNIE CASTLE HOTEL, FIFE

For Neil and Mary Blackburn, who own Fernie Castle Hotel at Letham, in Fife, objects being moved around are part of everyday life. While renovation was in progress, Neil was on top of a ladder in the midst of decorating a room when the paintbrush he was using fell to the floor.

In the meantime, a member of staff came into the room and placed some keys on the mantelpiece. Neil carried on working with another brush and then turned to find that the first brush had been placed on the mantelpiece while the bunch of keys had somehow attached themselves to his tool belt.

A young couple who stayed overnight complained that their bed had started shaking in the night. The Blackburns appear unfazed about this, and most of their guests do not seem to mind. Sometimes they even claim to have enjoyed the experience.

One lady who had retired to her bedroom in the west tower after a superb dinner was just about to fall asleep when there was a knock at the door. When she opened the door, there was nobody there.

The following night it happened again, but this time a lady came into the room wearing a green dress, and then disappeared through a wall. She also has the unofficial reputation of causing electrical faults in the building.'[60]

Unaccountable electrical faults in the building have affected anything utilising electricity. This is a common feature of paranormal phenomenon.

'Intelligent' Spirits is a term I use for the spirits of the departed who have awareness.

To affect physical disturbance as a notification of their presence, anything utilising an electrical current to make it function is easier to affect than trying to open or close a door or window for example.

Electrical appliances already have a power source, so Intelligent Spirits use their own energy *indirectly* by coupling with the electrical energies operating the appliances to then power or depower something. Whereas anything not directly driven by electrical energy requires a direct force to affect its behaviour, and this requires the utilisation of more external energy.

Lordscairnie Castle
Ghosts of Fife Castle Trail Ref: 23

Ghostly associations in brief
The Ghost of Earl Beardie

Visiting restrictions/fees
No restrictions at present, but care should be taken if crops are being grown in the field when visiting.

Directions
This Tower House Castle is situated some two and a half miles northwest of Cupar in an area known as Moonzie.

On the GOF Castle Trail from Fernie Castle turn right back onto the A92 retracing your steps back to the A913 junction. Take the right exit towards Cupar. Take the next left signposted for Moonzie and Lordscairnie Guest House and continue along this road.

photo by the author

The castle is not seen from the main road, nor is it seen along the first part of the approach towards Lordscairnie Guest House, but after around half a mile once over the rise of the Torr of Moonzie, this visually impressive structure appears in a field on the left of the road. It stands as a massive square slab of dark stone towering on the horizon to some sixty feet in height. These are the large heavy almost foreboding ruins of Lordscairnie. It is said to be the ancient seat of Earl Beardie, (Alexander, 4th Earl of Crawford who died in 1453)'[61] but the present castle wasn't built until after his death. It was built in 1495 by Sir Alexander Lindsay, the 7th Earl of Crawford. There is however, archaeological evidence to support dwellings here before then, spanning all the way back through the Iron Age to prehistoric times.

The following legend of Lordscairnie is a shared one with that of Glamis Castle in Angus. It is from the pages of *The Kingdom of Fife: Its Ballads and Legends*, an 1899 anthology written by Robert Boucher. The occasional Scots word or obscure reference makes it quite difficult to read in places so I have added descriptive footnotes and translations in brackets where applicable.

This is a wonderful old Scots story, a rare and atmospheric tale of great antiquity which I hope you will enjoy.

'Beardie – The Tiger-Earl

AMID the hills in the north of Fife, and about three miles from the County town [Cupar], stand the ruins of Lordscairnie, or, as it is commonly called, Earl Beardie's Castle.

> Grayly draped,
> With streaming grass, appears low built but strong,
> The ruinous donjon as a Knoll of moss,
> The battlement overtopped with ivytods,[xxiii]
> A home of bats, in every tower an owl.

For centuries it has stood the attacks of the ruthless fingers of Father Time, and, though now a mouldering ruin, it is still magnificent in its grim decay.

A rough, tumble-down, wild-catlike feudal knight was the builder of it, Alexander, Earl Crawford, a scion of the "antique race" of the Lindsay's, and traditionally great-great-great-grand-son — many times over — of Thor, the ancient Scandinavian deity, and therefore of Fornioter, the mythological King of the North[xxiv].

> Honoured and feared he was, but little loved;
> For e'en his bounty bore a show of sternness,
> And when his passion's roused, he was a Satan
> For wrath and injury.

He lived during the reigns of the early Jameses — that is, four and a half centuries ago. His contemporaries spoke of him as "The Tiger," on account of his ferocious disposition, or, as the early manuscripts have it, dictus Tigris qui totam Angvsiam in subiec Hom tenuit — because he held the whole of Angus

---

xxiii A clump of ivy.
xxiv A demi-god of Norway and an Elder of the Earth.

in thraldom. He was also nicknamed "Earl Beardie" from his great beard, though one authority states that he was well known by the designation of "Beard the best of them," referring to the irreverence which he entertained for King James's courtiers.

The Earl was one of those petty, though powerful, princes who, in those troubled times, ruled Scotland, and who, in mutual league, would brook no curb, and hesitated not in defying even the authority of the Sovereign himself. Foolhardy and braggart at times he seems to have been. When his great antagonist, the Earl of Huntly defeated him on Ascension Day 1452, at Brechin, through the treachery of one of his vassals, the Tiger exclaimed on reaching the Castle of Finhaven "that he would be content to hing seven years in hell by the breers o' the e'e" (i.e., the eyelashes) could he but pay back to his enemy, tooth for tooth, for that day's dishonour. On that occasion the Lindsay's soldiers were dressed in green; hence arose the superstitious proverb that;

> A Lindsay with green
> Should never be seen!

Apparently it was the Earls pride more than his power that had been hurt by this reverse, for soon after he stormed through Angus, launching forth his terrific vengeance on those who had deserted his cause or refused him their aid, devastating their estates, razing their strongholds, and leaving only desolation and ruin in his train. A few months later — the Douglases, who had been Beardie's staunchest allies, having meanwhile been compelled to lay down their arms — the Earl went Gibeonitishly[xxv] to the King, clad in old and tattered garments, bareheaded and barefooted, threw himself at his liege's feet, and with floods of tears and an avalanche of sobbing and sighing that choked back the pitiful petition, prayed for mercy, which the King in his clemency freely and frankly extended to him.

Thus the wild renegade knight was subdued and became "a faithful subject and sicker targe [a protective shield] to the King"; but the reconciliation was of very short duration, for the Earl died in September 1453, and was buried regid

---

[xxv] This is quite a subtle analogy. In biblical terminology the Gibeonites lived in the Promised Land before the Israelites who would have expelled them, but the Gibeonites put on worn out clothing as if they had done the same as the Israelites and come into the land themselves and the Israelites lived with them.

'prope pompd (with princely pomp) in the Greyfriars of Dundee, beside the ashes of his forefathers.

The good that men do "is often interred with their bones"; so has it been with the Tiger-Earl. What few redeeming features his lawless character possessed tradition has written in water. His repentance, sincere and self-reproachful as it certainly was, has disappeared in the mists of time, but tradition has cradled and nurtured, for generations yet unborn, the story of the Tiger-Earls Doomsday encounter with the Archenemy of mankind.

Let it be understood that Beardie was an adept at the "deil's buiks." [Devils books] We should say nowadays that he was an expert gambler — a gamester to overcome at dice and cards at the table was a task and a half indeed. In a moment of recklessness he had sworn that he would play at cards on the Sabbath Day with whoever should dare — ay, even though the Evil One himself were to appear.

It was the Ides of March when the Tiger threw his daunting challenge in the teeth of heaven and earth, and already one could faintly hear the pinion-flap of the equinoctial gales. A fortnight later the storm broke. The intervening days had been stormy ones, too, for the Earl. He had been raging through Angus on his devastating career, but things, somehow or other, had not gone so well with him, and he withdrew to the Castle of Glamis to recuperate. Still he felt dull — an evil destiny seemed ever to be dogging his footsteps as perniciously as his own shadow — and on the Sabbath following his return[xxvi] he retired after dinner to his well-appointed playroom for rest, — perhaps to listen to the battling storm without, which struck just then a chord responsive to his own ruffled feelings.

Scarcely had he entered the room when he became conscious that his was not the only presence there. Casting his keen eyes round the apartment, the fitful light of the tapers revealed to his steady gaze a man of towering stature, majestic countenance, and baleful eyes that seemed to burn with fire. Yet there was about him an air of stately melancholy, and Beardie felt that he stood face to face with the Chief of the Fallen Cherubim. No sound had heralded the stranger's entrance.

> In shape and gesture proudly eminent
> He stood — a tower; his form had not yet lost
> All his original brightness, nor appeared

[xxvi] The story of Lordscairnie is very similar to that of the legend of Glamis Castle. The author in this instance has Earl Beardie stopping off at Glamis on his way back to Lordscairnie as a subtle reminder of how the two stories in legend appear to be linked.

Less than an Archangel ruined, and the excess
Of glory obscured.
His blazing eyes, like two bright shining shields,
Did burn with wrath, and sparkled living fire,
As two broad beacons, set in open fields,
So flamed his eyes with rage and rancorous[xxvii] fire;
But far within, as in a hollow glade,
Those glaring lamps were set that made a dreadful shade.

He was apparelled in graceful attire, well befitting such a playroom as that which Beardie possessed. His mysterious and startling appearance, however, altogether discomposed the Earl, whose fingers involuntarily sought the hilt of his sword, while all the time he regarded him with riveted eyes as he would some venomous reptile.

"Nay! forbear, foolish knight! thou canst not injure me," said the Arch-fiend of the Powers of Darkness in his most mincing tones, and he favoured the Tiger with a look that might have withered a more dauntless man than he. "I have heard of thy vain boast, and now am I come to pick up the gauntlet which thou hast so ruthlessly thrown down. Until the shadows of night are fled away, and the cock proclaims the approach of the morning, so long, and no longer, shall this warfare of ours last."

"Amen!" grunted the Earl, for he despised the fiend more than he actually feared him. "When the shadows begin to fall aslant the earth towards the west, thou sayest, must we stop. So be it. I hold thee to thy word, and thou shalt fail, Auld Nickie-ben — thou shalt fail." Thus spake the Earl dauntingly, though racked with dark forebodings.

"And if thou failest— if thy attempt should prove vain, as I am sure it will," said Sathan with measured sarcasm, a sinister smile meanwhile distorting his countenance, "thou shalt be

...hurled headlong down
To bottomless perdition; there to dwell
In adamantine chains and penal fire."

The Tiger's lip curled with bitter scorn. "Great is your power, I ken," he replied. "Aft-times I've heard the douce [quiet], honest creatures hereaboots tell hoo [hereabouts tell how] they've heard ye rustling through the boar trees on

---

xxvii Long lasting resentment, deep seated ill-will

dreary wintry nichts, or flyin' [nights, or flying] on the wings o' the tempest, or hauntin' the lonely bypaths to lure poor benighted vagabonds to their destruction. Na, faith, Auld Nickie-Ben, thou art neither bleart [whining], nor blate [bashful], nor blind."

Beardie paused, and the Demon looked at him with an amused smile.

"I've heard the story, too," the Knight went on, "hoo ye played your spitefu' pranks, ye auld twa-faced scoondrel, [how you played your spiteful pranks, you old two-faced scoundrel] on Adam and his fair sweetheart Eve, in the bonnie gairden o' Paradise, an' a'maist [and almost] sent the lot o' us to everlastin' condemnation. Ay, an' just an 'oor or twa ago ye sklented [in just an hour or two you sided] your cursed jokes on my canty [lively], crouse [confident] henchman, guid Dauvit Bethune [good David Beaton[xxviii]], wha [who] never yet did onything [anything] or onybody [anybody] harm. He happened to hear your eerie drone coming along the dykeside, an' cam' rinnin' in wi' his hair standin' on end [and came running in with his hair standing on end] like a hedgehog's quills. Guidsakes! ye nearly frichtened the life oot o' him. [Godsakes! You nearly frightened the life out of him] My hert was wae for the honest carle." [My heart was always for the honest common people.]

A silence deep as death followed this harangue of the warlike Earl who seldom gave vent to such lengthy orations. Then Michael answered — "Nevertheless, you cannot gainsay the firmness of my conquests. Here I have come to avenge no injury. No! revenge is not in my line; 'tis a thing I scorn with implacable hatred. Use all thy powers, haughty chieftain; employ all thy arts, thy devices, thy strategy, but take heed lest thy over-weening peacockishness have a terrible down coming."

And so the strife commenced — fallen angel and fallen man, the immortal and the mortal, confronting each other in deadly feud.

Outside the wind howled furiously, ending ever and anon in a low and dreadful wail. The massive battlements quivered before the mocking ire of its rushing pinions, which startled the night birds and made them scream dolefully. But the combatants inside the castle heard none of these sounds. They shuffled and cut and dealt the cards; trick followed trick, and game followed game; they played and finessed and forced — silently, warily, unceasingly.

The hours sped past; seven — eight — nine. For a while they ceased playing, the odds, if anything, against Beardie. On his brow stood great beads

---

xxviii Cardinal of St. Andrews in the 16th century. Bit of poetic licence here as the Cardinal wasn't around for another 100 years after Beardie's death.

of perspiration. He rose, and walked to a side-table on which was a bell. He rung it sharply, and a servant instantly appeared. "Here, set afore us a flagon o' wine, an' tak' care ye dinna keep us waitin'." ["Here, set before us a flagon of wine, and take care you don't keep us waiting."]

The servant, instead of complying, stared in blank astonishment at his master, unable either to move or speak. His dumbfounded gaze wandered from his lord's perspiring face to the table upon which, at either extremity, lay the cards. At one end they were being toyed with by an invisible hand. Superstitious awe seized hold of him, as a faint mocking laugh smote upon his ear.

"Speak, knave! What's the matter wi' ye demanded the Earl, livid with rage. "Bring the wine at once, and some snaps."

The man hastily withdrew, and in a minute or two re-entered, bearing in one hand a massive goblet embossed with holy angels and filled with the choicest wine, and in the other a platter covered with the nicest home-made snaps, which formed a tit-bit with Earl Crawford. Nickie-Ben glanced at the angelic ornamentation on the flagon, and his fierce eyes flashed fire. The vassal in amazement retired.

"Queer churl that," remarked the Arch-fiend, the moment the door had closed. "One would think that he and I were great strangers. Ha! ha! ha! Tiger! Last week I helped him in his wolfish villainy while thou were at Brechin. Ha! ha! ha! He shall know more of me hereafter." And Auld Hornie laughed a horrid, unearthly laugh as he said this. "Better success this time, Sir. Knight, or may Heaven help you!"

The Earl grinned self-confidently. His pride was matchless. The effort, however, was too much. The hot wine and the hotter snaps went down the wrong road, and burned his throat. Springing to his feet with a yell of pain and rage, and an awful imprecation, he spluttered and cursed in turn, gnashing his teeth furiously together.

"Sit down, friend," said Nickie-Ben in his most mellow tones.

Beardie obeyed the injunction, and they set to again, as earnestly as before, deftly frisking the cards over the table. Many a time had the Earl played at cards, but never in such a game as this. Often had he lost, as often, oftener indeed, had he gained, but tonight the chances seemed so much against him that he began to feel irreclaimably degraded and ashamed of himself and with his embarrassment fled his satiety. He made a desperate effort to recover his lost chances.

It was a pitched battle, and no mistake. Midnight arrived, and still they played on — Beardie excited, anxious, and faltering; the Devil calm, collected, and calculating. Already Beardie was Satan's debtor to the tune of three games. There was no thought now of refreshment, no signs of a cessation of hostilities, no signs of wavering on either side. Soon after the Tiger won a game through a palpable mistake on the part of his opponent.

Once more the pack was dealt, and desperately, sometimes successfully, generally, 'however, the reverse, Crawford played his cards, determined to risk everything. His mind was exhausted and stupefied; he made frantic and reckless efforts to retrieve a position which was ere now irretrievably lost; and he felt dimly that, if his case was not to be worsened, he must trump every possible suit that was tabled, but only to be plunged deeper and deeper into the mire.

One — two o'clock arrived. They went on, wading knee-deep through cards and regardless altogether of time. Outside the tempest was howling with unabated fury. By this time the air of the room was stifling and insufferable; yet they ceased not from play. Silent they sat; nothing was heard save the patter of the cards upon the oaken table within and the angry blast of the storm without. What the Devil experienced in that infernal den we know not; he was as cool and self-possessed as ever. What Beardie felt we can but very feebly conjecture; his savage, tiger-like eyes followed every movement of his antagonist with ravenous torture. No sword hung now by his side — it had fallen upon the floor unheeded. Woe, unutterable woe sat upon his countenance, and he looked ages older; his cheeks had lost their youthful freshness and were hollow and bloodless; his eyes were bloodshot and glittered maniacally.

Three o'clock came, and he was then four games in arrears. His kestrel-like courage was forsaking him. He had sold his soul to the Prince of Darkness, and the Prince of Darkness was but claiming his own. He had battled with nature, and nature had overcome him. Oh! The inexpressible anguish, the torturing care! Oh! That death would swallow him up, and put an end to all this harrowing ghost likeness!

He sank into a chair exhausted. Opposite him sat the tempter of men, his face wreathed in a diabolical smile. What unspeakable agony the man was undergoing! His body was cool enough, but his head was on fire — was scorching, and the Devil grinned at the sight. With weary, tottering steps, Crawford rose to his feet and paced the room, striking wildly at the air with his Herculean fingers.

"Thou art losing time," the Evil One remarked scoffingly. "Sit down, man, and don't be a coward."

The magic words arrested Beardie, for he possessed all the proud daring and fearless propensities of his great progenitor, Thor the Thunderer, and did not like to be attainted with cowardice.

A weird-like stillness reigned in the room, broken only by the laboured breathing of the mortal. The birds of darkness, roused by the violence of the storm, fled hither and thither, gibbering loudly as they went. The Tiger sat panting like a wild animal at bay.

"Earl Crawford!" exclaimed the fallen angel, "thou hast desecrated the laws of Heaven, and art worthy of being hurled into the subterranean fires of hell. As an angel, fallen as I am, I was permitted to hear of thy unguarded vow. Remember, who plays with fire must be prepared for burns." Here he smiled vindictively and continued — "The stake, as thou knowest, is thy soul; who fights with the Devil barters neither more nor less. Shouldst thou win, the Prince of Darkness shall not grumble, nay, shall rather be the happier, for every soul that rejects him sends him nearer reunion with the companions of his youth. If thou failest — and it wants but an hour or two to daybreak — Heaven itself cannot help thee; thou shalt pay the penalty of thy rashness — thy soul shall go down, down, down to eternal damnation."

Here he stopped. Beardie had risen, but was silent. No wonder he turned deadly pale; no wonder he stood, as if the palsy had smitten him, and his members refused their office. It was more than he could bear. This prospective eternal misery was unmanning him.

Auld Nickie-Ben was not ugly; on the contrary, he might have been called passably good-looking, yet his face assumed a stern fierceness as he said, "Heaven and hell both demand that thy boast shall be requited. A couple of hours more and thy doom is sealed. Command, if thou wilt, the King of kings and all the hosts of heaven to thy aid; or wilt thou yield to me now?"

> There was silence deep, in the silence of sleep,
> Through all that lofty hall –
> An instant more, and, like torrent's roar,
> A sound through the silence broke;
> "Twas stern and loud, 'twas fierce and proud,
> 'Twas Lindsay's voice that spoke.

"Yield" he shouted defiantly. "Be your slave? No, never, though everlasting damnation stares me broadly in the face."

"I am sorry I spoke," returned the other sneeringly. Yet the tones were perceptibly mournful all the same, and they touched Beardie as stern words would not have done. He trembled.

So they set to again, man and angel, as before. The time sped on. Five o'clock came, and Beardie was one step nearer his horrible doom. He worked

— he toiled, but in vain — he gnashed his teeth in fury, but no headway could he make. Beads of perspiration burst upon his brow, and rolled down his hollowed cheeks.

At length long streaks of grey light showed themselves athwart [across] the eastern sky, proclaiming the approach of day. Still the whirling, whistling wind came rushing down the vale, and beat louder and more ragingly than ever against the castle. Boreas blew a blustering blast that shook the walls, "an unknown door was open cast," and the Arch-Fiend sang : —

Come, Spirits of Darkness, come!
And take your captive home;
His wild career is run,
We'll claim him as our own.

Ere he had finished, a company of hideous spectres entered the room. Beardie looked on perplexedly, nay, terror-stricken, so weirdly did they walk about the apartment. There might have been thousands of them, yet was there no overcrowding. On the face of each one pale death was stamped, and their sunken eyes glimmered with an unearthly wildness.

"These," said Clootie, "are my worthy disciples; dost thou admire them?"

For answer the Earl shook his head dolefully. His senses were shattered, lacerated, benumbed, and his tongue clave to the roof of his mouth. When he did regain his voice, he turned shudderingly from so horrid a sight, and cried supplicatingly –

"Leave me! Oh! Heaven have mercy."

"Not yet, not yet," replied Satan.

Crawford staggered to his feet and trembled at the gathering gloom, where only a few hours before haughtiness and lordliness had had so great a part. A thrill of bitter despair shook his powerful frame, and his unsteady, enervated fingers clutched eagerly at his unscabbarded sword which lay at his feet, and he rushed frantically at his antagonist.

"Back, madman, back!" cried the Prince contemptuously. "Woe betide thee; vengeance overwhelm thee! Back, I say; thou art doomed to unending torture, to Hell's destructive flame, whose interminable dominions are open for thee, to range through at thy pleasure. For thee there is — No hope of heaven, no word, no breath, thy hour is come— to death, to death !"

As the demon uttered the awful judgment, Crawford's hands fell limpless by his sides, and he dropped upon the floor a writhing and woeful mass of fallen humanity — chill, alone, forlorn.

The phantom game was over. Daybreak was at hand. Without the hollow winds shrieked wrathfully, and the ground rocked tremblingly. Upon the table the hour-glass had run its course, and the light of the tapers flickered and flickered away, and in the yard, amid the storm, the cock crew thrice. There was a fearful laugh from the Prince of Darkness, a crashing noise as if the heavens had fallen, and the chamber vanished.

> He is past, he is gone, like a blast of the wind.
> And has left but the fame of his exploits behind.'[62]

'According to legendary lore, Earl Beardie may still be playing cards with the devil in some corner of the ruin. If one has the luck to look in at the stroke of twelve.'[63] Another legend has Earl Beardie appearing at midnight on Hogmanay (New Year's Eve) – one for the diary!

When visiting these ruins it is not hard to imagine that something dark and sinister is lurking within, even during the summer months when bathed in brilliant sunshine it has an odd feeling attached to it. Not exactly a selling point, yet although it is rare to find castles coming up for sale this one recently has! As a point of interest and as an aspect of historical significance I have included the following details dated 2013 from a website of Edinburgh Property Consultants offering Lordscairnie Castle for sale. So if its atmosphere you're looking for then a historical bargain with a great deal of land could be had for a price cheaper than some two bedroom flats in St. Andrews:

Lordscairnie Castle, Moonzie, Fife
Offers in the region of £220,000

Lordscairnie Castle is an historic 15th century B listed castle restoration set in about 29.62 acres (11.99 ha)

SITUATION
Lordscairnie Castle enjoys an idyllic setting within the open countryside of north Fife. The castle sits in a sheltered position at the base of the Colluthie Valley and is surrounded by rolling hills and agricultural farm land.

The castle is highly accessible with the M90 nearby and Dundee only 11 miles to the north. Edinburgh's international Airport is only 40 miles away otherwise Dundee Airport has regular flights to London. Perth is also within an easy drive giving road links into the Highlands of Scotland for further sporting and leisure interests.

HISTORY

Lordscairnie Castle was built in the late 15th century (circa 1493 1498) [The actual date seems to be 1495] by Sir Alexander Lindsay, the seventh Earl of Crawford, who at the time was one of the most powerful noblemen in Scotland. The castle was an important centre for the Lindsay clans operations and aspirations in central Scotland enjoying a colourful history. The various intrigues include raiding of the castle, house arrests and conflicts with the Bishop of St Andrews. The castle was abandoned in the mid 17th century and was utilised by the local congregation as a church until the end of the 17th century. The castle has been unoccupied since then with ownership transferred to the Earl of Glasgow in the 1840s, then by a succession of local farmers before it became the property of the existing owner. One of the most enduring legends is that it is the hiding place for ill-gotten treasure but unfortunately, nothing of any significant value has come to light so far.

DESCRIPTION

Lordscairnie Castle is an L plan tower house from the 15th century. The massive walls are over six feet thick in many places and when restored it would be five stories tall, rising to a level of 65 feet. The restoration of the castle would provide an extensive floor area providing an excellent mix of living and bedroom accommodation. This is indeed a rare opportunity to acquire a piece of Scottish history and to form a unique home in an unrivalled setting.

GROUNDS

The grounds of Lordscairnie Castle extended to approximately 29.62 acres, or thereby, which are mainly in grass and also feature a large pond on the northern perimeter of the subjects. The pond features extensive reed beds and is home to approximately fifty different species of birds.

DIRECTIONS

From Edinburgh cross the Forth Road bridge into Fife and travel north on the M90. Turn off at junction 8, signposted A91 St Andrews. Follow this road to Cupar. On entering Cupar and travelling past Elmwood College on the left, turn first left onto the A913. Follow this road for approximately 2 miles and take the turning on the right hand side signposted for Moonzie. Lordscairnie Castle is situated on the left hand side approximately half a mile from the A913.'[64]

Dairsie Castle
Ghosts of Fife Castle Trail Ref: 24

Ghostly associations in brief
Passageway to Kemback House where legend tells a piper disappeared

Visiting restrictions/fees
Grounds only, and then with discretion as the castle is let as a private self catering destination for holidays, weddings etc. Best way to enjoy this castle is to hire it!

Directions
On the A91 between Cupar and Dairsie take the Kemback/Dairsie Bridge turn off. Follow this country road sweeping round to the right and this impressive castle will loom into view on the right just after driving through a farmyard.

On the GOF Castle Trail from Lordscairnie Castle go back to the A913 and turn left for Cupar, once in the town turn left at the T junction onto the A91 signposted for Dairsie. Travel through Cupar, then once out the town, after about two miles turn right at the Kemback/Dairsie Bridge turn off. Follow this country road sweeping round to the right and this impressive castle will loom into view on the right just after driving through a farmyard.

The restored fortified Castle of Dairsie spanning back to the 12th century was home to the early Archbishops of St. Andrews around the 13th century. It was meticulously restored from its 19th century ruins in 1992 by the current owner as a family home before letting out as a six bedroomed self catering destination for holidays and weddings etc.

A subterranean passage is said to span between Dairsie Castle and Kemback House around a third of a mile to the southeast. The pipes of a piper journeying along the passageway disappeared at the nearby River Eden separating the two estates. He was never seen again! The current occupants have had no experiences of the piper or any knowledge of ghostly associations.

Refer also to *Kemback*, p.165

Earlshall Castle
Ghosts of Fife Castle Trail Ref: 25

Home of 'Bloody Bruce' & an ancestral home of Ghosts

Earlshall Castle circa 1888

Ghostly associations in brief
Presence on the turret stairs, footsteps, ghost of Sir Andrews Bruce, ghost of an old woman, ghost of a serving woman, blue lights and the indent of a body on a bed.

Private residence. The castle is closed to the public. The gardens are open for visitors at certain times of the year. Check first before visiting. It isn't possible to view the castle at other times and privacy should be respected.

Directions

Off the A91 onto the A919 signed for Leuchars. The following gives further details:

On the GOF Castle Trail from Dairsie Castle back onto the A91 turning right for Guardbridge and Leuchars. Turn left at Guardbridge onto the A919 Dundee road. At the mini roundabout in Leuchars turn right and follow the Main Street, continuing straight on at the next mini roundabout junction, turn left just past the Norman church then right onto Earlshall road. The castle is along this road on the right.

This courtyard castle is situated in a wooded area three quarters of a mile from the village of Leuchars. It was built in 1546 by Sir William Bruce who survived the Battle of Flodden Field in 1513 and lived to the age of 98. He is commemorated in the Norman church of Leuchars. Also commemorated here is his great-grandson's wife who died in 1635 and is described as being "charitable to the poor and profitable to that house." Her temperament was it seems quite different to that of her son – the Joint Sheriff Depute whose ghost haunts the castle. He is Sir Andrew Bruce of Earlshall and was Joint Depute of Dumfriesshire in the mid-seventeenth century. He had a dark reputation, 'known to the Covenanters as 'Bloody Bruce,' his ghost is said to snatch at your ankle, in the gloaming, as you go up or down the worn turret stair that leads to the strange panelled hall with its painting of Princes and marvellous beasties.'[65]

His name comes through his reputation against the Covenanters. At Airds Moss and the Battle of Bothwell Bridge on the 22nd of July 1680 he captured Hackston of Rathillet and his men at Auchinleck shortly after fleeing from the battle. Hackston had been witness to the gruesome murder of Archbishop James Sharpe on Magus Moor in 1679.[xxix] Even though he took no part in its proceedings he was taken to Edinburgh and condemned to death. At the battle Bloody Bruce had also cut the head and hands off Richard Cameron – another Covenanter and took them for display to Edinburgh. The Privy Council in Edinburgh wrote: 'that Hackston's and Cameron's heads be fixed on higher

---

[xxix] Refer also to *The Bloody Murder of Archbishop Sharpe* p.195

poles than the rest.'[66] They were displayed as examples of the fate awaiting any who would dare follow the Covenanters cause.

The ghost of Andrew Bruce has been seen in 'Bloody Bruce's Room' of the castle and heavy footsteps have been heard on the stairwell.

This next story also relates to 'Bloody Bruce' and also concerns the stairwell. It occurred during a grand ball held within the Long Hall of the castle over two hundred years ago:

One of those attending; a woman in lavish dress was walking down a flight of stone steps within the castle with a candle in her hand lighting her way. Half way down her candle was blown out and she let out a large scream. Others in the vicinity alerted to her distress came to her aid, when they reached her it was discovered that one of the red shoes she had been wearing was missing. The stairwell and the immediate vicinity were searched but to no avail.

A number of years ago while workman were re-flooring one of the rooms within the castle they discovered a single red shoe under the floor. The shoe was consequently dated to the 18th century.

The 50 foot long hall is the Long Gallery, with wood panelled ceiling depicting various Scottish family coat of arms and mythical creatures of old. Also around the walls are over one hundred basket hilted swords.

On the 12th of February 1987 a team from Edinburgh arrived at the castle to make a video for British Gas. Later in the day the continuity woman was asked in passing by a member of the household if she had seen "any of the many ghosts that inhabit the castle." Her reply was quick and surprisingly to the positive. In the Long Gallery she saw a man standing by a suit of armour wearing what appeared to be an Elizabethan period costume. She viewed the figure for a few moments before it disappeared. Surprised herself at seeing such a thing she requested that her encounter be kept quiet from the rest of the film crew. True to her wishes the others were not informed and to this day – until now that is, they have probably remained unaware that she ever saw a ghost there.

Mary Queen of Scots visited here on a hunting trip from St. Andrews in 1561 and her bedchamber of the same name is haunted by the ghost of an old woman.

Strange blue lights have also been seen within the castle with no apparent source. The indent of a body appears on one of the beds as though someone had just laid down to rest, and a serving woman roams along the corridors.

Like so many other castles Earlshall nearly fell into ruin after being abandoned, but was bought by Robert Mackenzie in 1891 who commissioned Sir Robert Lorimer to restore it in 1892. He recreated the formal gardens including a large Topiary Lawn laid out in a 17th century style with chess pieces. This was just after he had restored Kellie Castle in the 1880s.

W. T. Linskill, author of *St. Andrews Ghost Stories* wrote a tale about a Castle called Lausdree in his famous work. This was a castle he has as being located near St. Andrews. But Lausdree Castle doesn't exist. Should we enquire however if a real castle set the scene for his story, then Earlshall Castle would be a prime candidate. Whilst it doesn't have the same capacity of ghosts and bogles as his fictitious Lausdree, there are a few associations that make for an interesting comparison. These and Linskill's story of Lausdree Castle will be found in my companion book *Ghosts of St. Andrews*, (2013), commencing on p.257

Part Two

The A-Z Collection
of Fife's Ghostly Haunts

'All the country between the Forth and the Tay grows narrow like a wedge eastward, even to the sea and it is called Fife, a district provided within its own bounds with all things necessary for the use of life.'

George Buchanan, *History of Scotland*, 1582

Paranormal Discovery

While this book is fairly comprehensive there are a great many more haunted locations in Fife than I have thus far been able to uncover. As a testimony to this, shortly after I thought I had finished this book I came across the website for 'Paranormal Discovery'. A Paranormal Research Team created in 2006 and based in Dundee. They have a number of investigations under their belt for locations I would otherwise have been unaware of. Katrina Dolan, one of the founding members and the team of researchers from Paranormal Discovery have kindly granted permission for me to share some of their findings here. I have listed the disturbances they mention for eight locations on their website for Fife. They have put a lot of work and effort into obtaining what they have received, not least in finding these locations, which is no mean feat. So I am very grateful in being able to publish some of their material. It is important also to direct the reader to their great website: paranormaldiscovery.org where further information about their organisation and many other investigations in other locations across Scotland may be found. The featured locations are:

Anstruther – The Dreel Tavern
Anstruther – The Scottish Fisheries Museum
Anstruther – Spindrift B&B
Auchtermuchty – The Forest Hills Hotel
Lathones – Lathones Inn
Leven – Regent Cinema
St. Michaels Inn
Tayport – The Auld Hoose

Paranormal Discovery is operated on a voluntary basis by founding members Katrina and her sister Natalie, together with a crew of dedicated researchers. They give themselves tirelessly to the cause of paranormal research and can be contacted through their website.

W. T. Linskill, author of the 1911 classic *St. Andrews Ghost Stories* writing about the work of paranormal researchers said in an article he wrote for the *St. Andrews Citizen*; 'Such investigations are continually going on, privately, day by day all over the world, although we may hear little about them. Sometimes they are ultimately crowned with success. All honour to such intrepid explorers – whatever line of investigation they may take up. The humblest efforts sometimes reveal the unexpected in most mysterious ways, far beyond the comprehension of most folk. Miracles have never really ceased, but continue daily in our midst, often unknown, unheeded, and unsolved. We have still very much to learn.'[1]

Anstruther

Anstruther or 'Ainster' as it is known locally is the largest of the East Neuk villages on Fife's coastline. Like all the villages in the East Neuk, tourism is the main industry since the decline of the fisheries.

The Dreel Tavern

photo by the author

The Dreel Tavern is situated on the High Street in Anstruther Wester. It has had numerous reports of paranormal activity over the years.

photo by the author

The following is the first of three reports in Anstruther by Paranormal Discovery based in Dundee who carried out an investigation here a few years ago. The following also includes some of the history associated with the building.

'It is a charming stone built 16th century property and former coaching inn. The building has links with King James V of Scotland and there is a plaque outside commemorating his visit to the town. The details on the plaque are said to be a watered down version of the story for tourists. James was supposedly carried over the Dreel burn by a local beggar maid. The promiscuous James paid her for her services, which probably included a bit more than keeping his feet dry, with a gold coin. The woman's greeting or benison "May Prick nor Purse never fail you" inspired the name of the first sex club in Scotland. The Beggar's Benison club was founded in Anstruther in 1732. Perhaps it is not surprising, then, that a previous psychic had the impression that the upstairs of the Dreel Tavern was once used as a brothel in times gone by.

photo by the author

Paranormal activity reported by staff includes:

Doors have been heard opening and closing by staff after closing time in the area near the toilets.

Brass plates have fallen from the wall in the pub without any obvious reason for doing so.

Movement and shadows have been seen by staff after closing the bar.

A man has been seen on more than one occasion sitting in the armchair in the guest bedroom. He was said to look like a pirate.

The shelf in the guest bedroom was witnessed by several people turning round but the ornaments on top of it did not fall off.

The bed in the guest bedroom is said to have moved during the night while the occupant was asleep in it.

A commotion/voices were heard at 3am by the occupant of the bed in the office. She thought it sounded like children playing.

The bed upstairs in the office is also said to have moved during the night while being slept in (both beds are situated under windows with window seats and which look out over the front of the building).

Footsteps have been heard coming from the top floor of the building when nobody was there to account for them.'

The tavern is full of historical character and charm with very hospitable staff. When I visited the tavern I was told about the ghost of an old man who sits at the window table by the tavern's entrance. He is known by the staff and locals simply as George.

The window table in the tavern
photo by the author

With the main tourist thoroughfare being along the harbour of the town, it could be said the Dreel Tavern is slightly off the beaten track, but then sometimes this is where the best places are to be found. It is only a few minutes' walk from Shore Street and the harbour, and is a gem of a tavern to either start or complete your trip of Ainster. Where else can you visit and enjoy your meal at the same table as a ghost! Andy Walker, the staff and George, will take good care of you here I am sure. The tavern is highly recommended for a meal and a drink in a congenial atmosphere.

Buckie House (Private Dwelling)

Just along the road from the Dreel Tavern is Buckie House, famous for its decoration of sea shells or 'Buckies' that cover its outer walls. The house also retains some of its ancient interior as an old fishers abode. One of the upper rooms has a small old wooden box bed set into a corner and an ornate shell covered ceiling set in much the same fashion as the exterior. It was here in the 1980s that the ghostly figure of an old man was seen by a couple not long after buying the property. It was believed the figure was of a fisherman who once lived within the house.

His name was Alex Batchelor, an eccentric of the 19th century who also covered his coffin in shells. Robert Louis Stevenson on visiting Anstruther as a child around the 1860s remarked on this house in his Fife Journals, commenting on the agreeable eccentric who covered his house with pebbles.

The shell covered room within the house has also been prone to those sudden bouts of coldness customarily associated with a great many hauntings.

photo by the author

Smugglers Inn

One night a number of years ago (1980s) a couple booked into the hotel for two nights, but sometime during the first night the couple packed up and left the hotel in a hurry. The next day a letter was found together with money for both nights. The letter explained they had a strange

photo by the author

experience and had to leave. The bed they slept in had apparently been moving around during the night with no physical cause.

Two local men on hearing this story ventured up to the room a few nights later. On this particular night there were no guests staying within the hotel, it was the end of season and the hotel was temporarily closed for cleaning. On opening the door of the room they felt an uncanny coldness and fled soon after when they heard an unaccountable noise from within the room.

Over the years the ghostly figures of more than one person has been seen in the Inn by members of staff and residents. Customers in the public bar have felt a presence and the sensation of someone, or something brushing past them when no one has been around.

Kirkgate Priory

This building now replaced by flats once stood close to the Ship Inn by the shore in Anstruther. It was haunted by the ghost of a prior who was found bricked up in a priest hole at the priory.

The Scottish Fisheries Museum

photo by the author

This is the second of the reports by Paranormal Discovery from Dundee, along with a little history they have written about the Fisheries Museum:

'The museum was opened in 1969 and is comprised of several historical buildings, two of which are 'A' listed buildings: a 16th century Abbot's lodging and a Merchant's house dating from 1724. Parts of the museum are also on the site of an earlier chapel, cooper's yard, and tavern. The site itself has historical links to Balmerino Abbey. Paranormal activity at the museum has been reported by staff and visitors alike.

Reports include:
A dark figure has been seen crouching down by a boat in the boatyard.

Footsteps have been heard after closing by staff standing in the engine room (the steps appeared to be from above in the Days of Steam room)

The door to the Cottage has been difficult to open and felt as if someone was pushing on it from the other side.

A general feeling of unease and of being watched in the Zulu gallery.

A child reporting that a 'spirit person' had been with the group as they went around the museum on a torchlight tour during a themed night.

Poltergeist type activity was experienced in the Days of Sail room when a certain pair of boots was moved into that room from their original place. The activity ceased when the boots were returned to the loft of the Cottage where they had been originally.'

Johnstone Lodge (Private Dwelling)

The lodge is on Chalmers Brae, just up the hill from The Ship Tavern and the Scottish Fisheries Museum. It is also known as The Green Lady's House. The Green Lady is believed to be Princess Titana Marama (1842 – 1898) from Haapiti, Tahiti. She has been seen wearing a green dress wandering around the building. She has also been seen standing with a spy glass in her hands looking out of one of the windows. She committed suicide after seeing her husband's ship sink during a fierce storm in the Firth of Forth. Since that time she has kept constant watch for ships to come in, waiting for her beloved husband. Her body was buried either at Anstruther or Kilrenny.

The lodge itself was built in 1829 with Edwardian additions and has a walled garden of an earlier origin.

The Spindrift B&B

The third report by Paranormal Discovery in Anstruther involves the ghost of a clipper ship sailor called Captain Smith in the Captains Guest Room and a woman in room 5. Further details will be found at: paranormaldiscovery.org

Arncroach

Kellie Castle
Including a haunted chamber and a menacing presence.

Refer to *GOF Castle Trail* p.43

Auchmuirbridge

The Apparition of a Girl
'Auchmuirbridge lies on the Fife border just to the east of Loch Leven. Bought by Ron Wanender and his step daughter Catherine Young, their restaurant here was formerly a Blacksmiths and is haunted by ghostly noises upstairs. Ron once

saw a fair-haired girl within the building and their Doberman dog was terrified when left in the centre of the room.'[2]

Auchterderran

Crisis Apparition

'A woman who was attending to an old man living alone in a cottage some distance from her residence, set out one evening to visit him. On coming near his house she saw him quite plainly standing outside the door, but he was only "as high as the key hole." She knew that this apparition meant that the man was dead, and on entering she found him dead in bed. – Communicated, D. R.'[3]

Auchtermuchty

The Royal Hotel (Former)

photo by the author

The building is located at 38 Cupar Road. It closed as a hotel in 2008 and remained empty until late 2012, when it became a kindergarten and café called 'Go Nuts Softplay Centre and Taste Café'. The site of the building was once an abbey and a cemetery.

A former owner of the hotel in the 1970s committed suicide in Room 4. Since that time the room has had a very oppressive atmosphere and has been subjected to cold spots and noises with no accountability. The former hotel's hallway also has a ghost and a presence has been felt in an upstairs flat.

The Forest Hills Hotel

This hotel was formerly the Boars Head Inn. I remember playing a gig here many years ago one lively Saturday night! The hotel is in the centre of Muchty, on the High Street. It was originally a coaching inn dating back to 1738 and hosts a number of ghosts and paranormal disturbances investigated by Paranormal

photo by the author

Discovery of Dundee as follows: 'A dark shadow-like figure was seen in the function room doorway by a member of staff after closing time. This caused him to swiftly lock-up and leave but was left with a horrible sensation of dread which lasted with him till he got home.

Glasses have been mysteriously thrown from the shelf behind the bar in the function room with 2 witnesses to this event

A woman in old-fashioned clothes (possibly Victorian) has been seen in the back bar area.

A male spirit in uniform has been seen regularly in the kitchen by a member of staff.

A loud noise has been heard by a guest. The noise appeared to be coming from the landing outside her room and sounded like something heavy being dragged along the floor. No other guests were staying in the hotel at the time.

People have also reported feelings of being touched.'

B936 Auchtermuchty – Falkland Road

Ghost of Jenny Nettles

Refer to *Strathmiglo Area*, p.236

Auchtertool

Anniversary Ghosts

The following is an 'anniversary' funeral procession that occurs each August in Auchtertool. It comes to us through the Rev. William Stevenson who was a Minister of Auchtertool in the late 19th early 20th century's. His work is *The Kirk and Parish of Auchtertool* and it was published in 1908.

'A lady who spent much of her youth in the parish, lately told the writer that in her childhood an old servant, a native of the parish, gave her an account of the tradition current in the district regarding this burial (that of one of the Skene family, who had been involved in the rebellion). The Earl of Moray of that day allowed the body of the deceased Skene, which had been brought from France, to be taken to Halyards; and from thence at the "mirk midnight," accompanied with torchbearers, old retainers of the family, bare the body by the "Lady's Walk" and straight across the field, according to their old burial custom, to the

Kirk of Auchtertool, where it was placed in the vault.... The narrator added this interesting and picturesque detail, that every year on the same night in the month of August a ghostly procession comes along the "Lady's Walk" to the Kirk of Auchtertool, bearing a shrouded coffin shoulder-high, and attended by a piper clad in the tartan of the Skenes, playing an ancient lament. No one of late seems to have observed this procession, or have heard the wail of the pipes, but it would never do for anyone belonging to the parish to doubt that it takes place as has been recorded.'[4]

Refer also to *Balmuto Castle* – just south of Auchtertool, p.79

Balcarres

Balcarres House

Refer to *GOF Castle Trail*, Colinsburgh, p.53

Ballingry

Crisis Apparition

In Skinner's book *Autobiography of a Metaphysician, being the life of Reverend James Skinner*, 1893 he relates the following:

'My grandmother had a belief in supernatural appearances as most people of her day seem to have had... she related the experience of a neighbour with whom both she and I were intimate. This man's wife had died a short time before. One summer morning he was lying in bed quite awake. One of his children was in bed beside him ill and shortly after died. He became aware of the presence of someone near, and looking up, saw his deceased wife, as distinctly as ever he had seen her in life, gazing calmly in upon them.'[5]

Balmerino

Balmerino Abbey

Sited in a picturesque area by the River Tay, the abbey was founded in 1229 by Queen Emergarde. The abbey was run by Cistercian monks whose attire was white cassocks. They had by all accounts a great wealth which afforded them many luxuries not in-keeping with the strict lifestyle they were supposed to be accustomed. An interesting feature of the existing ruins is a room crafted from large stone blocks that is only accessible through the roof, as there are no doors or windows exist within the chamber. It is believed that this was the dungeon of the abbey. The roof was covered by a large stone slab which was slid aside for access.

The abbey like so many others was ransacked during the reformation in 1558 which leant to its eventual disrepair and ruin.

The ruins are reputed to be haunted by one of the former inhabitants, that of an abbot who now wanders the grounds.

Boarhills

Craig Hartle

A beautiful area known as Craig Hartle forming a group of rocks on the shoreline a little to the north-east of Boarhills is reputed to be haunted by a small human figure, seen either on the rocks themselves or by a slight beach area near here.

This was the site where a ship called the Napoleon was wrecked in a thundering storm and high seas in the 1850s. No one on board survived that night. It was after that disaster that Boarhills became a lifeboat station built in 1860. The remains of which is now a cattle food store.

Refer also to Pitmilly, p.208

Buckhaven

Buckhaven College

The following is from James W. Taylor written in 1875: 'But the College of Buckhaven, what of it? Its name and site are still known. To the east of the village, and retired from the main road by a few feet, with a gateway formed of whales' bones, stands a two-storied house. This house still retains the name of "The College." In other towns and villages of Fife, you meet with buildings which were dignified with the high sounding title of "The College." Probably they were schools of a higher grade, where two or three branches of learning were taught. Whether this was the case with Buckhaven or no, one thing is certain, that in this house, for many years, was held the chief, if not the only school, in Buckhaven.'[6] He then continues; 'One who was a young alumnus of the College, "for he was born within its walls," supplies this account of its later history. It came, seventy or eighty years ago, into the possession of a sailor, who engaged in smuggling. The smuggled goods were concealed on the premises; and the gin, which was a principal article, often gave rise to drunken brawls. In one of these, the sailor's wife, whose name was Maillie, met with her death. Thereafter, her ghost haunted the spot. It became a dreaded place; and, instead of passing it in the dark, many, both old and young, within the last thirty years, preferred giving it a wide offing, by going down along the sands.'[7]

Burntisland

A Spectral Visitation

The following is a Christmas ghost story from the *Weekly Scotsman* dated 26th December 1896:

'My grandmother actually saw all the events related here, and told them to me a few weeks before her death.

Shortly after I married, my husband and I went to live in an old spacious house opposite Burntisland, about half a mile from the coast. The day on which these wonderful events happened was a wild December one. My husband had gone to Dunfermline on business, and the servants were all out, for one reason or another. So I was left alone for the first time in that great house. After an extra furious gust of wind, I was aroused by a noise at the door. On opening it I was startled to see four unknown men, dressed like seamen, march in without a word, carrying the apparently lifeless body of a young lad. They carried him upstairs into a small bedroom at the back of the house. They halted beside a large cupboard that occupied one side of the room, and, while two men held the boy, the other two moved a small camp-bed that was near beside the cupboard, and laid the boy gently thereon. Then all four marched out.

All this time I was watching, dumb with astonishment. Not a word had been spoken by them through the whole proceeding, and the few words I spoke were received in silence. A few minutes after the men left, a young lady, apparently about twenty-five, with a beautiful and expressive face, ran into the room. She was dressed in an antiqued style of dress of rich and elaborate material. I can yet remember every detail of the scene, so vividly was it impressed on my memory, although that was more than fifty years ago.

I was aroused by the sound of the girl speaking violently to the lad, who had just recovered from his faint or whatever it was, and I stepped forward to ask an explanation, when, to my horror, I saw the boy's face through the body of the girl. It was with an effort that I kept myself from fainting, but managed to seat myself in the corner of the room and await developments.

"Jack, Jack!" I heard her say. "He is coming. Hide yourself. He is within a hundred yards of the house."

"I cannot Agnes," he said, with a look of terror and fatigue.

"I am too weak, and there is nowhere to hide."

"Hide in here," she said, rapidly opening the door of the cupboard, and, pressing a spring at the back, revealed a dark opening.

"Quick now, my poor boy," she said, tenderly, helping the boy in at the same time.

She had just time to close the spring door and the door of the cupboard when the door of the room was opened violently, and a tall, stern-looking, black-bearded man strode in.

"Where is the boy?" he shouted. Receiving no answer, he took a small dagger from his belt and repeated his question. This time the girl firmly refused to give any information, so without a moment's hesitation, he plunged the dagger into her heart. Instantly all vanished, but before I could recover myself I heard a scratching proceeding from the cupboard and agonising cries of despair.

I tried to rise and go to the cupboard but in vain; my limbs refused to bear me. I fell back, and remembered no more until I awoke with my husband standing over me. When I was able I told him the whole story, and together we searched the cupboard. After much searching, we found the spring, and on opening the spring door discovered a few mouldering bones and a large but illegible manuscript. The affair was treated as a dream, until a caretaker was horrified to find himself chosen for the next spectator of the dire tragedy, when the house was pulled down and the site covered with wheat crops.'[8]

Refer also to *Kinghorn - The Ghost of a Green Lady*, p.169

Cameron House
(Private Dwelling)

The Secret Room

The following is another account of a hidden door with its secrets beyond. I received this account from Mrs Cawley, now living in California. This is the first of two accounts she gave to me concerning her paranormal experiences in Fife. Refer to Pittenweem and *The Grey Woman of the Church House in Pittenweem*, p.227 for the second.

Cameron House standing three miles south of St. Andrews on the Largo Road was bought in 1976 by a St. Andrews family called Cawley from its former owners the Church of Scotland. Standing within a walled garden it was used by the church as a manse after being converted from stables dating back to the 18th century. When they moved in there was a room in the attic measuring twenty feet by fifteen feet containing six lead tanks used for the storage of water from a nearby well. A few improvements needed to be made within the old church house so they replaced the electrics and installed a new water supply, with the lead tanks now becoming obsolete they had them removed. Once the area had been laid bare Mrs Cawley noticed a door in a wall behind where these tanks had been, it was about 5'6" in height and because access to it had been blocked by the tanks it hadn't been seen for a good many years. The door wasn't locked and creaked open, revealing a little room beyond. Within she found a quaint old fireplace and a built-in wooden bench. After this discovery she would come here to relax and sit on a bench reading for a time in its peace and quiet.

On one of these visits she decided to move the bench to another part of the room, on doing so she found hidden behind it a small black iron bed upright against the wall, together with a few aged gin flasks and bottles. The bed wasn't damaged in any way so she put it back together and found it fitted exactly where the bench had been, as if that had been its rightful place. From time to time she would go to this room and perhaps picture a servant or some other such person living here many years ago but not it may be added in a terrible amount of comfort.

From the height of the door and the design of the old iron bed she knew its origins were very old, perhaps from the 1700s.

It came about a while later that they had a girl staying with them from England. One afternoon during the course of conversation Mrs Cawley chatted to her about the secret room and its curious old bed. After becoming interested she decided to show it to her. Up the stairs they went to the top of the house, then through the old tank room to the door. When they entered Mrs Cawley with great surprise saw an old woman with grey hair and wearing a black dress, she was lying on a small iron bed and seemed very sad indeed, her companion at this point suddenly burst into a flood of tears, whereon the woman disappeared and they both rapidly left the room. When they next spoke of the incident Mrs Cawley asked if she had seen the same as herself, but it was found the girl hadn't seen any ghostly figure in the room at all, on the contrary, she had seen nothing but had immediately become attuned on entering the room to an inexplicable feeling of extreme anguish and loneliness.

Cash Wood

Ghost of Jenny Nettles

Refer to Strathmiglo Area, p.236

Colinsburgh

Balcarres House

Refer to *GOF Castle Trail*, Colinsburgh, p.53

Craigtoun Country Park

Craigtoun and the Mount Melville estate are situated a couple of miles south-west of St. Andrews on the Pitscottie road. The ownership of the lands at Craigtoun is today somewhat fragmented. This area, once all part of Mount Melville farm land comprises the Duke's Golf complex with an 18 hole championship course, a country park, a holiday park with lodges and caravans, and Mount Melville House, a late Victorian mansion built in 1900 for Dr James and Mrs Annie Younger. They were part of the famous Scottish Brewers based in Edinburgh. Younger Hall in North Street St. Andrews was donated by Annie Younger to the University in 1929 as a Graduation Hall.

Mount Melville House together with 47 acres of Mount Melville ground was bought by Fife council in 1947. The landscaped grounds were then turned into Craigtoun Country Park. For many years this has been a major attraction for locals and visitors to Fife alike. The park even hosted a couple of Live Aid inspired music festivals called Fife Aid in the 1980s.

The Dutch Village at Craigtoun

The grounds of the house have a number of follies, as well as landscaped gardens, all built by the Younger family to entertain guests. The unusual Dutch village is one such folly, a white walled mock village set in the middle of a boating lake. It was designed in the 1920s by the Younger's and has been one of the central features in drawing people to the park since it became public ground. The village has a boathouse, tower, pavilion, gatehouse and a long stone bridge spanning the land and the village.

The park is haunted by a tall dark figure standing near the entrance of this bridge on the landward side. The ghostly figure has also been seen within the fairly circular grass courtyard of the village which is flanked by white buildings and a wall. Nothing appears to be known about this solitary apparition and why it would be haunting this particular spot.

Craigtoun Country Park has always been a buzzing place for families – especially when the sun is shining. Like many others in St. Andrews I used to finish work of a summer evening and head for the park for a couple of hours. Apart from the ghost, the parks attractions also include a miniature renovated steam railway for rides around the park, a performance stage, crazy golf and putting, an Italian garden and trampolines etc. I always remember the small café in the middle of the Dutch village serving ice cream and tea. The area has suffered neglect over the years despite the volume of people visiting each year, but it has finally had a facelift and the park was re-launched in March 2013, after a major financial revamping of its tired looking services and is set once more to become the attraction it deserves to be.

Mount Melville House

The Victorian mansion of Mount Melville House which stands in the grounds was named Craigtoun House when Fife Council bought it and in 1949 they turned it into the local maternity hospital for St. Andrews and surrounding districts. It closed as a maternity hospital in the 1980s as it was proving too costly to run. Its loss was felt throughout the town as a piece of history where many were born closed its doors. The building lay empty for a time, until the council could find a use for it. It temporarily became a residential home for the elderly then closed its doors once again in 1992. The council retained the country park but sold the house to the American investor Kohler Co, the farm estate sold a massive 330 acres of Mount Melville land to them also. Kohler also has the Old Course Hotel and Hamilton Hall in St. Andrews. They turned the land into the Duke's Golf Course in 1995. The mansion was left empty for 16 years before redeveloped slowly began to breathe life into the old building again and 2008 saw it starting to turn it into a private luxury residence for golfers and guests.

When the mansion was a maternity hospital the hairs on the back of the neck of its occupants would often be alerted by its resident ghosts. A woman I spoke with who had a baby here when it was a maternity hospital told me that around lunchtime the cries of a baby were sometimes heard, baffling those who would search for its source. It was heard on occasions by the staff, patients and visitors alike and after eliminating the more obvious of sources no satisfactory explanation would ever been found in tracing its whereabouts.

The building is also haunted by a mother looking for her baby. Both had apparently died here when she was in labour and she now roams the large empty corridors in perpetuity, searching for the child she never saw whilst alive.

A place of this size and history will have a few other haunts and stories to tell I have no doubt. So many mansions find their end in ruins and decay. The mansion at Craigtoun is both imposing and beautiful. With a new lease of life from the high end golfing market its future as a building of stature is guaranteed for many years to come.

Crail

Balcomie Castle
Ghostly pipe music, the figure of a boy and a soldier.

Refer to *GOF Castle Trail*, p.39

Crail Castle
Apparition

Refer to *GOF Castle Trail*, p.42

The Devil's Blue Stane

photo by the author

Lying by the entrance to Crail Church the 'Blue Stane' has the same name and a similar history to that of the one to be found in St. Andrews[xxx] Somewhat larger than the one in St. Andrews, this being around 4 feet in diameter in days past villagers would kiss the stone before leaving the parish hoping for good fortune in their travels and for their safe return. 'Legend has it that it was flung at the church from the Isle of May by the Devil himself, but it fell slightly short. An impression may be seen in this rock which is believed as the story goes to be his thumb print.'[9]

[xxx] Refer to *The Blue Stane* in *Ghosts of St. Andrews* by the author, (2013)

Another account states:

'The legend runs that the arch-fiend, bearing some especial grudge against the church of Crail, took his stand upon the Isle of May, and thence threw a huge rock at the building. The missile, however, split during its flight into two pieces, of which the smaller one (bearing the impress of his satanic majesty's thumb) kept its intended course, falling but a few yards short of the church, while the other larger portion slanted off to the east and lit upon Balcomie sands both fragments remaining to this day (thumb mark and all), to give ocular demonstration of the truth of the story.'[10]

Yet another addition in a different account says:

'It is the local fetish, and Crail bairns used to kiss it in leaving the old town, in pledge of their return.'[11]

It was common for churches to be built on or nearby ancient sacred sites, with talk of the devil being a negative slant on whatever offering in folklore and belief may have been at the time. So the Blue Stane along with its cousin in St. Andrews more than likely marks such an ancient site.

Ghostly Eyes

The ghostly eyes of a woman are seen peering out of dark corners in the rooms of a house by the sea. The exact location is not known.

The Bothy

The V shape in the hill to the left is the end of the track from the road
photo courtesy of Joanne Finnigan

A mile along the coastal route from Crail toward Anstruther stands a small bothy by the ruins of an old fishing works known as the Pans. Built almost level with and standing only a few yards from the North Sea the bothy narrowly escapes the ravages of the high breaking waves battering and spraying the nearby rocks of the coastline. The bothy is only accessible either along a scenic coastal walk from Crail or Anstruther; or along a track from the main road and down a hill some 150 feet to the shore. Until the 1990s it survived as the last remaining inhabited place in the area, with no electricity or plumbed in amenities associated with modern day living.

photo by the author

Unfortunately this is what the bothy looks like today. I knew the occupants who once lived here and regularly visited them. It is a real shame this is all that is left of a place that until relatively recently had a family living within its walls. Lighting was from Hurricane lamps, water from the cow trough at the top of the hill, heating from drift wood along the shore, a record player powered by a car battery and rent of £100 a year! A dream home really. Many happy times were shared here between the Finnigan's who lived here and a few of us who enjoyed their company.

photo by the author

This overgrown track leads to the edge of a hill sloping some 150 feet down to the bothy on the shoreline. The bothy is around 200 feet away from the end of the track. On one occasion whist visiting I got off the St. Andrews to Leven bus on the main road by the track. It was about 2pm and a very bright hot sunny day with little cloud and no wind. I started walking along the track and once accustomed to the uneven changes in its surface looked up and saw the bothy straight ahead of me at the end of the track. It was clear in every detail. The small whitewashed cottage appeared level with the rest of the landscape on the horizon. The glistening sea behind forming the backdrop and both appearing slightly hazy from the heat of the sun's rays.

Nothing struck me as unusual about this at the time and no thoughts entered my mind as I wandered along, looking aimlessly at the surroundings, although something did start niggling me in the back of my mind, but I wasn't aware of what it was. Three quarters of the way along the track I looked up, and the bothy had disappeared from view, nothing seemed unusual about this as the track deceptively rises slightly at this point and obscures what may have been visible from a distance.

I visited the family and all was most enjoyable, but still something I couldn't quite place haunted the back of my mind.

The next weekend I visited again. Travelling by bus as before from St. Andrews, as it reached the same place at the head of the track by the roadside and slowed down to let me off I was struck by an obvious absence. The bothy wasn't on the horizon.

I realised then it wasn't possible to see the bothy from either the road or the track as it sat by the shore down a 150 foot incline at the other end of the track. It seemed the previous week I had witnessed something strange, but I had no idea at the time how what I saw could have been possible. To see a large inanimate object that had not appeared as some relic of a distant past, but of something still standing and looking no different. Other than it appeared some 150 feet above its natural foundation level was very odd.

Sometime later I found out how the phenomenon of mirages occur which explained exactly what I had seen and how it could have occurred. It also became a plausible explanation for how some of the ghostly phenomenon documented all over the world can appear as it does.

The Mirage Effect

Differences in temperature between layers of air cause differences in density. This in turn causes light rays to travel in curved paths. The light rays reach the eye as if they have travelled in straight lines – and as the mirage appears above or below the true image, it frequently appears magnified and with a greater clarity.

Cases have been known for whole towns to appear in this way, often many miles from where they actually are. In my case it was a cottage appearing some 150 feet above and correspondingly closer to its actual position.

People have also been seen and battles re-enacted in the sky. The latter phenomenon may have occurred many years previously. The explanation for this is more complex than that just mentioned above. They can be formed, unlocked and witnessed in the same manner as impressionistic ghosts (where the impression has left its mark on the space of the locality), coupled with the distortion of a mirage it causes them to appear in the sky. This doesn't take account of all sightings and can never be a definitive. While we may look for one line answers to cover what we look to understand, nothing in reality is ever black and white. Individual circumstance will always dictates the nature of the explanation.

Refer also to the nearby *Kilrenny* – Caiplie Caves, p.167

Culross

Culross has been a Royal Burgh since 1588. Until 1891 and the remodelling of the boundary of Fife, Culross was part of Perthshire. This charming little town is a step back to the 16th and 17th century, with its period backdrop of buildings featuring in a number of Hollywood films including the 2008 film *The 39 Steps*. The main source of income for the town today is tourism, but in times past income was from the export of coal which was both abundantly mined and salt from the local salt pans. In its hay day it was believed some 170 ships would birth at the nearby harbour to take these commodities away and in . The town has also had long Christian associations with the early Christian missionary St. Serf settling here in 520 AD.

Culross – Abbey

photo by the author

The Abbey, grounds and church are free to enter and are open all year round.

Ghostly Monks
The Abbey was founded in 1217 by Malcolm I, the Earl of Fife and became the home of the white robed Cistercian Monks whose ghostly figures have been seen in the grounds. The abbey itself fell into disrepair and ruin following the reformation of the 16th century. Still active and open to the public the Abbey Church which was restored in 1603 is now home to the Church of Scotland.

The Piper and the Secret Passage
The author David Beveridge in 1885 wrote about a piper and a secret passage under this

Abbey: 'Of Culross Monastery... the usual tale is recorded of mysterious subterranean passages and communications. In one of these a man is said to be seated on a golden chair, and has doubtless prizes of regal magnificence to present to the courageous adventurer who may succeed in penetrating to his secret retreat. The story is told of a blind piper and his dog who entered the vaults at the head of the Newgate, and was heard playing his pipes on his subterraneous march as far as the West Kirk, three quarters of a mile distant. But the gnomes or subterranean demons got hold of him, and he never again emerged to the upper air. His dog managed to effect his escape, but the faithful animal of course could tell no tales.'[12]

Stories such as Beveridge's will certainly have found their inspiration with W. T. Linskill, author of *St. Andrews Ghost Stories*. It is reminiscent of his story – *The Smothered Piper of the West Cliffs*. Linskill spent many hours searching for a similar network under St. Andrews Cathedral. He felt sure they existed but never found any and none have ever been found to exist. The discovery at the top of the Pends in St. Andrews of what he believed to be a subterranean passage had his heart racing – unfortunately it turned out to be a mediaeval latrine! The discovery of the mine and counter mine in St. Andrews Castle had a similar effect on Linksill, whether he knew it was a mine at the time is uncertain.

There are a number of legends around the Kingdom of Fife of pipers seemingly to have disappeared into caves never to return. They enter into the dark tunnels merrily playing their trusty bagpipes like musical potholers journeying to see if they can be heard above ground as they go. Occasionally their sounds would be heard in faint short bursts drifting through cracks or holes from way undergrounds some distance from the cave entrance itself......but then, nothing! The pipes would stop and they would never reappear again. Despite searches for them in these caves their bodies would never be recovered and whatever happened to these musical adventurers is never known, only that they never returned in physical form. One explanation is the pipes are so loud they caused a cave-in which would explain the sudden end to their playing and the lack of any trace of them.

Refer also to *Kemback*, p.165
Refer also to *Kilrenny*, Caiplie Caves, p.167
Refer also to *Kirkcaldy*, p.175

Ruins by the roadside just before entering Culross from the east.
photo by the author

Not much remains now of the chapel by the roadside. The chapel was built in 1503, possibly on the site of an earlier church. It is believed to have been the birthplace of St. Mungo, the more popular name for St. Kentigern. He was the Patron Saint and founder of the City of Glasgow where he died in 603 AD.

Figures have been seen flitting around these ruins. One in particular is that of a monk with plump figure and long hair. The wailing noises of a man have also been heard emanating from the ruins. The figure and the sounds of wailing are believed to be that of Brother Joseph Macgregor, who had served in the nearby Abbey from 1745 to his retirement in 1789. The story is told that ten years later on Hogmanay 1799 he had a vision of the chapel collapsing. After his vision the chapel seems to have borne the brunt of poltergeist type activity.

The altar in the ruins still exists
photo by the author

During sermons the pews began moving and candles were wont to light by themselves. Needless to say attendance by the congregation fell sharply amid talk of the devil himself possessing the chapel. Six months later on the Summer Solstice of 1800 the roof of the chapel collapsed with Brother Joseph inside. He was the only occupant in the chapel at the time.

Fevered superstition and the characteristic stories of the devil recounted under torture and duress did a great deal of damage to communities two hundred years earlier, and even in 1800 there were those who still believed in the propaganda put forth by both the Catholics and the Protestants against one another since the reformation of 1559.

A woman near the chapel was said to have heard Joseph denouncing the Devil's work and could hear him wailing as it collapsed and killed him. She said: 'I saw the cloven feet of the devile and his disciples on the chapel roofe. They danced and fornicated on the timberes and laughed as the roofe fell inwards. I heard the good Brothere wail during the storm as he denounced the devil's work.'

The chapel was excavated in 1926 exposing a two chambered building, and is now owned by the National Trust for Scotland. The chapel is open all year round and is free entry.

An Old Culross Premonition

The monk's vision isn't the only one to have been recorded in Culross marking tragic consequences. The Reverend Robert Wodrow, an eminent Scottish Historian writing in 1721-1722 says: 'Patrick Erskine, son of Colonel Erskine of Carnock told my informer that Mr. James Culbert, who had taken much pains upon him while alive, had more than once appeared to him in Culross, in Holland, and in New England, and had given many advices and excellent directions to him; That even when at the table in his father's house, he would have had visions and apparitions, and the company would have observed him change colours, and fall sweating; That when his mother died, he was for a long time peremptory she would not die: She was very low, and not to be turned almost in her bed, yet still he said she would not die, till some hours before her death she would be carried to another room for a change; and when that was moved, he fell a weeping and opposed it much, but was overruled. When inquired into the reason, he said that, several days or weeks before, he had, in vision, seen her taken into that room, and lying dead and straight in that bed. That still he had fostered the thoughts she would not die as long as she was in the other room: That now he saw his vision was to be accomplished, and he could not bear the thoughts of her being taken away, accordingly, she was taken into that room, and in some hours died. The accounts of these things are very strange, but I have them from the first hands.'[13]

photo by the author

This bright mustard yellow building is striking to see. Owned by the National Trust for Scotland the Palace is open to the public and opening times and entrance fees apply.

Russell Leadbetter wrote a Halloween article to the Herald, 31ˢᵗ October 2010 called *Scotland's Most Haunted, National Trust for Scotland "ghost audit"*. In this article about the Palace he says; 'Former head gardener Nick Hoskins recounts a "rather strange" experience in 1997: "A man in 16th-century clothing walked from the main door of the North Block of the palace into my bothy. I assumed it was a staff member or volunteer who had donned historical clothing – something we did quite often at that time – but when I got to the bothy there was no-one there. And no-one had been dressed up that day.

"It was an upper-class gentleman, and it was a bright sunny day at about 11am. I have no explanation for it. He was wearing baggy trousers, long socks, tunic, waistcoat and hat. It may have been George Bruce himself. I saw him as plain as day and went to see what he wanted."'

George Bruce of Carnock (1550-1625), a merchant and a coal mining engineer built this merchants house sometime between 1597 and 1611. As he grew wealthier he extended the building until it gained the name 'The Palace.' Its adopted name wasn't unfounded. It did have a royal resident, albeit brief when James VI visited in 1617. George Bruce took him to see his coal mining operation which ran under the Firth of Forth. When the King climbed a mine shaft and appeared in the middle of the sea he thought Bruce was trying to kill him and shouted "Treason! Treason!" The matter was soon cleared up with the simple explanation that this was where the coal was taken aboard ships. Reassured, the King sailed in a rowing boat that was waiting for him back to the shore. This mine was lost in 1625 due to a high storm but it was the first example of its kind.

The Palace has been restored to its original by the National Trust for Scotland with the unusual orange façade being its original colour. It has painted ceilings and a garden recreated to how it would have been in the 17th century. Effigies of George Bruce and his wife can be seen in Culross Abbey where they were both interred.

The Palace also has the ghost of a servant and the ghosts of two young women. Customary drops in temperature have also been felt throughout the building.

Culross Townhouse

Circa 1883

Built in 1626 with the clock tower being added in 1783 the Townhouse was once the seat of the local government here and housed the town's court and prison. In the days of the witch trials suspected 'witches' were believed to have been confined to the attic of this building, and areas of the building are said to be haunted by both a notorious Judge and by those he callously executed.

Cupar

The Royal Hotel

A large hotel once stood on St. Catherine Street in Cupar, directly across from the Sheriff Courts on the town's main eastern thoroughfare. Until its closure towards the end of the 1980s the hotel was a very popular place with tourists and locals. It especially filled every lunch time with magistrate and lawyer seated before the main lunchtime rush began. A testimony to how good the meals were.

It was built on the site of an old abbey graveyard and the ghostly figure of a tall monk that makes its appearance here has been witnessed by a few people over the years. The hotel was also the haunt of mild 'prank' like poltergeist activity and certain areas could get very cold.

G. L. Playfair in his *Haunted Pub Guide* of 1985 says: A Mr Watson of Dunfermline related that he had seen the tall figure of a hooded monk in October 1978:

'The figure was seen at times throughout the hotel, appearing also in the function room which could get unusually cold at times. On one occasion the assistant manager on opening a metal door to the room found it to be extremely cold, he also saw the monk standing within part of the building.'[14]

After I incorporated the above I found a more descriptive account than that of Playfair which seems to have been his source. It is given to us by Andrew Green in the 1970s:

'When the golfing centre of St Andrews gets over-crowded, Cupar, the county town of Fife, becomes an 'overspill area' to accommodate the supporters of the game and the Royal Hotel rings with the sounds of voices talking of 'birdies' 'putts' and 'pars'. Some guests staying in this 150 year old building and using the Function Room for meetings have been puzzled by the occasional drop in temperature but have usually ignored the cold sensation, accepting that radiators and central heating thermostats are not always reliable. However, one evening in October 1978, Mr. Watson of Dunfermline who is a regular guest at the hotel, passed the empty room and purely out of interest, peered in. The room was 'icy cold' and what intrigued Mr. Watson even more was seeing a figure of a tall hooded monk walk slowly and silently across the floor. The guest stood in the doorway for about half a minute puzzled by the appearance of another visitor in the empty room, especially as it was quite late in the evening. Still wondering about the incident he walked on to his bedroom and went to sleep.

A few weeks later one of the assistant managers of the hotel was switching off the lights prior to closing down for the night, when he reached the Function Room noticing that one of the lights was still on, he began to open the door wider to go in, but was shocked by the freezing metal of the handle. So intense was the feeling that he was unable to move, but through the partially opened doorway he saw the identical figure seen earlier by Mr. Watson. When the apparition reached the outer wall it vanished and the light suddenly went out. There is only one doorway to the room and that was occupied by the assistant manager.

This was the third occasion when the mysterious monk has been seen in the same locality and has been associated with the inexplicable movement of cutlery when the room was used for a special gathering. A brief comment from a local provides the probable answer to the haunting. 'The hotel is built on the abbey's burial ground'.[15]

The building has now been completely demolished and all traces of the hotel, abbey and graveyard have gone, leaving a large hole in the ground for new development.

A Spectral Dog

Sometimes the ghosts we see are not gory enough to become the stuff of horror films or spectacular enough to command the headlines of the local or national press. A great many – if not the majority of hauntings in fact seem almost trivial by comparison to say screaming sculls or phantom coaches, but they are no less real for all they are experienced. This next account is one such sighting with a simplicity typifying the tone the majority of sightings actually take. They are subtle, casual in appearance and quiet in their manifestation, causing no other anomalous activity to then take place. What struck me about this story was the way in which it was recounted. It shows how sceptical we can be of the paranormal until something happens to us personally, and how we can think we are the only one to experience it – perhaps discounting it as our imagination or not wanting to cause concern in others. Out experiences of this nature tend to take us quite by surprise, especially when it is not in a haunted castle or a haunted pub but in our own home. When it happens it can scare us, especially if it appears unexpectedly at close quarters. Despite our mind telling us it shouldn't exist, we know that whatever it is, like others who witness the same, there is no other explanation than to call it a ghost. At least in this way others will get an idea of what it is you are talking about even if they don't understand or are dismissive of your testimony.

The account is as follows:
A ghostly black dog made its appearance curled up in front of the fireplace within an old house in Cupar. Seen several times over a period of eleven years it only appears for a very brief moment at a time. One of the former occupants of the dwelling said to me: "If someone had told me about this kind of things I wouldn't have believed them, but there it was! I was in the living room reading the paper when I became aware of something by the fireplace, when I looked up there was a dog lying there!" As he told me he visibly raised his head back in surprise as if he was again seeing the animal for the first time. "It was only there for a moment" he said, "then it was gone. Is this what they do?" He queried.

He never told anyone about what he saw, until one day his wife saw the same thing and mentioned the apparition to him. Upon which he told her that he too had seen it. After this they both saw the animal a few times whilst living in the house. It never really alarmed them; it was more of a surprise than anything else when it appeared.

Sometimes it would fade half in so it was still transparent, and then fade away again. It always appeared in the same place and never moved.

A few years later a couple who were on holiday in Fife arrived at the house, announcing themselves as the previous owners, they explained that since they were in the area at the time it would be nice to drop in on the place they had lived in for around thirty years.

During conversation the couple were asked if they had a pet whilst living there, to which the reply was that they had a lovely black dog.

In the garden one day the bones of an animal were unearthed, which they believed to be the last resting place of the previous family's pet, who still visits its favourite resting place from time to time.

Telecom House
A few years ago this building was disturbed by the sounds of footsteps along the corridors. Doors opening and closing of their own accord and banging noises in the morning or early evening were also heard with no explanation.

Dairsie

Piper

Refer to *Dairsie Castle*, p.109

Dairsie Bridge

Ghostly white figure

Refer to *Kemback*, p.165

Dalgety Bay

Otterston Loch

Directions

Otterston Loch is just out of the eastern edge of Dalgety Bay off the A921 Aberdour road. The loch is easily missed as it isn't signposted. The road entrance is on the right before entering Dalgety Bay from the east and is signed for Cockainie and Crossgates.

Otterston Loch is a beautiful local fishing loch. The recently restored and architecturally awarded Couston Castle stands in the secluded south eastern bank as a private residence. Built in the 16th century this was home to the Reverend Robert Blair – a covenanter who was banished to the castle by Archbishop Sharpe and died there in 1666.

A simple haunting by day in a beautiful location, and by night?

David Beveridge writing about this loch in 1888 says: 'At Otterston Loch just north of Dalgety Bay is the ghost of a lady with a child in her arms, the victim of misplaced affection.'[16] Although we could hazard a guess in a number of directions as to what this misplaced affection could have been, he doesn't unfortunately give any other details as to what it might have constituted.

Directions

On the eastern most edge of the town take the last road towards the shore off the A921. Signposted for Dalgety Bay and Hillend Industrial Park. Then take the first left following the signs for the church.

Commanding beautiful viewed over the bay the church is maintained by Historic Scotland, this ruinous church dating back to at least 1178 is all that remains of the original village of Dalgety.

photos by the author

The village stood just back from the shore on a rise overlooking Dalgety Bay on the eastern edge of the present town, which was only developed as a new town in 1962.

The church was altered in the 17th century for protestant worship with emphasis away from the altar to the pulpit.

Despite losing its roof in 1830 it continued to be used for burials and its graves now span over 800 years of history. The church Beadles or 'lay officials' of the church were prone to staying here overnight, keeping a lookout for body snatchers. This elaborate stone seat adorned with skulls, on the western side of the church wall is where a Beadle would have sat. The date at the top of the seat is 1685. It is just down from the main entrance and any coming through would have had a rude and fairly scary awakening.

The haunting of this Kirk is believed to occur every August/September when 14th century pirates from England revisit the church they plundered all those many years ago. This band of rogues on pillaging the area defeated the Sheriff of Dunfermline and his officers sent to stop them. They were eventually overcome in their rampage by men sent by Bishop Sinclair of Dunkeld who were staying slightly to the north in the village of Auchtertool at the time.

Dunfermline

Dunfermline Abbey/Palace

The current abbey of Dunfermline is a Church of Scotland Parish church built in 1821 incorporating the ruins of a Benedictine Abbey which was built on this site in 1128 by King David I. Parts of this abbey still remain and was itself constructed on an even older structure from the 11th century. Like so many Catholic buildings the Benedictine Abbey fell into disrepair following the reformation of 1559/60. The ruined abbey is believed to be haunted by a ghostly figure wandering its grounds and the walkway between Monastery Street and St Catherine's Wynd is haunted by a procession of monks.

The abbey is open to the public and has no admission charge. The site also has the ruins of an 11th century Royal Palace, with no less than 22 Kings, Queens, Princes and Princesses being buried here. King Robert the Bruce who gave support to William Wallace is possibly the Abbey's most famous occupant. He was buried here following his death in 1329 – however he was buried without his heart. This was removed from his body and embalmed. It was then taken on a crusade to the Holy Land led by James Douglas. When it eventually found its way back to Scotland instead of being reunited with his body it was buried at Melrose Abbey in the Scottish borders. The stone marking where it was buried has the words 'A noble hart may hae nae ease, gif freedom failye,' meaning; 'A noble heart may have no ease if freedom fails.'

The Abbot House

Of this house, Roddy Martin in an article for the Scotland Magazine in 2004 says; 'The Abbot House in the Maygate sits beside Dunfermline Abbey which dates from the 12th century. Ten years ago it was lovingly restored, and it has since become a heritage centre. While the repairs were taking place, however, strange things occurred. An architect working on site claimed to have vividly seen a figure wearing robes [a Benedictine monk] emerge from one of the stones in the wall. A member of the Abbot House staff insisted that somebody unseen had tripped her on the staircase. A young boy, one of a group with learning difficulties, refused point blank to go down the same staircase, and visitors often comment on the sudden drop in temperature.

A visiting clairvoyant who had never been there before spoke of a room full of children in the east tower, saying that it was accessed only by a one-way staircase. On investigation, it turned out to have been the room used for sick orphan children who were taken there when they were not expected to recover.

Do not let this put you off visiting as most people find the Abbot House a friendly place. The one sensation you do, however, come away with is that you have not been alone.'[17]

The Abbot House dates from 1460 and was once the administrative headquarters for the Benedictine Abbey. Today the house is a Heritage and Cultural Centre where you can take a tour of the building in the company of the resident ghostly monk appearing in physical form to speak of its history and heritage. It also hosts concerts and historical re-enactments and has a café to relax and continue the tranquil atmosphere of the area after wandering around the Abbey and Palace grounds.

Alhambra Theatre

Built in 1922 the theatre staged many productions before it was turned into a cinema then in 1965, like so many theatres of the day it was turned into a bingo hall. With ever changing times in 2005 the building had a major restoration and refurbishment to transform it once again into the theatre it was originally designed to be. It is now a major attraction for large productions and a cultural asset to Dunfermline with a great deal of character and no shortage of atmosphere.

The theatre has the ghost of a projectionist who appears in the projection room together with an unsettling feeling. There is the ghost of an Italian opera singer and the ghost of a woman wearing a black cowled dress. Footsteps have also been heard on the stairs, and numerous other sounds witnesses have been unable to account for over the years.

Coal Road

A Victorian policemen was seen on the Coal Road by Pittencrief Park in 2007. He was standing by the wall.

Northern Hospital

Many years ago this building was a work house for the poor, it is reputed to be haunted by unknown apparitional figures and the cries of a baby. Much in the same way as the former Maternity Hospital of Craigtoun just outside St. Andrews, where both staff, patients and visitors alike had all sometimes heard the unaccountable cries of a baby.

Pitreavie Castle

Haunted by a headless highlander, amongst other apparitions.

Refer to *GOF Castle Trail,* p.81

Izatt Avenue Housing Estate

'There is a ghost in Alice Cox Walk in the Izatt Ave. housing estate.* She was a district nurse. She knocks on doors and switches lights off & on.'[18]

(*Izatt Avenue is around half a mile to the north west of the Castle)

Dunino

Dunino Church and Dunino Den

Dunino Church was built in the early 19th century on the site of a medieval church built in 1240 and consecrated by Bishop David de Bernham. Sibbald in 1710 mentions about 'the church of Dininno belonging to St. Salvator's College'[19] [St. Andrews], it was a Catholic church until the reformation, standing until at least 1791.

Druids well and stairs

photo by the author

The church is now the Church of Scotland. The earliest Christian settlement here appears around the 11th century with the Culdee Monks, but its history as a spiritual centre with religious significance spans back to a far greater age, over many thousands of years.

The site of this church and its pagan origins is on the top of a rolling hill overlooking Dunino Den, a very picturesque wooded valley walk running through this area. A rocky crag juts out to a height of around twenty feet from the narrow stream of the Kinaldy burn below. On its top is a stone well, known as the

Druids Well, some three feet in diameter with a surround of smooth flat stone marking its perimeter at ground level.

A few Celtic engravings can be found on the rocks overlooking the burn. A 15 foot Celtic Cross along the cliff face is also etched into the rock, and probably spans back to the 10th century. This was a hallmark of the Culdee church which was primarily monastic Celtic Christianity.

There have also been very recent additions etched into the rock face, including a green man, a Celtic trinity and Celtic knotwork.

The Culdees were sympathetic of the old traditions but they laid the ground as a bridge between these old beliefs and the new religion of Christianity; integration rather than coercion

Stairs from the Burn to the Druidic well
photo by the author

and suppression. Unfortunately the might of the Catholic Church around the 12th century enforced the practices of the latter and looked to dominate the kinsfolk of the time away from their age old traditions.

Celtic knotwork of recent origin
photo by the author

What the Culdees appreciated, the Catholic impositions missed. Pagan considerations by decree of Christian terminology became synonymous with a primitive race of heathens, and if they didn't conform to the Catholic ways they were daubed heretics. A legacy that has stuck in the minds of many today not realising the word Pagan is *not* synonymous with Satanism as the church would have all believe, there is no correlation whatsoever. The association is the church's own perversion of an earth based way of being not necessarily tied to any religious belief or doctrine.

To be a Satanist means adherence to the Christian ethos and to then promote the antithesis of those values. When there is no Christian ethos there is no conflict. No archetypal heaven or hell in paganism and no god or devil as seen through Christian eyes.

A way of being doesn't necessarily require the promotion of a formalised doctrine for it to have value and for it to sustain itself for hundreds if not thousands of years. Survival utilising the simple awareness of the changing seasons and being in-tune or in touch with the elements – the land, the sea the air, the heat of the sun and fire were all crucial factors for survival, but that doesn't mean these were primitive people. Far from it; if the values between the primitive and the civilised are based on the complexity of their religion, there is something far wrong. Paganism is an umbrella term for many things. It is simply a collective term, and one not restricted by orthodox religious dogma or any contrived or coercive antithesis.

According to some sources there are around 300 million Pagans in the world today – not quite the minority the 'popular' church would have any believe, and if they were indeed to be believed – that would be a lot of Satanists!

Ancient Celtic Cross
photo by the author

Not a great deal can be seen now of the Celtic cross inscribed on the rock in the valley of Dunino Den. Even in the last 30 years it has lost a lot of its markings. Especially the upper part of the circle its horizontal extending arms. Its placement here by the Culdees was certainly to integrate if not overshadow existing beliefs, as the Culdees were looking to convert those of the pagan traditions, but they weren't looking to desecrate. The effect of whatever unification the Culdees were looking for however was primarily lost with the stamp of suppression served by the Roman authorities. The new religion had arrived and so too the Culdees were brought under the control of Canonical rule.

The natural magic of the people of Fife would never be the same again. The Celtic Cross in the Den which at best could be suggestive of symbolising a coexistence of Culdee Celtic Christianity with older beliefs, was shattered with the construction of the Roman church on Dunino Hill in 1240. Built on a sacred site it knew the only way to convert the people was to adopt their sacred spaces in a bid to then administer their beliefs. Consequently today, the cross in Dunino Den is seen as being as much a symbol of Christian graffiti defacing the values and respect for the older ways of being, as it is an early depiction of the Christian faith in Scotland.

A modern day sculpture in the rock face of the Green Man
photo by the author

The original significance of this area may not be forthcoming to the archaeologist or the historian who might attribute the more pagan elements to it "possibly being used for religious or ceremonial purposes," with no notion as to what that might have entailed other than the usual calls of 'sacrifice' or worship of old gods. Many find the time so distant and the evidence so scant that speculation covers too wide a field, so no one can know what these old beliefs comprised. Fundamentally this is true, but there are clues which can be discerned to the ceremonial practitioner and more importantly the sensitive to the earth's energies. As these later two are not the same.

To give an indication indicative of a different logic, and to make sense of why this attractive but fairly unassuming area has been a contended spiritual seat for thousands of years. The site of both the hill top and the sacred area in Dunino Den both have very strong natural energies, these are conducive to a 'between the worlds feeling' and this makes complete sense to its nature and purpose. Everything

Another modern day sculpture
photo by the author

in this Den is a microcosmic display of natural perfection. It is a place so vibrant and full of life. The Den lends itself to those qualities conducive to the frolicking of earth spirits and undines, all under the protective and watchful gaze of their elders. Such is the good nature and temperament of this unique and very special Den.

There is a sense here that everything is in order, and that you are never alone; a sense you are certainly being carefully watched or closer the mark, being closely observed and even scrutinised.

Dunino Den

photo by the author

By day at least this does not appear to be in a menacing way and is actually quite welcoming in the respect it both commands and gives when it is acknowledged; albeit on an unconscious level for most. By night however, I have a feeling things can be quite different, and unless invited, this is not a place for humans to roam with any degree of security or comfort.

Phantom Village

The following story about this Den was related by James Wilkie in his 1931 book *Bygone Fife* and typifies the possibilities of this 'between the worlds' haven. A place where occasionally the realms of existence appear to one another and a partial interaction of them both can take place. When these visions of transformation happen the everyday world is temporarily abandoned, as a new backdrop creates a different scene to meet with the eyes of the unsuspecting recipient. This is the closest any can come to being a time traveller, as the standing stones we see dotted about the countryside mark these areas where time overlaps – especially at the crossing of ley lines marked by stone circles. They are also very conducive to the promotion of paranormal phenomenon as the energies they utilise and concentrate are the same as those utilised by the phenomenon itself. They form a focus for the manifestation of many varieties of paranormal incidences to occur, as well as conveying many benefits to the physical constitution and especially the spirit itself.

'Some years ago, when many of the roads in the east of Fife were still used by but a few, a visitor to the district chanced to ride from the south coast to St. Andrews by that across the uplands. He had heard of Dunino Church, and knew something of its associations. He therefore resolved to make a detour to visit it. A somewhat rough track leads down to a bridge across the Pitmilly Burn, not yet united to her sister streams. Thence there diverges a broad and well made path, cut into the hillside and climbing among the trees to the Kirk and the manse. Leaving this for the moment he continued on the level track round the flank of the hill, and saw before him on the farther side of the stream a picturesque hamlet. Some of the cottages were thatched, some tiled; but all were covered with roses and creepers. In front a strip of garden, stretching to the burn, was trimly kept and full of old world flowers; behind it took on more the nature of a Kail – yard. At the east end, on slightly higher ground, a smithy closed in the prospect save for the trees that shut out the farther windings by the Den.

No sound broke the stillness of the summer noon but the flow of the burn. At one or two of the doors there stood an old man in knee–breeches and broad bonnet, or a woman in a white mutch and a stuff gown, while in the entrance to the forge the smith leant motionless on his hammer:-

"It was as though life's nurse in nurses fashion had lulled the world to sleep."

Peace brooded like a benediction over the hollow. Half in a dream he turned and climbed to the church, nor, as time pressed when he had seen it, did he return that way.

No sense of the abnormal had occurred to the intruder. He encountered no living thing till he had passed back to the high road. All was solitude.

A year or little more elapsed ere the wanderer came thither again. It was autumn, and tints of russet and gold were stealing into the colour of the woodlands. This time he was accompanied by a companion to whom he had told the story of his glimpse of "the most old – world hamlet in Fife." Where he left the highway they diverged from it, and crossing the bridge prepared to sketch the Arcady to be revealed.

The cottages were gone.'[20]

A footnote to this story states 'The author is informed on excellent authority that there were at one time at least three or four cottages and a blacksmiths shop at the place described. It is said these were taken down. "Sometime last century."[21]

I stayed at Stravithie House for a season many years ago and frequently took to wandering through these woods. On one occasion in the height of winter I went for a stroll along the path to the Den and the sacred site by the stream. The snow was thick on the ground, when I felt sure I must have been by the circular well on the promontory of rock by the stone carved steps I could see no sign of the well with the snow being so deep. I crouched down and wiped away some of the snow. Part of the stone well appeared, I continued, and as I did so the curvature of the well went around me. I then realised the water had frozen and I was crouching on top of it. With visions of falling through to the depths below where I would surely be lost, I gingerly moved off the ice trap I had inadvertently found myself on. Thinking myself lucky to be alive, it wasn't until a number of years later that I found it was less than three feet deep. So it doesn't appear to be a well for gathering water from the depths, more the characteristics of an ancient fresh water basin which is in-keeping with purifications before descending to the sacred stream below.

Dura Den

Ghostly white figure

Refer to Kemback, p.165

East Wemyss
MacDuff's Castle and Caves

Apparition of a woman

Refer to *GOF Castle Trail*, p.60

Falkland

The Covenanter Hotel

This centuries old Inn is situated in the Square along the High Street by Falkland Palace. In the early 17th century it was the coaching Inn for the village.

A number of hotel websites list it either as being a traditional Scottish hotel called The Covenanter Hotel, or as an Italian restaurant with a few rooms called Luigino's. So when I visited this hotel I wasn't sure what to expect. On arrival I was pleasantly relieved to find it was called The Covenanter Hotel, and on speaking with the proprietors – a local Falkland family, it was turned back into a Scottish hotel and restaurant 18 months ago. The building has a lot of character and this is reflected within the building itself. It is situated in an ideal location and with its own charm it offers traditional Scottish fare. When its hospitality, its conviviality and its ghosts are added to this, it is a hotel I highly recommend.

So what of the ghosts to be found here? The building is haunted by a young woman who has been seen over many years in the bedrooms. She has been attributed to Mary Queen of Scots and not just because of her staying on occasion at the Palace across the road. A story runs that Mary had an affair with someone who lived here when she was visiting the Palace and that somewhere in the attic of the building her lover hid an engagement ring for her.

During my visit I found the ghost of Mary is not the only ephemeral occupant to haunt this building. A boy has been seen running up and down the stairs and recently another presence has been felt by a psychic of an older lady roaming the building. This recently drew some publicity to the building with national papers covering the story. If you stay here you may be lucky enough to witness one of these apparitions for yourself, although like many places, the staff don't like thinking about them too much. With working here every day they are not sure how they would react to seeing something of a supernatural origin.

Falkland Estate

The nearby Falkland Estate just down the road and in easy walking distance from the Hotel also has a ghost that is known to the locals of the village as a White Lady. She has been seen over the years gliding through the woods.

There are mixed feelings about the woods here and the ghostly inhabitant who roams them. They are avoided by some, while others have no qualms about taking their dogs for a walk in them at night time. Ghosts are an interesting phenomenon on the psyche, with perspectives completely changing about them once they have been seen. A local man who saw the White Lady was so feared at what he saw that by all accounts he never left his house at night for years after the incident. There is little requirement for exaggeration here. We each react differently to what we experience, and once we have, our opinion of them is never the same again as the impact on the mind is so lasting.

Falkland Palace
Apparition of a woman

Refer to *GOF Castle Trail*, p.88

A912 Falkland – Strathmiglo Road

Ghost of Jenny Nettles

Refer to Strathmiglo Area, p.236

B936 Falkland – Auchtermuchty Road

Ghostly female figure in white

Refer to Strathmiglo Area, p.236

Fife Ness

King Constantine's Cave

The oldest ghost in Fife is to be found here. Sometimes called 'The Devil's Cove' this Cave is situated by the most easterly part of the Balcomie Links Golf Course near Fife Ness, which as a point of interest is the seventh oldest golf club in the world. This small caved used now it seems as a watering hole for the stray golfer was named after King Constantine, who a great many years ago renounced royalty and became a monk residing within the cave. He eventually died here in the hands of the Danes around 874, and his ghost is said to make its appearance at the entrance here. Golfers beware!

Fordell Ruined Mill

All that remains today of the Mill
photo by the author

This is a place avoided by many after dark, and even during the daylight hours some are apprehensive of approaching it alone. The path through the woods runs close to the ruins but very little remains of the mill today. Major landslides

of the bank over the years have resulted in whatever was left of the building collapsing creating piles of moss covered worked stone lying as rubble and half buried in the earth. Part of the Mills wall is still intact but nothing else is recognisable.

Situated east of Dunfermline and just to the north of Dalgety Bay, follow the B916 north from Dalgety Train Station past the cemetery on the right and the nursery on the left. After a few more metres go down the rough gravel road on the right. At the end follow the track into the woods by the course of the Fordell Burn along Fordell Glen some 500 metres. The ruined village mill will be found just to the left as the path begins to curve in a horseshoe away from the burn.

Fordell Mill was built some time before 1511 and features in an Edinburgh charter of James

IV. The mill has had extensive use over the centuries and has been reconstructed on a number of occasions. A stone panel above the ancient entrance door has the date 1585 with the present ruins showing building work from the 18th century and later.

'The story runs that after the Battle of Pitreavie in 1651, Cromwell's victorious troops were quartered in the surrounding district. The Fordell miller had a squad of soldiers billeted with him who, despite his pleading, continually molested his wife and daughter. In desperation, the miller poisoned his unwelcome guests and fled.

A picket of soldiers was sent to avenge their comrades, but being unable to find the miller, hanged his assistant Jock instead. To this day, it is said, at certain times and seasons he hangs there still, the branches creaking dolefully as his body swings to and fro. On some moonlight nights, Jock's ghostly corpse, with agonised face and staring eyes, can be seen in the branches.'[22]

A slight variation of this story from J. C. R. Bruckner in 1881 is as follows:
'The story goes that a corporal and four soldiers, who were quartered at the mill, behaved in a disagreeable manner towards the miller's pretty wife, and still prettier daughter, and that the man of flour freed himself of his unwelcome guests by poisoning them. A party of soldiers was dispatched by Cromwell's officers to avenge the deaths of their comrades by hanging the miller on the nearest convenient tree.

The miller had, however, been apprised of this intention, and, under pretence of business, decamped, leaving his foreman "Jock" to impersonate him till his return. It is, of course, needless to say that the foreman was seized and hung in the place of his master. The tradition proceeds: "Ever after people avoided the place, and no one ventured to pass after nightfall, as 'Jock's ghost' was always visible at midnight hanging from a tree near the mill.'[23]

Grangemuir

Mansion House and Grounds

J. W. Jack in 1914 wrote: 'Repose was utterly banished from the family mansion of Grangemuir in consequence of a strange unaccountable noise which invaded the ears of the inmates…. The sounds resembled those produced by a barefoot person hastily running from one apartment to another…

This spectre continued its nightly visits, under the title of Baff Barefoot, till the beginning of the nineteenth century, when the house was razed to the foundations, being superseded by the splendid mansion which presently stands about a furlong to the northward of the old site; but for a certain reason, not a single fragment of the old building was applied to the new.

There are also stories of ghosts "flitting" with the material or contents of the old house.'[24]

In the grounds there is a grouping of old ash and elm trees not far from where the old mansion house was sited, they are said to be haunted by the ghostly figure of Baff himself. The legend of Baff was extant in the early 1800s with stories and warnings not to pass these trees after midnight for fear of the ghost that dwells there.

The present mansion was built in the 18th century as a hunting lodge for a branch of the Douglas family, a number of them being buried in the burial grounds of nearby Dunino church.

Jack was quite right, none of the original building was used in the construction of the new building, and it was through the fear that the ghost would be transferred with the fabric to the new location, causing it to continue its escapades in the new dwelling. This alone gives an idea that whatever the actual extent of the disturbances in the original building, they were not looking for them to be recreated. This was certainly an idea, but reality works in many mysterious ways and it didn't work.

The haunted main stairway
photo by the author

Occupants a number of years ago once again heard ghostly footsteps pacing the long dark corridors and stairs within the house. Although this building is in a different location to the former, it would appear being on the same grounds has been enough for the disturbances to be maintained. There were also brief cold spells in the house, sometimes accompanied by a breeze, which would blow through the corridors when the windows and doors were all fastened quite shut.

The legend of Baff Barefoot or 'Buff' Barefoot as he has also been recorded, more as a nickname with buff meaning bare or naked, tells of how in the 17th century a maiden who lived in Grangemuir House fell in love with Baff. He was a sailor by trade who had been shipwrecked off the Fife coast. Soon after their meeting however he was destined to go back to sea, but with promises to her of his return. While he was away Baff's brother tried courting the maiden, but his advances were to no avail, so smitten was she with her sailor man. So bitter and angry at her rebuttals and jealous of his brother he plotted their mutual demise.

Baff wrote her a letter saying that he was coming ashore. That night she excitedly went to Doocot Hill to greet her lover as this was the meeting place in his letter. When she arrived however it was not Baff that greeted her but his brother. He greeted her with murder in mind and shot her where she stood. He had intercepted Baff's mail to her and fabricated a letter of his own, purporting to be from Baff himself. He put in writing how he was to come ashore and wanted to meet with her on the Doocot Hill.

He planted the letter on her, and upon her body being discovered the forged letter from Baff was found on her person. He was dully found guilty and sentenced for the crime. He told her he would return to Grangemuir House and sure enough to this day he seems to have kept his word as he runs through the house looking for the whereabouts of his true love. The reason for him being bare footed isn't known, but it would appear he roams the estate looking for her also and not just the house. Although his footsteps wouldn't be heard running on grass in the estate his ghost has been seen by the ash trees so there are more than just footsteps at work here. Perhaps there are those who have heard footsteps themselves on the gravel driveways with no apparent source? So he was never confined to the old house which makes sense of how his footsteps have been heard in the present house.

Grangemuir Estate is now a thriving woodland chalet park for holiday makers. Spread over 18 acres of well kept lawns and tranquil forestry walks, it is a popular holiday destination. The house was bought by two lawyers a number of years ago who spent some £400,000 on the property trying to do it up, but they finally went bust. The latest owner who also has the caravan park at Kilrenny is gradually working to bring it back to its former grand country house stature. As he says, time is the only factor as it is such a large project.

Isle of May

photo by the author

Grangemuir is not the only place to have the sound of footsteps – albeit these ones are wearing shoes.

Robert Sibbald the Scottish Physician and Antiquarian writing in 1710 says: 'This small island of rock one mile long by a third wide is a nature reserve lying five miles south east of Anstruther in the Firth of Forth. Many migrating birds including terns and puffins live on this rich isle under supervision of bird watchers and members of the reserve. Built in 1636 the lighthouse on the island warning shipping of its presence is the oldest of its kind in Scotland. The architect of this forty foot high tower after a visit to the isle was drowned on his return journey to the mainland in a great storm, believed to have been created by witches who were later burnt for their grave misdeed.'25

Ever since his death his ghost is said to haunt this lighthouse. I spoke to a couple of men commissioned to carry out work on the lighthouse a number of years ago and they reported how on numerous occasions they had heard footsteps climbing the stairway of the lighthouse. They waited for the originator of the sounds but nobody was ever forthcoming. When they later checked, it was found they were the only on the island at the time.

The island also has a vague ghostly figure that has been seen momentarily by the thirteenth century ruins of St. Adrian's Priory. 'It was the canons of this Priory that established the Augustinian Priory of Pittenweem after leaving the island. They built it in dedication to St. Adrian, who was one of the early saints of Fife. He built a monastery on the island and was killed here, or rather slaughtered along with many other monks, some say upwards of 600 by the Vikings in 875CE, making St. Adrian a martyr. The island became an important place for pilgrims to gather for blessings and healing, with no less than 3000 visitors to this small island each year over a period of 200 years. James IV was one of those pilgrims, visiting the island on at least five separate occasions.'26

Kelty

Blairadam Forest
The following report is from the Dunfermline Press, 9th October 2008:

'Rosyth family see ghost in Kelty woods
by Graham Gibson,

A ROSYTH man is in a state of shock after stumbling across what he believes is the ghost of an old miner while out walking with his family in Blairadam Forest, Kelty.

John Wilson (32), a joiner, of Daniel Place, had the spooky experience while visiting the forest with his wife and three children when they stopped near an abandoned mine to take family photographs.

Mr Wilson said, 'I put the pictures on the computer but never looked at them for a year.

"It was only when I went to sort them out a week ago that I noticed something odd.

"I went to crop the pictures to get rid of the rubbish and I noticed something odd in the tree line behind the kids."

John is adamant that there was no-one else present at the time though does recall his dog was greatly agitated at nothing in particular, which at the time the family put down to an unseen rabbit in the bushes.

He reckons the photos appear to reveal the presence of a long-deceased miner and, although not a big believer in the afterlife, what John saw in the photograph has certainly made him think twice.

"I think it looks like on old miner wearing a flat cap and an old coat.

"I'm not a big believer in ghosts but I was going through my head trying to explain it and it's all I think it could be."

John is familiar with the area, having played there as a child and remembers vividly searching for the entrance to the mines which closed in the early 20th century.

"I used to stay in Kelty and spent a lot of time in those woods," he said.

"I know that's near where the old Blairenbathie mines used to be.

"I used to go looking for the entrance shaft when I was a kid and I'm sure kids do the same these days."

John is under strict instructions from his wife, Karen, to keep the photograph hidden from his three children, Holly (11), Derryn (5) and Kyle (3).

"My wife told me not to show it to the kids as it might scare them.

"They are still quite young to be dealing with such things."

Private Kelty Residence

Social media groups such as Facebook are now the most popular forms of global interactive communication to share our experiences with others. The following is a brief post from Janice McFarlane of Kelty which I found both honest and down to earth. With it being written with a distinctive Kelty/Fife colloquialism I have translated it for those not versed in the broad Scots tongue!

Posted on Facebook 29th September 2012

'Ma hoose in Kelty when I was a bairn! 102 Centre St! Loads of Kelty folk have stiries aboot the auld man who used to watch oot

'My house in Kelty when I was a child! 102 Centre Street! Loads of Kelty folk have stories about the old man who used to look out of the

the window keeping an eye on the bairns climbing the tree in the front garden! I saw him when I was wee apparently when I was in the front room. Neighbour doonstair cudnae get their bairns to ever settle in the front room!'

window, keeping an eye on the children climbing the tree in the front garden! I saw him when I was small apparently when I was in the front room. The neighbour downstairs couldn't get their children to ever settle in the front room!'

Kemback

Kemback sits in a most beautiful gorge, amid high cliffs and woodland. The road of Kemback winds along the route of the Ceres Burn, following the high cliffs to the left along to Pitscottie to the south.

The area here known as 'Dura Den' is world renowned for its fossil fish, discovered here in 1859.

Some are still existent here although most have now been removed. The following story from the Peoples Journal 1907 concerns a White Lady who haunts the locality:

The White Lady of Kemback
'It is said that one of them [the family of Schevez of Kemback] suffered persecution for nonconformity. He had to leave the house and hide in a cave still seen high in the rocks of Dura  Den. It was winter. His wife carried food to him, tying her shoes on heel to toe in going to confuse any pursuer. She was taken, and refusing to betray him, was hanged over Dairsie Bridge and beheaded. Tradition identifies her with the White Lady of Kemback, whose headless effigy in stone lies in a wood near the house, and after whom a room in the mansion house itself still bears the name

of the White Lady's Room. But some antiquaries say the effigy is that of Mario te Olifert, Lady of Kemback in the 15th century. We prefer the popular tale.'[27] Her ghostly white figure now haunts Dairsie Bridge and the roadway along Dura Den.

Another story from the same copy of the People's Journal above concerns a piper and a cave network said to span between Kemback House and Dairsie Castle.

'There is a tradition that a subterranean passage ran from the house [of Kemback] to Dairsie Castle, underneath the river [Eden]. When the present laird was a boy there was a very old woman who said that her grandmother told her that when some alterations were being made, the mouth of this passage was discovered. A wandering piper was induced to go into the hole and play his pipes, so that the direction in which the passage went might be discovered.

Kemback House

The piping below ground led to the river's edge and ceased. The piper did not return, and after allowing what they considered a reasonable time, the people built up the mouth of the hole.'[28]

Kemback House, a large 18th century country mansion and a private dwelling is situated to the north-east of Kemback village.

The restored fortified Castle of Dairsie is around a third of a mile to the north-west of Kemback House. This beautiful castle built by the early bishops of St. Andrews around the 13th century was meticulously restored from ruins in 1992 by the present owner. It is now available to hire as a self catering destination for holidays, weddings etc.

Dairsie Castle

Refer also to *Dairsie Castle*, p.109

Kilmany

Within the parish of Kilmany, the lands of Rathillet were the property of the family name Hackston. They had been granted the lands in the 13th century by King Malcolm IV. In the 17th century it was home to Hackston of Rathillet, a covenanter present at the murder of Archbishop Sharpe in 1679. He paid for the crime with the most gruesome of executions in Edinburgh and in remorse haunted Sharpe's former residence at Strathtyrum House by St. Andrews.[xxxi]

The area known as 'Ghouls Den' in Kilmany is situated near the A92 Dundee to Glenrothes road, 5 miles from Newport-on-Tay. The Fife Herald and Journal of 1904 reported: 'This romantic ravine lies a little to the north-west of Kilmany Cottage with its pretty walks, little waterfalls and overhanging rocks.... "White Ladies" and the shades of the departed (who found Kilmany so beautiful that they haunt it even yet) are to be seen, it is said, after nightfall by those who have the courage to venture at the witching hour within its sombre depths.'[29]

The Parochial Directory for Fife and Kinross of 1861 on describing this area says; 'Immediately north-west of the hamlet of Kilmany, and in the course of the Motray, is a very romantic dell, which appears to have been formed first by a trap-rock disruption, and afterwards by the action of running water. Its banks have been planted with trees, and walks made through it, which renders it easy of access; and its little waterfalls and over-hanging rocks present a very picturesque and interesting scene.'[30]

Kilrenny

Caiplie Caves

Among the many interesting sights to be found along the route of Fife's coastal footpaths are the caves of Caiplie, situated between Crail and Cellardyke. The caves look out to sea; across to the Isle of May and have an association with St. Adrian mentioned above. Set a little back from the sea in the surroundings of green grass and gorse. Varying in both size and depth the entrances to some of the smaller caves are half hidden and access may now be impossible or at the least dangerous. The largest cave is known as the Chapel Cave and one of the smaller caves is known as the Hermits cave; after an old man who lived here with his cat and dog before the Second World War. Remnants of the entrance fixings of his primitive dwelling are still in place. The caves are a natural formation of sandstone, carved from the sea, with expansion from being used for different purpose over the years.

[xxxi] Refer also to *The Bloody Murder of Archbishop Sharpe* p.195

These caves were mentioned in the New Statistical Account of Scotland (1791-1799) and read as follows:

'There are some remarkable caves or coves, as they are sometimes called, situated in the eastern part of the parish and close by the shore... They stand at present several feet above the high-water mark, and rise to the height of 30 or 40 feet. There are likewise to be seen in the interior of the caves, artificial cuttings and chiselled crosses, which indicate that at some period they have been used as the abode of men... There is no tradition regarding them, except that there is a communication belowground between them and the house of Barnsmuir, situated nearby half a mile from the shore, where it is said that a piper was heard playing beneath the hearth stone of the kitchen; but these days of delusion have passed away.'[31]

The 'artificial cuttings' mentioned in the above were for a pigeon doocot around 170CE and the 'chiselled crosses' refer to incised crosses from when the caves were a place of early Christian worship in the 9th century, 'when Adrian with his company together came to Caplauchy.'[32]

Kinaldy

'The Bivy' and a St. Andrews Legend

A few miles south of St. Andrews there lies a quiet woodland area by Kinaldy Farm known as 'the Bivy'. During the summer of 1980 a party of people from the Air Training Corps in St. Andrews went camping in these woods by the farm. At around 3am one of those gathered decided to pull a prank on the others. Dressed in an RAF great coat and wearing a balaclava he started rattling tents and making noises to scare them. Succeeding in this, those he had awakened began searching for their mysterious intruder. One of those who began to search heard something moving through the trees toward the edge of a field and followed the sound, but was soon called back to the camping area. The prankster on hearing someone moving toward him waited for him to appear through the trees then heard him change direction back toward the campsite. He was about to start on behind him when he noticed something. It was a small red figure amongst the trees; only about three feet in height and about fifteen feet in front of him. Surprised he stood motionless and viewed the strange figure who seemed to be dressed in what looked like a hooded one piece jump-suit. The small red creature walked with purpose straight passed without even a glance or acknowledgement that he was there.

Somewhat bemused by this he went to the campsite and made his presence known to the rest of the party. Confessing it was he who had attempted to scare them, he then explained about the mysterious figure he had encountered. It was then found that this figure was what one of the others had followed through the forest.

To this day he is still bemused by the small figure in red, there was no explanation to account for it as it was far too late for a child to be wandering through the woods alone at this hour and despite all the commotion they all caused, it showed no sign of fear and appeared to completely ignore all of them as it went about its business in the dead of night.

The Kinghorn to Burntisland A921 Road
and the Green, Grey and White Ladies!

The Ghost of a Green Lady

The apparition of a female figure dressed in a green robe is seen by the memorial to Alexander III on the Burntisland road. Her name is Yolande and she is the wife of Alexander who roams the area looking for her long lost husband.

photo by the author

'Although Alexander's castle is long gone from Kinghorn, there are still reminders of him here. A memorial was erected to him beside the road to Burntisland to mark the spot from which he fell to his death, and it is said that the green robed ghost of his young wife Yolande still searches for him here. And just outside the east end of Kinghorn Parish Church, built in 1774, is a partial wall and stonework that once formed parts of a church dating all the way back to 1243. An aisle from the earlier church was also incorporated into the 1774 church. It is remarkable to think that Alexander III would certainly have worshipped in this earlier church.'

Alexander III was crowned King of Scotland at Scone Palace in the 13th century. Yolande de Dreux, the Comtesse de Montfort was his second wife. On the 18th March 1286 only five months after they were married, he was travelling back to Kinghorn Castle (no longer in existence) on horseback. When darkness fell and stormy weather loomed the Kings horse faltered and he was thrown over the cliffs to his death, which is why the green clad widow still searches for him yet.

William Skene in 1871 gives two more accounts as to the nature of his death:

'There are two stories currently told of how the king [Alexander the Third] came to his death. The first is, that the king had been returning on horseback at night to Glammis Tower, his castle, above Kinghorn. His horse shied and threw him over a high cliff, which rises abruptly and almost perpendicularly from the level sand below to the height of about 150 feet, along the summit of which the path on which he was riding held its course. He fell with his head upon a rock, and died. This rock is known as the King's Stone.

The second story is that the king was passionately fond of hunting, and rode a high-spirited horse. Thomas the Rhymer told the king that the horse would be his death, but the king would not believe him. One day an archer shot an arrow, which glanced from a tree, struck the horse, and killed it. The horse fell dead upon the Kinghorn road, and the king said to Thomas the Rhymer, "and how can your prophecy come true?" However, some months after the king was travelling that way on another horse, which shied at the appearance of the bones of the first horse, and threw the king, who was killed in this way.'[33]

The monument is only yards away from a bus stop on the same side of the road towards the Kingswood Hotel and is haunted by a Grey Lady haunts both the bus stop and the local service buses.

The Ghost of a Grey Lady

The following is from a local online magazine called the Kirkcaldy Book:

'She appears on cold dark evenings as a shadowy figure waiting at a bus stop across the road from the Kingswood Hotel, Burntisland. Local gossip states that the Grey Lady once lived in a cottage behind the Kingswood Hotel and that she hanged herself from a tree on the Kinghorn Road. Others have an unkind dig at the bus company and say the Grey Lady died while waiting for a bus. The Grey Lady has been spotted by a passing motorist. Antoinette Blanchard recalls a chance meeting with the phantom. As her father drove around the corner at the Kingswood Hotel he slammed the breaks on to avoid a grey figure standing in the middle of the road. When he jumped out of his car to look for the woman she had vanished.

photo by the author

She has not been seen recently but in the early sixties she was the talk of the bus garage. One night a bus stopped and picked her up. It was the last run of the night along the coast road. The bus arrived at the infamous stop around midnight. The bus stop was dark but the driver caught sight of a figure in the glow of his headlamps. He pulled the bus up at the stop and the shadowy figure stepped onto the bus. The conductress watched as this middle aged woman dressed in grey sagging clothes climbed onto the bus and made her way upstairs. The conductress rang the bell and the driver started on his journey. The conductress climbed the stairs to take the fare but there was nobody there.

She rang the bell and stopped the bus at the next stop. She explained to the driver what happened and they both searched through the bus, but there was no sign of the mysterious woman. They were quite shaken by the experience and told the story when they arrived back at the garage. After that reports came in at regular intervals about sightings of the Grey Lady standing at the bus stop. A conductress from that period confided in me that the last late night run along the coast was unpopular with the bus crews. The apparition became a good excuse for not wanting to go on that run. The shift was so unpopular with the bus crews that the company cancelled it.'[34]

Only a matter of yards from this bus stop is another apparition known as the 'White Lady' at the Kingswood Hotel.

The Ghost of a White Lady and the Goose of Kingswood Hotel

Kingswood Hotel just along from both the haunted monument and the haunted bus stop is itself haunted by a White Lady known as Jenny, who wears

photo by the author

a long flowing beautiful white Victorian dress. She has often been seen flitting about the building. There have also been reports – especially in Victorian times of a phantom goose that pecked at the young girl who lived there when it was a private residence. It has also been known to attack others over the years.

The Old Manse of Kinghorn

While this is not a ghost story, it nearly became one!

'The said old manse was the residence of the famous Rev. John Scrimgeor, of whose wife a grim old story lingers in the lore of the parish. It seems that Mrs Scrimgeor had been buried while in a death-like trance, and that she was restored by the attempt made by an avaricious sexton to remove the rings from her clay cold fingers. "She never smiled again," runs the story.'[35]

Kinglassie

The Ghost of 'Green Jean' (Private residence)

In the first section on the tour of Fife's many haunted Castles I reproduced a letter about a 'Green Jean' at Pitcairlie House near Auchtermuchty and that it was one of two letters I had received regarding an apparition by this name. As I mentioned in the other account the two stories concern different locations and don't appear to be related other than for two striking similarities, both apparitions are called Green Jean and both met their end by falling from buildings.

The following is this second letter and pertains to Kinglassie House from Pat Cowieson in Dundee 5th March 1989 and reads as follows:

'Dear Sir,

With reference to your letter in the Courier this week I thought you might be interested in the haunting at my aunt's former home.

She used to live in Kinglassie House, Kinglassie, Fife, and moved there in 1953. The house is about 350-400 years old and is haunted by 'Green Jean'.

A few weeks after my aunt and uncle moved into Kinglassie House they went for an evening stroll and met the minister, Mr Able, who asked them if they weren't afraid to walk around and go back into the house in the dark. That was the first they had heard about the ghost and they never saw nor heard anything themselves in the years they lived there.

However my parents, my sister and I went to stay with them in May 1953 when my sister was just six weeks old. My mother, sister and I slept in one of the front bedrooms while my father slept in a smaller bedroom. In the morning my mother commented on how the dog – a Labrador – had paced the landing all night and had even tried to open the bedroom door and also how cold and windy it had been. Up until then my parents did not know about the ghost. My aunt then told my parents that it hadn't been windy and that the dog had been shut up in their bedroom all night.

My aunt had three dogs during the time they were in Kinglassie and none of them would stay in the house alone. They had to be left at the lodge at the foot of the drive. One of them even went as far as half chewing through the heavy latch kitchen door in an attempt to get out.

After my mother told my aunt about her disturbed night Mr Able and another minister came to exorcise the house and this seemed to quieten things down for a while.

However my aunt's mother (also my father's mother) took very ill while she was living at Kinglassie. My father was sent for and my grandmother died in an early evening of 1955. After everything that had to be done was done my aunt, uncle and father were told to go and get some sleep. But 'Green Jean' had other ideas. Doors rattled, wind whistled, handles turned and nobody got much rest. It seemed to take a death in the house to make the haunting more active. One morning when my sister and I were still young and staying at Kinglassie we came downstairs and one of us asked who the strange lady was who came into our bedroom during the night. Neither my parents nor my aunt and uncle had gone into our room after we had gone to bed. Nobody seems to know who 'Green Jean' was or what happened to her although the minister, Mr Able, who is now dead thought that she may have fallen to her death from the balcony in that front bedroom.'

Pat Cowieson

The minister's account of her falling to her death seems to be taken from the general legend about 'Green Jean' in this part of Fife rather than holding down any further validity. Also with Green Jean being a generic name for an unexplained ghost it explains why there appears to be a number of them in the area. Further information has proved difficult to ascertain but I found an account published in 1903 by a Dr Rorie in the Fifeshire Advertiser which pertains to the original Kinglassie House on the grounds nearby to the present building and seems to involve poltergeist type disturbances in a similar manner to those described by Pat in the above account.

'The Kinglassie Deil. The locus of this unearthly visitant was the old manse of Kinglassie, now demolished, which stood on the other side of the road from the present one. His presence was heralded by a loud noise in an upstairs room "as if a cart o' stanes had been coupit on the floor." The cause of the disturbance was never satisfactorily accounted for, but while the noises occurred they naturally caused great annoyance to the inhabitants of the manse. On one occasion the minister and his Kirk session assembled at night, with coal and candle-light and an open Bible on the table, to wait for and lay the ghost. One member of the session professed great disbelief in matters supernatural, and, as it was a cold night, had taken off his boots to warm his feet the more satisfactorily at the fire. Suddenly the terrifying noise occurred upstairs, and the unbeliever burned his feet very badly through trying to hide in the chimney. Told me by an old inhabitant, aged 80 in 1808.'[36]

This would suggest the presence transferred itself to the new building when it as build. Being of the 'classic haunting' variety rather than the psychokinetic phenomenon from say an adolescent, it points to an intelligent force or being that is certainly looking to attract attention to itself. It is looking to be acknowledged. Whether it is trying to communicate or unsettle would take a medium to ascertain. Communication always has a far greater affect, and serves a greater purpose in finding out more about the reasons for the disturbance than a minister going in cold as it were, not being able to communicate. When not knowing what it was that was causing the phenomenon, it is all too easy to put occurrences down to malevolent means when in actual fact a plea for help is often the deeper motivation. It is often the case that disturbances can subside for a time following a blessing for the more dramatic house exorcism. They rarely work long term. Queen Mary's House in St. Andrews is a prime example of this. A minister walks in, says a few prayers, sprinkles a bit of holy water and job done! – Until that is, it all comes back and in the case of Queen Mary's

House, Kinglassie House and many other cases, they do come back. Typically their return is marked with activity more pronounced than it was before any blessings took place.

Refer to Pitcairlie House for the first letter, p.90
Refer also to the end of the introduction for further details of 'Green Jean' p.8

Kinkell

Kinkell Castle
Haunted by the Apparition of Lady Kinkell.

Refer to *GOF Castle Trail*, p.36

Kirkcaldy

Bell Craig – Cave, the sound of bagpipes
'Tradition affirms that there issued from a cave in the Bell Craig "an air from heaven or blast from hell" which enabled persons who imbibed it in proper measure to foresee future events. To this rock then the wizard [Sir Michael Scott] is believed to have resorted on particular occasions for inspiration. Within the memory of many, belated travellers, on passing the Crag, are reported to have experienced very peculiar sensations. All traces of the cave are now obliterated, that portion of the rock having been used as a quarry, and several stately buildings have been erected out of the walls of the wizard's cave.

About a century ago[xxxii] a drunken piper, returning from Lochgelly Fair, was arrested by the intoxicating vapour. Instead of availing himself of the propitious moment to learn the probable duration of Christmas doles, penny weddings, and other customs in which it may be supposed a person of his calling would be especially interested, the infatuated mortal only testified his exhilaration by a tune upon the bagpipe. ... A signal punishment, however, awaited him for the unhallowed use to which he had applied the divine afflatus. The instrument with which he had perpetrated the profanation was destined, alas! never more to pass from his lips. The night was stormy; but the louder the wind blew, the louder did the enchanted bagpipes sound along the strath. Such a piping was never heard either before or since. . . . Nor did the music cease till sunrise, when a peasant going to his work found the piper lying dead at the mouth of the cave, with the chanter between his lips. It rests on what the Ettrick Shepherd would have called excellent authority, that the Spectre Piper is still heard, on very stormy nights, playing a coronach on the Bell Crag -

---

[xxxii] Beginning of the 18th century

"In a windy unworldly tone,
To mortal minstrelsy unknown."' [37]

Council House
The Scotsman 4th May 1994 reported: 'A council tenant fled his flat and demanded to be re-housed after a series of unexplained incidents. A previous occupant confirmed he too had had strange experiences while living there.' [38] The location has been kept private.

17 Oaktree Square - Poltergeist Activity
The following was the subject of an extensive book with a famous photos on its cover of a girl flying in mid air, apparently having been thrown out of her bed. The house was the scene of purported poltergeist activity.

Between February and September 1958 17 Oaktree Square a two storied corner house was disturbed by poltergeist activity. It was reported in the Dundee Courier and the Edinburgh Evening News in 1972 [39] that: 'windows opened of their own accord, drawers would jump open, footsteps, bumps and scuffling noises were heard, and sometimes during the night between the 11th and 12th of September a wardrobe and chair in one of the bedrooms had moved. The room had been checked at 2:30am with no sign of anything unusual and nobody had heard anything during the night. In the morning though the discovery had been made and was reported by a twelve year old girl.'

The Journal of the Society for Psychical Research has the following about the haunting:

'A council type house.
2 stories, at corner.
A covered passage runs between it and the adjoining house.
Period. February – September 1958.
Phenomenon – Intermittent.
Windows opened of their own accord, drawers jumped open, bumps and scuffling noises heard. On one occasion (Sept 12) a wardrobe and chair were found moved in a bedroom, apparently of their own accord. Signs of damage. Cracks found in ceiling of covered passage underneath a bedroom, which were repaired as dangerous by Burgh workmen.' [40]

Another detail of this case stated that Mr Shanker Ram, his wife and five children had to leave the house because of the strange happenings (no details given) which were also experienced by a neighbour.

British Heart Foundation
Situated in Kirk Wynd the cellar is haunted by the ghost of a girl. The story has it that she was hit by a horse and cart many years ago and killed.

The following are two brief accounts of public houses in Kirkcaldy, together with similar experiences in St. Andrews 2013 and one in Edinburgh in 1998 manifesting attributes of the same activity.

One of the most common disturbances in public houses is for the taps of the gas and beer pumps to be turned off. Upon asking a publican if they have had any paranormal activity they might immediately say "no", then hesitate slightly and say "well maybe", and proceed to describe how the pumps are switched off. A great many have this problem and there is never any natural explanation to be found. For whatever reason it would appear to be one of the easiest methods for a presence to attract attention alongside electrical disturbances.

John Marini's establishment The New Inn in St. Andrews is a classic example of current activity in this regard. It actually happened when I was present. It was mid afternoon on a Saturday in September 2013. I went down to the cellar with John after the barmaid had called over to say a tap had been switched off and sure enough it had been. These taps are not electronic, you have to physically turn them on and off, and it is not possible for it to happen of its own accord, yet it is often occurring a few times a day. The only access to the cellar is through a hatch on the floor behind the bar, so they so they know when someone is down there.

Feuars Arms
At the Feuars Arms this also happens with an uncanny regularity. It seems the pumps are turned off during the night when nobody is in the building. Other classic activity taking place is also in this cellar, with objects moving around, the sound of a woman singing and further unexplainable noises accompanied by customary cold spots.

The Feuars Arms is an atmospheric Victorian/Edwardian public house located appropriately in Bogies Wynd – another name for a ghost.

A personal account from a public house in Edinburgh
At Whistle Binkies, a popular music venue and bar just off the Royal Mile in Edinburgh, I was once asked to attend of an afternoon in 1998 while they were closed to see if I could shed any light on the disturbances there. When I arrived I informed them I didn't want to know the nature of these disturbances until I

had gone round myself to see if I could pinpoint anything. Knowing beforehand can often generate too much of an expectancy. Not a method for everyone but I find it can 'sometimes' work to good effect. Before I began looking round I went to the toilet in the vaulted basement. Whilst washing my hands I looked up and there standing motionless and staring at me through the mirror from the corner of the toilet was a figure. It was a tall slim gentleman wearing a top hat and long black coat or suit. I turned round to see him and he had gone. When I went back up stairs I said "I think I have just found your ghost." The spot he appeared was directly beneath one end of the bar which as it turned out seemed to be the location for the focus of the activity in the bar. It would become very cold at this spot, and the taps along this stretch with annoying regularity would also be turned off in the middle of service. The bar staff were forever having to go down to the cellar – albeit reluctantly at times to turn them back on. After a little investigation I found this building had been the residence of the notorious Judge Jeffries and this is the ghost I saw in the mirror. He was known as the 'hanging judge' in Edinburgh in the 17th century for his disposing of Covenanters. A difficult and persistent ghost his restlessness spirit is one of the most famous or infamous in Edinburgh. He also haunts Greyfriars Cemetery in Edinburgh where in death he found additional fame. He is buried here in one of the crypts, and he is associated with extreme poltergeist activity taking place here by physically attacking those wandering the graveyard; especially along the Covenanters Avenue which was affecting those who entered so badly the gates had to be locked to stop anyone entering.

Betty Nicol's

Betty Nicol's on the High Street in Kirkcaldy has also had phenomenon – although slight. The sound of a chair moving across the floor, a candle appearing to relight itself and another – a tealight, found to be still lit in the morning when they only have a burning time of a few hours.

Ladybank

Melville House - Poltergeist Activity

Private residence

In April 1989 I received a letter from a lady in Dalbethie concerning Melville House, located at Monimail, a couple of miles north of Ladybank which reads as follows:

'Dear Mr Falconer.

In answer to your letter in "Scots Mag," April 89. I don't know if Poltergeist Activity comes into your research? My father had an interesting experience concerning poltergeist activity, he was Mr K. M. Mylne who was headmaster of Dalhousie Castle Prep School in Midlothian and in the early 1950s he decided to move the school to Melville House near Ladybank. During the first term, while sitting writing in his study, his button was pulled off his jacket and things were thrown at him in the bathroom. The boy's clothes were pulled off the hooks in the changing rooms while they were playing football and clothes neatly placed in drawers were all rumpled up etc. My father told them it was just practical joking to stop any unnecessary alarm.

He asked a member of the Edinburgh Psychic Association to visit the house, a woman duly obliged and after sometime maintained the disturbances were due to an elderly man who had lived within the house at one time and was objecting to the "Youthful invasion."

My father asked the Bishop of St. Andrews to come and exorcise the house – which he did – and the activity stopped – but for a while there was quite a lot of activity.

It would be interesting to know if there has been any more activity as others moved in, as the School has been closed now for about 20 years.

Hope this information is of interest and I am sure your research will lead to much interest.

Yours Sincerely

Mrs Jean Gibb'

In the 14th century this was the site of Monimail Tower which was then incorporated into the present building when it was built in 1697. The house has had a number of different occupants over the years George, 1st Earl of Melville was its first occupant. In the Second World War it was used by a secret Auxiliary Unit with Polish troops on standby in the event of an invasion. Following the war the Melville's sold the property in the 1950s to Dalhousie Castle Prep School for boys – the school Mrs Gibb's father – Mr K. M. Mylne was not only the headmaster of, it was he who decided to move the school to Melville House. With the disgruntled presence making itself known almost immediately after they had taken up residence, as Mrs Gibb says; 'During the first term, while sitting writing in his study, his button was pulled off his jacket and things were thrown at him in the bathroom.'

It is possible the disturbances focused around Mr Mylne – although I imagine far from exclusively - because of his decision to bring the school to the building. From Jean's letter he would play any activity down with the boys, dismissing it as practical jokes being played. As she says 'to stop any unnecessary alarm,' but it would be interesting to find if any at that school at that time had independent experiences they might have been too frightened to speak of, for fear of not being taken seriously.

The house was a boy's school for around 20 years. The Council then ran it for a time as a home for the handicapped and a centre for young offenders. Around 1999/2000 it began changing hands again with a few failed projects and is now a private residence.

Largo Law

photo by the author

A Local Ghostly Legend
Standing 948 feet above sea level this hill commands an unbroken view of Fife's landscape and over the Firth of Forth to Edinburgh, North Berwick and the Lammermuir Hills beyond. Its peak is known as the Devil's Chair and folklore has it that this hill was created by the Devil himself. It was also believed that the hill had a secret gold mine hidden within its depths.

A ghost was said to have appeared on this hill years ago to a shepherd, laying down certain conditions the ghost made a promise to disclose the whereabouts of a gold mine. The shepherd though never found the mine and was struck dead on the Law because it seems he had broken the conditions.

The story is related her as follows:

'A great many years ago, a ghost made its appearance upon the spot, supposed to be laden with the secret of the mine; but as it of course required to be spoken to before it would condescend to speak, the question was, who should take it upon himself to go up and accost it? At length a shepherd, inspired by the all-powerful love of gold, took courage and demanded the cause of this "revisiting," etc. The ghost proved very affable, and requested a meeting on a particular night, at eight o'clock, when, said the spirit:

> "If Auchindownie cock disna craw,
> And Balmain horn disna blaw,
> I'll tell ye where the gowd mine is in Largo Law."

The shepherd took what he conceived to be effectual measures for preventing any obstacles being thrown in the way of his becoming the custodian of the important secret, for not a cock, old, young, or middle-aged, was left alive at the farm of Auchindownie; while the man who lived at Balmain was in the habit of blowing the horn for the housing of the cows, was strictly enjoined to dispense with that duty on the night in question. The hour was come, and the ghost, true to its promise, appeared, ready to divulge the secret; when Tammie Norrie, the cow-herder of Balmain, either through obstinacy or forgetfulness,

"Blew a blast both loud and dreads," and I may add, "were ne'er prophetic sounds so full of woe," for to the shepherd's mortal disappointment, the ghost vanished, after exclaiming:

"Woe to the man that blew the horn
For out of the spot he shall ne'er be born."

In fulfilment of this denunciation, the unfortunate horn blower was struck dead upon the spot; and it being found impossible to remove his body, which seemed, as it were, pinned to the earth, a cairn of stones was raised over it, which, now grown into a green hillock, is still denominated Norrie's Law, and regarded as uncanny by the common people.'[41]

If you stand on Norrie's Law it is said the horn may still be heard on dark windy nights. Around 1819 a cyst was found on Norrie's Law which contained some silver artefacts; namely a suit of armour, shield, sword-handle and a scabbard. This may have been the location for the ghostly figure of a knight who haunted the area for many years and seems to have been especially active in the 1800s.

Lathones

The Inn at Lathones

The website for this Inn carries the following; 'The history of the Inn goes back over 400 years. The Stables, being the oldest part, is today our bar where The Grey Lady (resident friendly ghost) and her horse reside. The front house was built in the late 17th century and is watched over by a wedding stone placed above the fire place as its lintel.'

When I visited this Inn in 2013 I found the staff very helpful and friendly. A member of staff even tidied up the Stables for me so I could take a photo for this book.

Greg Jenkins, the assistant manager of the Inn for the past 8 years spared some of his valuable time to speak with me about the paranormal incidences at the Inn. The latest being an elderly lady with mediumistic abilities who felt a dark presence in the Stables around August 2013.

In January 2013 Greg and another member of staff heard a glass smashing in the bar. They went through to the bar to see what had happened and broken glass was found behind the main bar in the opposite corner from the glass shelf it had previously been sitting on. The shelf is by the entrance door. It wasn't possible for it to have travelled that distance without physical means. When they came through and saw this they then saw the bottles on the shelf at the back of the bar moving as if something was brushing past them, dislodging them and turning them on the shelf.

The Stables function room
photo by the author

Although 'the Stables' is popularly known as the haunted location of the Inn the Side Block facing the main road is actually where a lot of the activity takes place.

Side Block built in the 1970s
photo by the author

Built in the 1970s it is the upstairs that appear to be mostly affected. Housekeepers have refused to go up there. Open shutters have been found closed. Doors and windows opening and closing and the electrics are often affected. Televisions turn on by themselves, and lights turn on when nobody is around. One staff member made the bed then saw the imprint of someone lying down on it. Room 9 seems to be especially affected by activity.

The New Block
photo by the author

The new block was built in 2005 and is also prone to activity. Two years ago, an elderly couple were staying in that block. The lady thought her husband had got up during the night but he was still in bed, there was a strange person in the room.

The grounds are all part of a 400 year old farmstead and were formerly part of a drovers Inn. When Paranormal Discovery a paranormal research team I feature on a number of occasions throughout this book visited the Inn in 2007 they were given a report that fire tools around the fireplace were swinging to and fro and also that they were moving from one side of the fireplace to the other. A baby was heard crying in the upstairs office and a grey swirling mist appeared above the resident's beds.

A915 St. Andrews – Leven Road just by Lathones Inn.
Greta Boyd who we met earlier in reference to Kinburn House has experienced a number of paranormal occurrences mainly based in St. Andrews such as poltergeist activity, a disappearing car, the aforementioned ghost of Kinburn House and the following account which happened on the main road just past

Lathones Inn. The account of Kinburn can be found on p.33 and the others in my companion book *Ghosts of St. Andrews*.

The following account was when she was travelling by car along the A915 St. Andrews – Leven Road just by Lathones Inn.

"I was on my own travelling to Lundin Links to meet some friends. It was a dark October night, cold and very drizzly. I wasn't thinking about anything in particular as I drove along, the visibility had been cut down a little due to the rain but nothing hazardous. At around 7:45pm just past Lathones Inn I noticed standing in the middle of the road on the white lines the figure of a young man with his right arm stretched out in front of him, as if to motion me to slow down or stop. He had shoulder length bushyish blonde hair and was wearing what appeared to be blue denims; the sleeves of his shirt were rolled up and his face expressionless. I thought there had been some kind of accident as I can remember thinking how odd it was for him not to be wearing a jacket as it was pouring down. I slowed down but as I approached he completely disappeared in front of me, as if he just faded away!

My next memory was driving into Lundin Links a short while later. I can remember seeing a man with a suitcase in the village but that was my first memory after the experience.

The first person I spoke to after this was my boyfriend who thought it may have been some kind of warning, so the next day I got the car checked over to which it was found that one of the tyres had a bulge and could have caused a blow out.

A short while after this whilst driving along the same road with my boyfriend we were nearing the same spot when we saw there had been a serious crash involving a lorry. It was a bright, warm day and standing in the middle of the road on exactly the same spot as the figure I had seen previous was a policeman, with arm outstretched in the same manner and wearing a shirt with the sleeves rolled up.

On the day of the crash I had been held up in St. Andrews for a while and believe that if we had been on schedule it may have been us that would have been involved in this awful crash!"

Letham

Fernie Castle Hotel
The Ghost of a Green Lady

Refer to *Fernie Castle Hotel*, p.95

Leuchars

Earlshall Castle
Numerous ghosts and ghostly activity

Refer to *Earlshall Castle*, p.110

Leven

The Regent - Leven Community Cinema
Built in 1922, Fife Today on the 19th October 2004 ran the following story about this Cinema in the town. Titled 'HAUNTED "HOUSE!"' it ran as follows:

BINGO players looking for supernatural luck might find themselves sitting in the right place in Leven.

That's because Gala Bingo Hall on Commercial Road is home to a ghost who just can't seem to stay away from her beloved game!

Joan Martin, duty manager, said the building's phantom – an old lady – had been sensed by staff many times in recent years. But, much to Joan's amazement, she actually saw the ghost walk straight through a solid door.

Joan said: "I was sitting in the office when I spotted the woman on our monitor camera.

"I thought it was a member of staff – we were closed at the time – and I buzzed the door.

"But then she walked towards it and straight through it. I thought: 'How did you do that?'

"Nobody came into the office, so I went through to the foyer to have a look and there was nobody there."

The monitor did not record film, so no evidence of this apparition exists, but other staff need no convincing because many have encountered the phantom lady. In fact, Carol Smith, from Buckhaven, seems to be her particular favourite. "She whispers for me," said Carol. "I've never heard her shout on anybody else.

"Nobody believed me at first, then one day when I was at the book sales, she was quite loud and my colleague Sylvia heard her."

Carol joked: "It was just as well because I thought I was going off my head! Now when I hear her I just think: 'What do you want now'?"

The lady also makes her presence known in other ways, explained Sylvia Cunningham, duty manager. She said: "She smells of rose petals which have been soaked in water. The smell is quite strong and twitches your nose – it can make you sneeze."

Although staff say the hair on the back of their neck rises when the ghost comes near, they describe her as a mischievous spirit. And she occasionally makes them jump, especially late at night when they close the old theatre building.

Sylvia said: "You go upstairs to check the rooms before locking up and, in the silence the hand-dryer in the ladies' toilet goes off!"

Staff have no idea who the lady might be, but suspect she was once a regular customer.

A few years back a clairvoyant visited the hall and sensed the spirit of an old lady who wore a brown coat and handbag.

Joan concluded: "Many elderly customers practically live in the bingo hall during winter because they save on heating, get a cheap lunch and have a chat with friends.

"I thinks she probably could have been a customer who misses the bingo. She can't stay away!"

Lingo House
The disappearing riding boots!

Lingo House is a large white country mansion just off the B940 north east of West Lingo. James Wilkie in his Bygone Fife mentions: 'There hung till recently in the house of Lingo, which once belonged to the Priory of Pittenweem, a portrait of General Dalzell, "with his bald head and his beard to his girdle," although these lands only came in the family a few years before the '45. Beneath it were suspended the great riding-boots of him who, with Grierson of Lagg (Scott's Sir Robert Redgauntlet) and wild Bonshaw, Sir James Turner and Claverhouse, peopled the inferno of the Whigs. Legends yet linger concerning these boots. On nights when the moon shone in fitful gleams, as the clouds scudded over the sky, or when the stars of winter alone burned in the heavens, they would disappear from their accustomed place. Out on the moors that of old comprised the Boar's Chase flew a ghostly steed, the boots striking spurred heels into its flanks, and the feet of a bearded phantom filling them. It was the shade of the fierce old cavalier in wild pursuit of invisible Whigs, as in the days when word was brought in of an unlawful gathering in some remote hollow,[xxiii] and the general buckled on the broadsword, ever by his chair, and leaped on his ready bridled horse, calling on his men to follow.'[42]

Refer also to Kinkell Castle for the location of where he has been known to roam when the boots disappeared, p.36

[xxiii] This is referring to meetings at the castle.

Lochgelly

The white horse and a mole!
Loch Gelly is situated just south of the village inheriting the same name, and means – the 'shining waters'. The loch sets the scene for a couple of interesting paranormal quarks mentioned by Simpkins quoting F. A. Rorie in his book *Folklore of Fife* in 1914. He says; 'Animal Ghosts. The old house of Powguild, which stands beside Loch Gelly, boasts of a white horse which haunts its precincts. As it is close to the loch, the horse is perhaps a variant of the water-kelpie.

The garden of the same house has another and a smaller ghost -a mole or "moudie-wort." An old woman who lived there, and was a great lover of her garden, vowed on her death-bed that she would return to her garden and live there in the shape of a moudie-wort. Certain it is that some of the later dwellers in the house have hesitated to interfere with stray moles which are conducting digging operations there.
RORIE, F. A.'[43]

Lomond Hills
(Also known as the Paps of Fife)

photo by the author

'Lomond Hills Easter and Wester. These isolated heights were called by the old Highlanders "Wallace's Goals," because the national hero was held to be capable of jumping from the one summit to the other. The Wester Lomond, which is the higher of the two, being 1713 feet high.'[44]

The Fair Haired Ghost

On the lonely beautiful Lomond Hills wanders the fair-haired ghost of Jenny Nettles who died on these hills with her child after being betrayed by a soldier at Falkirk Palace. This is referring to a story and location slightly further east than the hills themselves.

Refer also to *Strathmiglo area*, p.236

Saved by a Ghost!

'A wonderful vision seen during the dispersion of a Field-conventicle[xxxiv] held in the year 1674. There was a meeting on Lomond hills, where John Wellwood, a young man, both grave and pious, and of good understanding, preached to the meeting; there came a party of the Life Guards, commanded as I heard by David Masterton of Grange, younger; the meeting was on the hill; the troopers essayed to ride up to them, I suppose between sermons, the people stood on the face of the brae, and the soldiers shot bullets among the people, with carabines and pistells, and as I heard, charged five or six several times; but though the balls lighted among men, women and children, and went through some of their hair, and broke upon stones beside them, yet hurt none, which was observed as a wonder to all present, the soldiers seeing the people stand still, and not stir, were forced to retire.

It was affirmed by some women who stayed at home, that they clearly perceived as the form of a tall man, majestic like, stand in the air, in stately posture, with one leg as it were advanced before the other, standing above the people all the time of the soldiers shooting.

The wrytter hearing of this afterward, did write to ane honest man in that country to send him notice of the certainty of the vision, and the above said relation was returned in write to him, but the women knew not of the soldiers' onset till the folk came home, to whom they told the vision that several of them had seen all the time. LAW, note, p.96.'[45]

Lundin Links

The Skeleton draped in seaweed!

Mr Archie Dunbar, his wife and their eleven year old daughter visited St. Andrews in 1970 during the British Open Golf Championships. Due to this busy tournament they were unable to find accommodation in the town and decided to try further afield. On reaching Lundin Links they took up residence in a small red sandstone hotel by the golf course overlooking the 18th green. At

---

[xxxiv] An unofficial religious meeting

the end of an enjoyable week the family retied to bed for the last time as they were leaving the next day. Just after going to bed, Archie, deciding to go to the bathroom got out of bed and made his way across the room to the door. He got to about a foot away from the wall when, to his horror and disbelief between himself and the wall there appeared a skeleton draped in seaweed. Terror-stricken he screamed and fled in his pyjamas to the corridor where on hearing the yell the startled occupants of the other rooms came into the corridor to see what had happened.

The time he said was around 11:30pm, no rational explanation could be given for this bizarre phantasm and the proprietrix was also unable to shed any light on the matter.

The building has since been demolished due to a fire occurring at a later date, with no trace of the hotel now visible.

Lundin Links Hotel

photo by the author

Another case concerning Lundin Links also deals with a hotel. Formerly known as the Emsdorf Hotel, the building is reputed to be haunted by a former housekeeper by the name of Miss Cameron who resided in the building in the earlier half of the 20th century. Described as being a very pleasant and benign spirit, she's been seen and heard on a number of occasions.

1988

Mr David Tong, a former owner of the hotel in the late 1980s told me when I visited the hotel in 1988 she sometimes makes an appearance in the afternoon at ten past four, wearing a grey satin dress and a creamy coloured lace shawl she walks down the stairs to the ground floor, along a corridor and disappears through a wall. Not always seen her footsteps can be heard in the reception, where the lights turn themselves on and off by unseen hands.

Windows in the hotel open and close by themselves and various guests staying in room 22 have felt it to be exceptionally cold. This was her room and is where she is reported to have died.

Mr Tong never had the fortune of actually seeing her himself but has had some form of contact with her, albeit indirectly, starting around the mid 1980s when he took over the hotel.

Miss Cameron in the 1930s outside the hotel

On refurbishing the honeymoon suite he found himself being very particular about the colour and design of this particular room, feeling that everything within had to be correct. A while later an elderly woman having visited the hotel for a great many years asked Mr Tong if she might look around and see what changes he had made. When taken to the honeymoon suite she suddenly exclaimed – "THAT'S MISS CAMERON!" She had seen her standing in the room wearing the same dress mentioned above, somewhat taken aback she explained to him that she was a psychic and had also known Miss Cameron when still alive and that the favourite colour of the former house keeper was the one he had chosen for the room! This left him in no doubt that Miss Cameron's influence had affected his judgement during its refurbishment.

Her influence has been felt by him at other times as well. Mr Tong sung to me part of a song he began singing and humming on occasion just after moving in. Later he was informed by the psychic that this had been her favourite song and guests in the building to this day have sometimes heard the ghostly voice of a woman singing this very same tune. Sheet music on the piano has been whisked away by the unseen hands of the former house keeper when the music being played has not been to her liking.

25 years later – 2013

The photograph of Miss Cameron was given to the hotel by a former resident who knew her. I visited this hotel for the first time in 25 years at the end of September 2013 to take a few photos for this book. I was greeted in the building by a lovely pleasant young woman called Darlene Murray, who has worked in the hotel for a number of years now. Whilst she was kindly making coffee, I asked her if the ghost of Miss Cameron was still active in the hotel. What follows are a few of the numerous incidences in the hotel she proceeded to relay to myself and Bob Miller, who drove me around Fife for these three days in September taking photos.

She said Miss Cameron tends to appear whenever there is a change in the hotel. It could be anything from a refurbishment, to the re-arranging furniture, an incoming or outgoing member of staff. The latest incident at the hotel had literally only occurred a few days before I arrive at the hotel in September2013. Following her last day of work Janette one of the staff members was about to leave the hotel for the last time as a member of staff. She was waiting on the ground floor for another staff member Rebecca when she heard doors closing and keys turning. Thinking it was Rebecca she anticipated her imminent arrival. Just then, she felt someone physically nudging past her arm, as if a person had just brushed passed her, but there was nobody else was around. Shortly after Rebecca appeared and they left the hotel. It had been Miss Cameron locking up.

A lot of the incidences are subtle, in-keeping with its most apparent nature. Mr Tong had spoken of lights being turned on and off, Darlene spoke of lights in the building flickering and televisions turning themselves on in unoccupied rooms. Rebecca I mentioned just now as being the one Janette had been waiting for was in the kitchen one day when utensils hanging on the wall started rattling. This could be put down to a very slight earth tremor, and other incidences could be put down to this or that – however outlandish they begin to appear to be, but it is the sheer frequency of these disturbances by independent people – staff and residents, that is more than just suggestive of non physically means, especially when there is no plausible physical explanation for most of it. The following is one such incident.

When Darlene was a housekeeper here she was checking the rooms on the top floor and in room 23 she found dirty cups on the table, even though the room had been unoccupied. This could have been an oversight by the cleaners so she took the dirty cups away and went to get fresh ones. When she returned to the room with the fresh cups however – they had already been replaced and there had been no one else around who could have done that – physically at least. Miss Cameron had been doing her work for her.

This room is next door to number 22 – Miss Cameron's old room. Interestingly Darlene said there doesn't seem to be much disturbance in her old room. On the other side, room 21 is a different matter and is considered to be an eerie room, one she doesn't enjoy entering. Two years ago two women shared a twin room and next morning complained at reception they had not got much sleep in the night due to the night porter. They said the porter had been walking back and forth along the corridor. They could hear keys and received a knock on the door. It took a while for one of them to get to the door and when they did no one was there. After relaying this to reception they were informed the hotel doesn't have a night porter – but they do have a ghost.

Over the years there have been a few staying at the hotel who knew Miss Cameron many years ago. She was a very pleasant woman and always very precise which is something Mr Tong also mentioned about her when he said she always appears at 4:10pm walking down the stairs to the main hall and entrance way. It is possible she took a break in her room after lunch and came down at that time shortly after afternoon tea would have been served.

There is a very peaceful air in the hotel although it can be creepy when no one else in around. Many things have happened here which individually are relatively easy to dismiss. As with so many cases it's the regularity of Miss Cameron's displays which keeps staff and residents alert. I spoke of Mr Tong's experiences and asked if the piano was still in the hotel, the humour was apparent when Darlene pointed out I was standing next to it. I think I was actually leaning against it at the time and could sense Miss Cameron having a wee chuckle to herself.

This is a lovely hotel with a benign ghost who is also there to look after you and is thoroughly recommended, especially for their great evening meals, where it is unlikely you will be able to say with any certainty that all present are of this earth.

photo by the author

As a point of interest being so close to this hotel, a few yards west of the Lundin Links Hotel is the former Lundin Links Stone Circle. Turn left out of the hotel onto the A915 then first right after only a few yards down Woodielea Road signposted for Lundin Ladies Golf Club. On the third fairway of this course are the remains of a large stone circle. Only three stones are now present. In the 1700s early curiosity rather than archaeology found stone cists with bones which are now lost. Each stone is up to an impressive 18 feet tall. Generally if you ask permission from the course staff at the starter box – a white building to the left of the car park, they will willingly let you wander the short distance down the side of the course once it is safe for you to see them closer. They are well worth a visit and represent quite a rare attraction. At the starter box they will give you a handout which you can read as you walk to the stones that gives further details about them. They are very impressive and are not only the largest in Fife as the handout suggests; unfortunately the photo doesn't do them justice, as they are some of the tallest stones to be found.

Standing stones are markers for ley lines running like a web of energy across the surface of the earth like a mesh of straight lines, each with a field of energy around 6 feet in height and 4 to 6 feet in width. These are powerful energy conduits and are intensified at the point where two or more ley lines cross with the collective energies being enhanced and more powerful. Often these crossings are marked by stone circles such as that which remains at Lundin Links. These centres have many beneficial qualities for physical health and mental wellbeing. They are also the merging points of otherwise intangible realms, and paranormal activity at these places is relatively commonplace phenomenon for those able to perceive just beyond the mundane barrier of physical reality.

The A915 road out of Lundin Links to Kirkcaldy is known as Standing Stane Road and travels in a straight line from Lundin Links to Leven and again from Windygates to Kirkcaldy. It follows the course of a ley line marked by standing stones which if you keep your eyes peeled you shall occasionally see on the side of the road. They are not very tall, but there are a number of these along this stretch.

Markinch

Balbirnie House

This is a country house hotel haunted by a ghost along with the ghost of a dog in the library.

Balbirnie Stone Circle

Just off the north east outer edge of Balbirnie Park is an ancient stone circle comprising 8 stones with burial cists in the middle known as the Druid's Circle. From the A92 running north along the western edge of the park turn right onto Star and Kennoway road, then into the Balbirnie housing estate where the circle will be found alongside this road. The circle was moved to here in 1970 by Historic Scotland when the A92 was being redeveloped. So the energies are not the same but it is worth visiting if in the area.

Magus Muir

Gruesome Deaths and Phantom Coaches

Phantom coaches are a perpetual talk of the town when it comes to the ghosts of St. Andrews. There have been various sighting over the years alongside even more reports of the unmistakable sounds of a coach and horses being heard in the still of the night. The locations have been in the quite outlying areas towards Strathkinness and around the precincts of the old town itself, especially along the cobbled east end of Market Street. Near to where the old Tolbooth once stood which saw various body parts being displayed from executions here and elsewhere. The occupants of these large black coaches range from Archbishop Sharpe and Cardinal David Beaton, to Hackston of Rathillet. All are being driven to hell with the Devil beside them as their final companion!

The following is a most gruesome episode in the history of this area with a culmination in horrific and graphic displays that St. Andrews and the surrounding shire have never forgotten.

While we make light the notions of phantom coaches and speculate upon their occupancy it is easy to forget the causes of how such macabre spectacles can come into manifestation. The Devil takes on many guises, and when the righteous convictions of man contrive to enact the most abominable of atrocities in the name of God. In this there is none more delighted in both their accusations and actions in knowing there is only ever one winner in the outcome of fate - the Devil himself.

On the morning of Saturday 3rd May 1679, a most ghastly murder took place at Magus Muir. A lonely wooded spot sited half a mile from the village of Strathkinness and three miles from St. Andrews. The following is the story of that fateful bloody day and the consequences to befall those involved. Included here also are some passages written in some detail from the time with a personal graphic account from Hackston of Rathillet following his involvement.

The Bloody Murder of Archbishop Sharpe

Archbishop James Sharpe

Two land owners – David Hackston of Rathillet and his brother-in-law John Balfour of Kinloch (Known as Burley) and seven other catholic covenanters set out in the morning with the intention of conspiring against William Charmichael, a former magistrate of Edinburgh, who after being promoted by the Protestant Archbishop Sharpe to Sheriff Depute of Fife had constantly set himself against them with brutality and extortion. They assigned themselves not to kill him but to severely chasten him for his involvement in their persecution.

After being given information he was to be hunting at Tarvet Hill that morning they rode at full speed. On arrival they found their plans thwarted as Charmichael had been notified of possible danger by a shepherd and had immediately fled in safety to Cupar some six miles away. Unknown to the party at the time a far bigger fish was about to fall into their hands.

A woman who believed in the cause of the covenanters discovered that Archbishop James Sharpe was journeying his way back from Edinburgh after conducting business and had briefly stopped in Ceres to visit the minister there. The woman sent her son to notify the party that Sharpe's coach would at some point during the day be in the vicinity of Magus Muir. The unexpectedness of this somewhat revelatory news didn't help to serve them in the situation about to unfold. Sharpe was not the original intention of these men, however their grievance against Charmichael although strong, had been slight in comparison to that for the Primate of Scotland. One year earlier James Mitchell, a fellow covenanter had been tricked by Sharpe into confessing he had conspired against him six years previously, making his confession on the promise his life would be spared, Sharpe never kept his word, and in a display of how ruthless he could be he had Mitchell executed.

The covenanters felt the scenario now being presented had been guided to them from a divine source, raising them to near hysterical fever. The prospect of the Archbishop appearing over the horizon was leading them to an almost inevitable conclusion, and the weight of what they were about to do would cause repercussions they will also have been aware of. They chose Hackston to be their leader, although he hated Sharpe, he could not let his judgement influence him like the others as his was a personal matter against Sharpe and not a matter of the cause, so he declined the offer. Although wanting no part in the proceedings he could not stand in the way of the others so John Balfour took up the position himself. So it was then, with mixed feelings and no planning the party now led by John Balfour rode to Magus Muir in anticipation of the arrival of Sharpe's coach.

It was midday when he appeared over the horizon of Magus Muir. Sharpe was accompanied on this particular journey by his eldest daughter, four servants, a coachman and a postilion. Once the coachman saw the band approaching on this lonely moor nothing could be done to evade them.[xxxv] A pistol shot was fired through the window of the coach missing its target, then once stopped the servants were restrained and the horses cut loose. It was then demanded that Sharpe leave the carriage, but refusing to comply with their demands they fired further shots into the carriage and thrust their swords at

---

[xxxv] Refer also to the companion book *Ghosts of St. Andrews*, (2013) by the present author: *The Spectral Coachman and the Postilion*, p.111

him where he sat. Badly wounded and bloody he eventually emerged falling to his knees.

This depiction of Sharpe's brutal murder appeared in an early newspaper; 'The Manner of the Barbarous Murder of James, Late Lord Arch-Bishop Sharp of St. Andrews, Primate and Metropolitan of all Scotland, And one his Majesties most Honourable Privy-Council of that Kingdom; May 3. 1679.'

In the above plate Sharpe is depicted just in front of the coach dressed in black, with his left hand raised as gun shot was fired at him, and in the bottom right, Isabel Sharpe is seen pleading with the men.

Hackston during the frenzied bloodshed was still mounted on his horse some distance away, like a mysterious highwayman watching the maddening slaughter with his cloak covering the lower half of his face. Sharpe begged them to spare his life that theirs may be spared also, but with the death of James Mitchell in their minds and by virtue of who they had before them, they ignored him. At one point it seems Hackston even tried to intercede but to no avail, and amid the panic and the adrenaline of the moment his daughter Isabel Sharpe in great distress implored and pleaded with the persecutors to stop harming her father. With this she was seriously wounded herself in the merciless attack for her trouble. Entreating them to stop, her father raised his left hand as they fired yet more shots and plunged their swords into his bloodied body as he then slumped forward and lay still.

Following a post-mortem and a report by four surgeons, in all there were sixteen great wounds found on his body. In his back, head, one above his left eye, three in his left hand that he raised in desperation and a shot above his right breast which was found to be powder.

Before the perpetrators fled 'they took nothing from him but his tobacco-box and bible, and a few papers. With these they went to a barn nearby. Upon the opening of his tobacco-box a living humming bee flew out. This either Rathillet or Balfour called his familiar, and some in the company not understanding the term, they explained it to be a devil. In the box were a pair of pistol balls, parings of nails, some worsit or silk, and some say a paper with some characters, but that is uncertain.'[46]

As famous as the above account of the tobacco-box and its contents is, there is another account of the box which sounds all the more plausible, as the one above is from a catholic perspective. 'they found on the bishop a box with some pistol-ball, threads of worsted, and other odd things in it, which they knew not what to make of.'[47]

A stone pyramid cairn stands in the woods at Magus Muir marking the spot where the Archbishop met his end.

After this barbaric display the descriptions of the perpetrators were given to the appropriate authorities, and a major hunt ensued for their capture with a reward of 10,000 merks for the apprehension of any involved. Andrew Guillan a weaver from Balmerino was one of the first to be found and slain, although it was believed that he, like Hackston had taken no part in the actual murder. At his trial in Edinburgh 'it was noticed that he endured the torture he was put to with a great deal of courage. In cutting off his hands the hangman, being drunk, or affecting to appear so, mangled him fearfully, and gave him nine strokes before he got them off. He endured all with invincible patience, and it is said, when his right hand was cut off, he held up the stump in the view of the spectators, crying as one perfectly easily, "My blessed Lord sealed my salvation with his blood and I am honoured this day to seal his truths with my blood." After his body was hung in chains for some time, some people came and took it down for which the country about was brought to no small trouble. On May 27th, 1684, "The council granted a commission to the earl of Balcarras to pass sentence of banishment on the persons who took down Andrew Guillan's body from Magus-muir, as being owners of the horrid murder of the Archbishop of St Andrews."'[48]

While Andrew was originally from Balmerino he lived at Magus Muir. He was a sympathiser for the covenanters cause, but it was by the unfortunate circumstance of already being in the area that was to be his downfall on this day. For all his suffering following the murder of Sharpe as relayed above, the account in the *History of the Sufferings of the Church of Scotland* of 1829 concerning Andrew Guillan writes of the actual part he played that resulted in his gruesome death:

'…all his share in the action was, that being called out of his house [by the covenanters], he held their horses, and was witness to what was done.'[49]

He had found himself not only in the wrong place at the wrong time but had been killed as an example of the wrath against the covenanters and the fate that awaited all who dared join in their cause.

In a nearby field Andrew Guillan is remembered on a tombstone with this inscription:

A faithful martyr here doth lye

A witness against perjury

Who cruelly was put to death

To gratify proud prelate's wrath

They cut his hands ere he was dead

And after that struck off his head

To Magus Muir then did him bring

His body on a pole did hing

His blood under the alter cries

For vengeance on Christs enemies

His head was displayed in Cupar but this stone marks where his body parts were hung by chains. The site of the grave is also close to where he lived and worked as a simple weaver, so those who knew him in the area would have certainly seen the aftermath of his death in Edinburgh. So it may not have been so much sympathising covenanters who set free what was left of his mutilated remains bound in chains, but sympathising friends who couldn't bear to see the horror of his fate in being hung and not buried. His ghost is said to roam the area around his grave.

The Horrors Awaiting David Hackston of Rathillet

A little over a year after the murder of Sharpe, on the 22nd of July 1680 the Joint Sheriff-Depute of Dumfriesshire; Bruce of Earlshall[xxxvi] and around 120

[xxxvi] This is Bloody Bruce. So named for tracking down the Covenanters and from an incident at the Battle of Bothwell Bridge on the 22nd of June 1679 where he cut the

Dragoons found and surprised Hackston and his men at Airds Moss, a moorland in East Ayrshire. The ensuing conflict resulted in the capture of Hackston.

The following which is said to have been written in his own hand is a graphic account of his capture and what then followed in Edinburgh as relayed from the ages of Wodrow in 1829.

Hackston's Account

'I was stricken down with three on horseback behind me, and received three sore wounds on the head, and so falling saved my life, which I submitted to. They searched me, and carried me to their rear, and laid me down, where I bled much, where were brought several of their men sorely wounded. They gave us all testimony of brave resolute men. What more of our men were killed I did not see, nor know, but as they told me after the field was theirs. I was brought towards Douglas. They used me civilly, and brought me drink out of a house by the way. At Douglas, Janet Clellan was kind to me, and brought a surgeon to me, who did but little to my wounds, only stanched the blood. Next morning I was brought to Lanark, and brought before Dalziel, lord Ross, and some others, who asked many questions at me: but I not satisfying them with answers, Dalziel did threaten to roast me; and carrying me to the tolbooth, caused to bind me most barbarously, and cast me down, where I lay till Saturday morning, without any, except soldiers, admitted to speak to me, or look at my wounds, or give me any ease whatsoever. And next morning they brought me and John Pollock, and the other two of us, near two miles on foot, I being without shoes, to where that party, which had broken us at first, received us. They were commanded by Earlshall. We were horsed, civilly used by them on the way, and brought to Edinburgh, about four in the afternoon, and carried about the north side of the town, to the foot of the Canongate, where the town magistrates were who received us; and setting me on an horse with my face backward, and the other three bound on a goad of iron, and Mr. Cameron's head carried on an halbert before me, and another head in a sack, which I knew not, on a lad's back; and so we were carried up the street to the parliament-cross, where I was taken down, and the rest loosed.'[50]

Although like Andrew Guillan he had not actually taken part in the murder, he found himself an accessory nonetheless and suffered the same fate.

---

head and hands off Richard Cameron and took them for display to Edinburgh. Refer also to *Earlshall Castle* home of Bloody Bruce, p.110

His ghost haunts Sharpe's old residence Strathtyrum House[xxxvii] in remorse of the events of that day in not being able to prevent what occurred. Hackston knew Sharpe, it was said: 'Hackston was the tutor for a cousin's children [of Sharpe], and had been made responsible for disbursements made by Sharp (from a forced sale of property for rents owed him).'

As graphic and sickening as Hackston's account is, it is still slim to the gruesome reality of the manner in which he was to spend the last moments of his life, as the arrangements for his death were laid out and followed in detail. They were drawn up by the Privy Council so as to inflict the most painful death as possible on Hackston. Both the arrangements of his actual death and what was then to befall his body was recorded in great detail as follows:

'That his body be drawn backward on a hurdle to the Mercat Cross; that there be an high scaffold erected a little above the Cross, where, in the first place, his right hand is to be struck off and, after some time, his left hand; then he is to be hanged up, and cut down alive, his bowels to be taken out, and his heart shown to the people by the hangman; then his heart and his bowels to be burned in a fire prepared for that purpose on the scaffold; that, afterwards, his head be cut off, and his body divided into four quarters; his head to be fixed on the Netherbow; one of his quarters with both his hands to be affixed at St. Andrews,[xxxviii] another quarter at Glasgow, a third at Leith, a fourth at Burntisland; that none presume to be in mourning for him, or any coffin brought; that no person be suffered to be on the scaffold with him, save the two bailies, the executioner and his servants; that he be allowed to pray to God Almighty, but not to speak to the people; that Hackston's and Cameron's heads be fixed on higher poles than the rest.

Privy Council.'[51]

Refer also to the Ghost of Hackston, *Rathillet* p.229

[xxxvii] Refer also to the companion book *Ghosts of St. Andrews*, (2013) by the present author: *Strathtyrum House*, p.205

[xxxviii] They were displayed in St. Andrews at the Tolbooth, also known as the Town House. This was a double storied building that stood in the middle of Market Street toward the Mercat Cross. It once housed a Charter of the town from King Malcolm II and a very large axe used for royalist executions at the tolbooth in 1645. It was pulled down in 1862 and was not replaced by another building. Its removal extended the street to what it is today.

Although not being present at Magus Muir on that day, five of the covenanters caught at Bothwell Bridge were 'hanged' in chains on Christmas Day 1679 at Magus Muir for not speaking up about the identity of the perpetrators. Their bodies were left there to rot away as an example to others for nine years. At Magus Muir there is also a grave to these men in a field not far from that of Andrew Guillan's stone.

A Foreboding Atmosphere at Magus Muir

It isn't surprising something supernatural should be associated with this location. Having this bloody piece of history attached to its name lends a strange eerie atmosphere and along with the ghost of Guillan the bodies that languished here for so many years linger even on bright summer days.

As the mind is cast back to that fateful day in 1679 with Sharpe's death and the fate of the Covenanters it becomes a reminder of how all found themselves caught in the horrors that conviction and circumstance. The isolation of this moor known afterwards as 'Bishop's Wood' appears all the more desolate when it is realised how close it is to the slim haven of Strathkinness, yet still distant enough that none could hear the shouts and screams.

Reports of the Phantom Coaches

The coach that drove Sharpe to his death has been seen a few times between Strathkinness and St. Andrews careering along the road from Magus Muir. As with other cases of phantom coaches around the British Isles, the Archbishops coach when heard traditionally foretells death or some other adequately auspicious misfortune.

Another with a connection to the Phantom Coaches being passed down by the annals of legend is David Beaton who we have already met as being one of the more regular ghosts to haunt the Castle of St. Andrews:

Cardinal David Beaton and the Devil
(East Sands)

"Have you heard how the Cardinal's coach goes by,
At the dead of night when the tide is high?
And the moon has hid, and the wind is shrill,
And all the city lies dark and still?!"[52]

A story or rather a legend of the Phantom Coach posted in the National Observer in 1893 concerns Cardinal David Beaton and the Devil.

'Whenever the tide is full on the East Sands between midnight and the first hour of morning David Beaton drives down by the old Abbey Wall into the Sea. They are many that have seen his white face pleading at the coach window; he cannot speak – mutely he must implore your prayers; for the Devil sits with him and holds him by the arm. His outriders are skeletons, his coachman is headless, and thus he drives to his doom.'[53]

This is a reference to his coach travelling down Abbey Walk and Abbey Street to the East Sands in St. Andrews.

Another legend tells how this spectral coach and four is seen passing through the area, vanishing in a puff of blue smoke and leaving only the reek of sulphur.

W. T. Linskill in his usual manner relates to us three stories concerning the Phantom Coach; two stories of the Strathkinness to St. Andrews Road where one ends its journey in St. Andrews Bay, and a third giving mention to a Phantom Coach also being seen in St. Andrews Abbey Walk.

Phantom Coach Locations
Along with Linskill's locations for Sharpe's Coach and Beaton's Coach finding its way to the Castle Sands. There are other locations that Phantom Coaches have been reputed as either being seen or just heard. The list of all the locations including those above is as follows:

Strathkinness – St. Andrews Road
    In St. Andrews:
    Hepburn Gardens
    Argyle Street
    South Street
    Market Street
    Abbey Walk
    The Pends
    Castle Sands
    East Sands
    St. Andrews Bay (non-specific location)

With such a profusion of locations it is more a case of where hasn't the coach been seen or heard in St. Andrews than where it has been, although it will be noted there is nothing random here, the reported locations of the coach with unidentified occupants are all from the direction of Magus Muir running towards St. Andrews Bay.

The Body Snatchers

Before we take our leave of that bloody day when Sharpe met his end on a desolate moor and the relentless Protestant hounds tracked and tortured the Covenanters and any connected with the Covenanters deeds. In the Holy Trinity Church in South Street there stands a large black and white marble tomb. Erected by Sharpe's son, it marks where Archbishop Sharpe was interred in 1679. In 1725 the tomb was raided and it was rumoured at the time his body had been taken. Generations would pass before any would know for sure if this were true. In 1849, with 124 years of rumours and speculation the tomb was opened, his body was missing. To this day no one knows who was responsible for its removal or what then happened to it. So with a twist in the tale, is the Phantom Coach carrying the corpse of Sharpe to his former dwelling once he had been killed at Magus Muir, or as the Catholics supposed at the time, in having him in league with the Devil, with no resting place on hallowed ground is it indeed like Beaton carrying him to Hell.

For accounts of the coach at these locations in St. Andrews Refer also to my companion book *Ghosts of St. Andrews*, (2013)

Milnathort

Burleigh Castle
Haunted by the ghost of Grey Maggie.

Refer to *GOF Castle Trail*, p.85

Milton of Balgonie

Balgonie Castle
Fife's most haunted Castle and currently haunted dwelling.

Refer to *GOF Castle Trail*, p.68

Moonzie

Lordscairnie Castle
Ghost of Earl Beardie

Refer to *GOF Castle Trail*, p.97

Newburgh

The Cross 'is situated upon the high ground, in an opening of the Ochils which forms a pass from the valley of Strathearn into the central portion of Fife. This cross is said to have been broken in pieces by the Reformers, on their way from Perth to Lindores; and nothing now remains but the large square block of freestone which formed the pedestal. This stone is 3 feet 9 inches high; 4 feet 7 inches in length, by 3 feet 9 inches in breadth at the base; and 3 feet 4 inches in length, by 2 feet 8 inches in breadth at the top. There are several holes or indentations on its different faces, which tradition says were nine in number, and in which nine rings were at one time fixed. There is no appearance of any socket in which the cross had been fixed; so that it must have been placed upon the surface of the stone, without any other support than that of its own base. No remains of the broken cross are to be seen in the neighbourhood. Cant says that the pieces were removed by the inhabitants of Newburgh, and built into some of the houses of that town. This cross, like that at Mugdrum, was dedicated to St. Magridden, who appears to have been the patron-saint of the district, and to whom the church of Ecclesia Magriden, or Exmagirdle as it is now called, in Strathearn, was also dedicated. It formed a girth or sanctuary for any of the clan Macduff, or any related to the chief within the ninth degree, who had been guilty of "suddand chaudmelle," or unpremeditated slaughter. In consequence of this privilege, any person entitled to take advantage of it, and requiring its security, tied to the cross, and laying hold of one of the rings, punishment was remitted on his washing nine times at the stone, and paying nine cows and a colpendach or young cow; the nine cows being fastened to the rings. What peculiar or occult quality was considered to dwell in the number nine, we do not pretend to be able to explain; but we see the privilege only extended to the ninth degree of kindred, the stone contained nine rings, the oblation offered to St. Magridden was nine cows and a colpendach, the washings were nine, and a powerful spring called the Nine wells, where it is supposed the ablutions took place, still takes its rise at no great distance from the cross. This spring, or rather collection of springs, is copious, and of the purest quality, and being collected together forms a considerable stream, which has lately been profitably employed in the operations of a bleachfield.* A short way west of the pass in which stands the cross of Macduff, and on the slope of the Ochils, is a small cairn of stones, known by the name of Sir Robert's Prap. It marks the place where a fatal duel occurred about the close of the 17th century, between Sir Robert Balfour of Denmiln, and Sir James Makgill of Lindores.

The privilege of the clan Macduff is said to have been often claimed, not only by the direct members of that powerful body, but by others who considered they were within the privileged. Among the persons who are said to have claimed the right, and to have had their claim allowed, were the laird of Arbuthnot, for being concerned in the murder of Melville of Glenbervie, sheriff of the Mearus; Spens of Wormiestim, for the murder of one Kinninmond; and Sir Alexander Moray of Abercairney, who had been concerned in the slaughter of one Spalding, in the year 1397. It was on all occasions necessary when the privilege of Cross-Macduff was claimed, that proof should be given of consanguinity within the limited degree; and where in any case the claimant failed in establishing his right, he was instantly put to death, and buried near the stone. There were formerly several artificial cairns and tumuli around the cross, and one rather larger than the rest about fifty yards to the north; but the progress of agriculture which has brought the ploughshare over the fields around the cross, has now removed all traces of them. These tumuli were supposed to have been the burying-places of those who had been executed here in consequence of failing to establish the necessary relationship; but no attempt has ever been made to ascertain the truth of this report. "Superstition," says Cant, "forbids the opening of any of them; no person in the neighbourhood will assist for any consideration, nor will any person in or about Newburgh travel that way when dark, for they affirm that spectres and bogles, as they call them, haunt that place." With the removal of the traces of the graves, it is probable that the superstitious fears attached to the spot will also disappear, if they be not already among the things that were.'[54]

Pitmilly

Pitmilly House circa 1870s

The Poltergeist of Pitmilly House/Hotel

Rumours of the hauntings of Pitmilly have always been riff in this area. So much so, that although the building no longer remains it is still a well ingrained feature in the minds of many through the localised landscape. Having heard from third party sources over the years that many people having stayed or dined within its walls have felt, heard or seen things that were quite unaccountable, I often wondered if any of these witnesses were still around to back the qualification, or if it is just all rumour and conjecture, having more to do with urban myth or folklore tradition than fact. Without firsthand testimony it is easy to see how folklore of a topic so easily digestible can steadily build, and how such statements can become accepted without any quantifiable substance to back them up. This is much in the same way as the ghost train of the Tay Bridge which features later in this book.

Bangs during the night, toilets flushing with nobody present, footsteps, strange noises, smashing sounds with nothing found broken, sounds of furniture being moved or dragged across the floor, and a strange ghostly figure wandering the grounds were all features of apparent disturbances here over the years. They were coupled with the apparition of a 'Green Lady' who was said to glide along the corridors of the house. By all accounts she was an occupant some two or three hundred years ago, perhaps one of the wealthy Moneypenny family who dwelt here for many centuries.

Although St. Andrews is around 5 miles from Pitmilly, I have found the mysterious goings on within the building have never faded from the memories of those who remember tell of it being haunted when it was a hotel. A local woman from St. Andrews I spoke with about the house in the late 1980s told me she had a few meals in the restaurant there during the 1960s. She relayed to me some of the phenomenon mentioned above as recounted by staff working at the hotel at the time. She also described the building as being one of the coldest and creepiest places she had ever known. The latter was a sentiment shared by many of the time I spoke with, and who had spent time in this building for a meal or function. The sense people had about Pitmilly was very similar to the feelings others I have spoken with had about Kellie Castle featured in the GOF Castle Trail. The sense of dread or foreboding, the cold atmosphere, and that unaccountable but tangible creepy sensation – these shared commonalities all point to something really not quite right. It could be argued any building with character and age could convey the same, but not many buildings have this kind of effect no matter how dramatic their character. Perhaps it was down to the thought of it being haunted that exacerbated these feelings of tension and negativity. Whatever it was that triggered these feelings, they were very real for those who experienced them and it is rare to find so many sharing the same about the same location.

In the mid 1990s I met an elderly woman in St. Andrews who saw the apparition of the 'Green Lady' when she had an anniversary dinner here one evening. She was just on her way back from the toilet when she saw a woman in a long dull looking green dress standing at the far end of the hallway. She was quite tall and leaning slightly forward. I asked her age but she said she was looking at the ground and had long dark curly hair which obscured her face. Straight away she was gripped by fear and ran into the room where she and her husband were having dinner. Without sitting down she grabbed her husband by the arm and ran out of the hotel. Somewhat startled by her behaviour he managed to pay for the meal and they left "that haunted hotel" for their home in St. Andrews. She never returned to Pitmilly and kept the ghost quiet from her family. Her only comment to them of that night was she had not felt well during the meal, and they had to leave early. If Pitmilly ever arose in conversation she would never recommend any to go there, with nothing more said they probably thought it was something to do with the food, but she wouldn't promote any further discussion about the place.

For seven centuries Pitmilly House was the seat of the Moneypenny family (originally spelt Monipenny), they had many royal connections and exerted considerable influence. They were granted the first charter for the land by

Thomas Prior of St. Andrews as the Moneypennies of Pitmilly in 1211, a title they held until the late nineteenth century. They always held high ranking positions not only in Scotland but also in France. One of the most famous was David Moneypenny due to his involvement in the assassinations of Cardinal Beaton at St. Andrews. He had come to the aid of Leslie when they gained entry to the Castle of St. Andrews and killed Cardinal Beaton.

All that remains of the site today are the lodges on its perimeter and a large square wall amid fields and woods that once housed part of the gardens. E. J. G Mackay in: A History of Fife and Kinross. 1896 wrote 'The road from Crail to St. Andrews makes an unusually sharp turn at Pitmilly; the country people remark that there is always shelter at one part of it or another, as there are walls presented to each of the cardinal points.' He continues :

'Wind – Pitmilly'
"'Blaw the wind as it likes
There's beild[xxxix] about Pitmilly dikes." [55]

I later found the full version of this poem recounted by author John Geddie two years earlier in 1894 as follows:

'Across the Pitmilly Burn –
the Brook Puttiken of the Crail charters.
Blaw the weather as it likes.
There's beild aboot Pitmilly Dykes.
Having outflanked the Kenly Burn,
on whose banks no stone could we find
upon another of the palace of Inchmurtach,
where the Bishops of St. Andrews were won't to feast
the kings who came here to hunt the boars.'[56]

The Palace of Inchmurtach was believed to have been situated on the spot where a Doocot now stands. The large rubble stone Doocot was said to have been built from the stones of the Palace in 1600. It is situated around half a mile north west of Pitmilly and can be seen in a field of Kenlygreen Farm just south of the village of Boarhills, directly opposite the Boarhills turn off from the A917.

[xxxix] A place of shelter.

The St. Andrews Citizen dated 16th December 1967 mentions the final end for Pitmilly House:

'Pitmilly House', now in the course of demolition will go down in history, not so much for its age-old associations with the ancient Moneypenny family, but as the haunt for some years of a more than usually active poltergeist. Its malicious pranks had been complained about by the owner of the house at the time, the late Captain J. W. Jeffrey and a number of inexplicable incidents culminated in the mysterious fire of 1938. Twenty rooms were set alight one afternoon and the investigating insurance company could find no rational solution for the outbreak beyond the fact that the fire could not be started accidentally. On the other hand, they were satisfied there was no one in the house to whom they could attribute the fires. They paid the damage of some £400. Now, the last glimpse of the ancient house will be recorded by T.V. film cameras, with particular attention to the magnificent old fireplace which still awaits removal to some other mansion house. Let us hope the poltergeist whose devilish appetite seemed to have been started by the fire has not been hibernating in the fireplace!'[57]

The paranormal disturbances at Pitmilly seemed to have reached their peak between the years of 1936 and 1940, the same period in which small mysterious fires were started. Poltergeists are renowned pyromaniacs. Although thankfully it is not always a feature of this kind of activity stemming from an unseen source, it does form one of the more notorious and possibly the most malicious of their many traits. Crashes were heard, beds and bedclothes moved, large pieces of furniture moved, a bell rang of its own accord, and vases were thrown and broken.

In 1929 the house was put up for sale, an advertisement placed in the *St. Andrews Citizen* dated Saturday June 8th 1929[58] is most informative for its description of the old mansion at that time so is worth reproducing here:

'The Mansion house of Pitmilly, near St. Andrews

FOR SALE BY PRIVATE BARGAIN.

Pitmilly House adjoins the St. Andrews-Crail highway (5 miles from St. Andrews and 3 miles from Crail). Railway Station at Boarhills (1 mile).

The house contains 4 Public rooms, 9 Bedrooms, 2 Dressing rooms, 4 Bathrooms, 6 Servants Bedrooms, Gun room, and ample kitchen premises, all in excellent condition, and recently completely modernised. Electric lighting throughout the house and offices with powerful plant. Central Heating. Gravitation water supply. Telephone, large steading with commodious Garage and Stabling accommodation. The Policies are very attractive and include a highly productive enclosed garden, with good range of Vineries, &c. 4 suitable lodges and other accommodation at the steading for employees. A portion of Pitmilly Den will be included in the sale with access to streams and beach for fishing, boating, and bathing. Adjoining grass parks may be purchased if desired.

Actual purchase at Martinmass first.

For further particulars apply Maxwell and Dow, solicitors Anstruther, Fife, from whom cards to view may be obtained, and with whom offers may be lodged.'

***

Pitmilly House was duly sold. Details about the new owner and the activity is now included here. But firstly by way of a brief introduction to what follows, having grown up in St. Andrews, vague rumours of the mysteries of Pitmilly have always captured my imagination. Along with the feelings people have had in this building which collectively makes for important testimony, meeting someone who had seen the ghost of the Green Lady at Pitmilly was a real pleasure for me. So I wanted to capture something here of the essence of Pitmilly, something of the enthusiasm others also share for its mysteries. Author and scriptwriter Lorn Macintyre conducted research about Pitmilly a few years ago which was published by Priormuir Press in a booklet called *Pitmilly House, Poltergeist Manor* in 2011. Rather than quoting excerpts from his valuable research and which I highly recommend obtaining,[xl] Lorn has kindly granted permission for me to include an article he wrote a year later for the Scotland Review on the 20th December 2012 about Pitmilly House which complements his earlier research.

Following his publication in 2011 a Society for Psychical Research (SPR) member Tom Ruffles wrote a review of his work for the SPR, which includes valuable additional information having not been covered by Lorn. With this

---

[xl] Available as a Kindle at only £2 at the time of writing

Tom has very kindly given me permission to include his review here also, which I have reproduced below Lorn's article. Between the article and the review they enhance the booklet without detracting from the value of its own content, whilst also conveying the essence of Pitmilly I was looking for, complete with details of its history, its inhabitants and its paranormal associations as detailed by early researchers from the SPR in London.

Christmas at Pitmilly, the house where things happened at night
By Lorn Macintyre

20th December 2012

Why was Captain John Jeffrey staring at the table at which he and his wife with their two children were sitting in the elegant old mansion of Pitmilly, near Kingsbarns in Fife? Had the butler placed an item of silverware that didn't belong at a Christmas feast? But it wasn't something set down by a human hand that was preoccupying the captain.

The previous week, a flaming coal had manifested in the centre of the dinner table. That Christmas of 1932, as he waited to be served, the former captain in the 13th Hussars was asking himself fearfully: what next?

Heir to an Edinburgh brewing fortune, John Jeffrey was starting to regret purchasing the mansion two years previously. Two aspects had attracted him. He had been born in Pitmilly House, and the details of sale promised the most modern amenities: 'Electric lighting throughout house and offices with powerful plant; central heating, gravitation water supply, telephone' etc. Pitmilly was the former seat of the Monypennys, one of the oldest of Scotland's prominent families, with William, 1st Lord Monypenny, crossing to France in the train of Princess Margaret of Scotland in 1437. Pitmilly had been leased to Lady Gordon Cumming, who had spent much money modernising it before the Jeffreys purchased it.

For Captain Jeffrey, residing at Pitmilly was a luxurious life of a gentleman of leisure. There was a Daimler at the door, a large staff to feed the family of four, and to keep the log fires blazing. But flames would come from more than log fires, and events threatened to put the family in physical danger and to make Pitmilly House notorious in the annals of the paranormal.

The Monypennys and Jeffreys gave me access to family archives and memories so that I could write up the story of Pitmilly House, called 'Poltergeist Manor' by Harry Price, the controversial psychic investigator. As a youth Ivan, Captain Jeffrey's son, remembered the appearance of the first flaming coal on the table at which the family were dining. Ivan recalled: 'Things disappeared, never to be seen again...Ornaments used to crash on the floor; pictures used to fall off walls...Hot coals made their appearance in different rooms and set fire to curtains...fires started in different places at once...My parents called in a gentleman of religion who came and exorcised parts of the house, and holy water was sprinkled in several places...' This was Bishop Wilson from St Andrews. The bishop was sitting with his hat on his lap by the drawing room fire when it was whisked into the flames. At this same fire a visitor left her gloves to dry, and when she returned to check them, she saw that they were being held up in front of the flames, filled out as though on someone's hands.

But what was being exorcised? Charlton Monypenny, the previous owner of Pitmilly, denied that his ancestral home had a resident ghost. He had leased the house to Lady Gordon Cumming, wife of Sir William Gordon Cumming. The Sporting Times called him 'possibly the handsomest man in London, and certainly the rudest'. But he was also fearless, a big game hunter who had served with distinction in the Zulu War. He was a rakish figure in society, having abandoned his Scots accent and acquired a fluency in profanity in English and Hindustani. His brother Alastair Gordon Cumming kept on his mantelpiece the skull of an Arab slave-trader he had killed in Portuguese Africa. As a trophy he carried the man's blackened finger on his watch chain.

Gordon Cumming was found cheating at baccarat (a banned gambling card game loathed by Queen Victoria) in the notorious 'Tranby Croft Case' when the monarch's heir the Prince of Wales was taking the bank. Made to sign a paper pledging never to play cards again, Gordon Cumming took his accusers to court, thereby implicating the prince, after Edward's mistress Lady Brooke (known as 'babbling brook') had spread the story of the Morayshire landowner's cheating in London society. Having lost the court case and become persona non grata in society, the aristocratic cardshark retreated to Pitmilly House, where he called his desperately unhappy wife Florence, an American cotton heiress, a 'fat frump', caring more for the pet monkey he carried about on his shoulder.

Had Gordon Cumming been dabbling in the occult at Pitmilly, and created a demonic presence? Or were the destructive manifestations coming from Mary, Captain Jeffrey's unhappy daughter, isolated from her peers by her haughty mother? Poltergeist activity has often been associated with energies emanating from children. But the presence in Pitmilly House seemed intent on driving out the Jeffrey family. Ivan recalled: 'On my first leave during the war...I was greeted by a Chinese bronze ornament which sailed across the hallway and impinged on my tum-tum...'

On Thursday 7 March 1940, a major fire broke out in Pitmilly House, affecting around 20 rooms on the ground and first floors. An 83-year-old woman who had been in service with the Jeffrey family for four generations had to be rescued from her room. It would be the first time that an insurance company would pay out for arson by a non-human agency.

In July 1942 William Randolph Heart's American Weekly published an illustrated article with the headline: 'No rest in the Mansion. Mean Plot of Incendiary Spooks'. A maid – obviously an actress – is seen by an overturned table, a candlestick on the floor, bombarded by objects flung by no human hand. Pitmilly's reputation had crossed the Atlantic.

Terrified by the spontaneous fires and airborne objects, the Jeffreys had been driven out of Pitmilly House at considerable financial loss. It became a country house hotel, and a Welsh newspaper magnate woke to witness his clothes being tipped from the drawers. When he opened the door, fire was running for yards along the corridor wall, but without leaving a mark.

Pitmilly failed as a hotel, and in 1967 the mansion was sold to a local farmer, who demolished it. However, Pitmilly House's reputation endures in paranormal websites, and the 1947 play by Frank Harvey Junior, 'The

Poltergeist', was made into a horror film, 'Things Happen at Night', the following year.'

As I mentioned before Lorn's article the following is a comprehensive review of his booklet by SPR member Tom Ruffles, which is also available on the SPR website[59] and is reproduced here with his kind permission:

Pitmilly House, Poltergeist Manor. Priormuir Press, October 2011. ISBN-13: 978-0956768124

Reviewed for the SPR by: Tom Ruffles

Lorn Macintyre, who gave the opening talk to the SPR's 2011 conference in Edinburgh on Pitmilly House, has produced a pamphlet containing information about this large residence and the strange occurrences that were said to have taken place there in the late 1930s and early 1940s. It is a useful supplementary background source for anyone interested in this enigmatic case, but unfortunately it has not drawn on the file held in the Society for Psychical Research's archives which contains much relevant information that has never been published. The case was initially investigated by Lord Charles Hope, and the extensive, if barely legible, notes he sent to the SPR's Research Officer, C V C Herbert in 1940 are a key resource for anyone delving into the Pitmilly affair.

Pitmilly House, which stood between St Andrews and Kingsbarns in Fife (tel. Boarhills 30), had long been in the Monypenny family, but their declining fortunes obliged them to let it to tenants, including the rakish Sir William Gordon Cumming and his unhappy American heiress wife Florence. It was bought in 1930 by Captain John Arthur Jeffrey. He and his wife Alison had two children, Thomas Ivan, born in 1915, and Mary Elizabeth, born in 1924. At the time the poltergeist outbreak became publicised, the family was living in the house together with a couple of elderly female servants (Hope is vague about the help as he discounted their involvement), a Swiss governess and a Danish daughter-in-law, Vibeke (or Vebike, Hope cannot make up his mind). Thomas was in the forces and mostly away from home at the time.

The large number of poltergeist-like phenomena which occurred in the house during the Jeffrey years, were recounted by Ivan (as Thomas called himself) in a programme on the brand-new Radio 4 in 1967. The first, when he was "comparatively young", was a piece of coal which appeared on the table in the middle of dinner. According to Hope's notes, the phenomena started in about 1936 (escalating in late 1939), but Ivan was 21 in 1936, so if Ivan's memory is accurate, events began earlier. When on leave during the war he saw a Chinese bronze ornament sail across the hallway and hit him in his "tum-tum", as he quaintly put it. Other events he recalled included valuable ornaments discovered upset or broken, pictures falling off the walls, items falling off mantelpieces, and things disappearing that failed to return. A wardrobe crashed to the floor, hot coals appeared in random places and set fire to curtains. Fires started in several different places at the same time. Visiting psychics also experienced phenomena and an "exorcism" carried out by a visiting clergyman had no effect.

In March 1940 an extensive fire broke out, affecting some twenty rooms, and the claim settled by the insurers was later used as evidence that the insurers had recognised poltergeist activity. Phenomena were not though confined to the family. From 1942 to 1946 the house was requisitioned, and soldiers had odd experiences, not least seeing the ghost of Captain Jeffrey, who had died in July 1941. By now word was getting out and an article appeared in the American Weekly in the US in July 1942 entitled 'No Rest in the Mansion'. While not named, this was clearly about Pitmilly House. Yet there seemed to be no long-established history of paranormal occurrences because Charlton Monypenny, the previous owner, was contacted by the press and claimed in ambiguous terms that "since my grandfather went there no-one has seen or heard anything except fancy on the part of someone". That may mean that there were suggestions of strange happenings that were attributed by the sceptical Monypennys to imagination. Even if there were, they would not have been on the scale of those reported during the Jeffrey period.

James Herries, a Spiritualist and reporter on The Scotsman, wrote an article for Psychic Science, published in the October 1942 number, in which he referred only to "a Scottish mansion house". He had visited Pitmilly House on 19 March 1940, staying overnight and adds the details that there were a couple of affable dogs in the house. He conducted interviews, and while he gives a useful overview of events, Hope in his notes calls him "very gullible". Herries held a séance with a Glaswegian direct voice medium, Mrs McCallum. There were some strange voices, but no other results.

Hope visited the house on 28 April 1940, but before this he had discussed Pitmilly extensively with the Jeffrey family lawyer, Gilbert Hole, of Gillespie and Paterson in Edinburgh. Hole was acting for the family in the insurance claim and had himself witnessed events, including vases in mid-air, which had scared him. Herries's article also refers to "an Edinburgh professional man" who had given him information, and this is Hole because both Hope and Herries recount a story (Herries without naming his informant) in which Hole was sitting in an armchair with an ashtray containing several used matches, and when he looked down he found that these were arranged along the arm of the chair.

As a result of Hope's lengthy account, Herbert asked W H Salter, the SPR's Hon Secretary, if it would be worth going to Pitmilly House himself, as Hope was keen for him to make the trip. Salter thought it would be, if Herbert could be there at the same time as Hope (despite wartime conditions Hope employed a chauffeur, who did a bit of sleuthing for his boss on the side), but there is no further correspondence on the matter so it looks as though Herbert never made it.

Harry Price devotes a chapter to the case in his 1945 book Poltergeist over England. To maintain confidentiality he calls it "Poltergeist Manor", which gives Macintyre his subtitle, though the way Price phrases it suggests that the sobriquet was coined earlier (it is not used by either Hope or Herries). Price refers to a "professional man", who had given him full reports, the first in 1940, and this again is Hole, as the matchstick story is reused, with the information that prior to the matches being arranged on the arm, Hole had been thrown to the floor with the chair on top; presumably he had picked up any fallen matches so would have known that they were in the ashtray when he sat back down. Hope's less dramatic version is that at some point prior to the lined-up matches incident, Hole had been sitting talking to a policeman when he was pushed over. For a solicitor, Hole seems to have been astonishingly indiscreet, and one has to wonder if he egged things on in order to be at the centre of attention.

Price too lists an extensive range of phenomena. Incidents included furniture sliding around by itself; ewers of water in bedrooms constantly emptied onto the beds; heavy fire-irons rattling themselves and when tied up managing to jump apart, leaving the string knotless; a heavy wardrobe tilting at an angle of forty-five degrees but not falling over, in defiance of gravity (presumably on the occasion Ivan Jeffrey recounted, gravity won); and a heavy bronze vase which once shot through the open front doorway "at an incredible speed", changed direction through ninety degrees, and came to rest in the garden, all in front of witnesses.

If this was the object that hit Ivan in his "tum-tum" and it was going at any speed, he would have known about it as according to Price the vase weighed about 15lbs. There were numerous fires, but conversely on one occasion the owner thought he saw a fire on his bedroom carpet yet after beating it out found no trace of damage. 'Exorcisms', to use Price's term, were conducted unsuccessfully by both Roman Catholic and Anglican clergy (the latter according to Herries an Episcopalian who merely held "some kind of service"). Price said at the end of the chapter that he hoped to be able to follow up the case personally, and Macintyre suspects that the result would have made a companion piece to The Most Haunted House in England, as The Most Haunted House in Scotland. Macintyre speculates that it may have been Price who leaked the story to American Weekly. Price was certainly aware of the article as he cited it in a footnote.

The Jeffrey family sold the house and it became a hotel in 1947. It was finally demolished in 1967-8, at the time of Ivan's broadcast. The Monypenny and Jeffrey families and their relatives and friends had a stock of stories from the house's heyday, like the bishop who came to conduct an 'exorcism' on a cold day sitting in front of the fire and having his hat leap from his lap into the flames. A woman dressed in green was seen in and around the house. One particularly bizarre story had a pair of gloves being held up to a fire, as if filled by invisible hands. The same witness, walking down the stairs, saw the portraits lift on their chains and rotate. During the period of the hotel, bottles of sealed alcohol mysteriously emptied, the seals left intact.

The house was referred to by G W (not F W, as Macintyre has it) Lambert in a 1964 paper in the SPR's Journal, 'Scottish Haunts and Poltergeists II', calling it "Pitmillie" (which he probably took from Hope's notes, which also refer to "Pitmillie") and noting its proximity to the Ochil fault. He links the bulk of phenomena at the house to the sorts of effects that occur with earthquakes, there having been a number of them locally in the period 1936-40, the very years in which events at the house were at their height. Lambert famously proposed hydraulic pressure caused by underground water action as a mechanism for poltergeists and was here seeking another type of natural explanation, though rotating paintings and levitating gloves would have been beyond its scope.

Macintyre notes that Frank Harvey Junior's 1947 play The Poltergeist and the 1948 film based on it, Things Happen at Night, have their origin in Pitmilly House (the film was not a Hollywood production as Macintyre states, but was made at Twickenham). The film acknowledges Price in a preamble: "The characters and incidents in this film are entirely fictional, although all persons interested in poltergeist phenomena must necessarily be indebted to Mr Harry Price for his research work in that field." Coals feature extensively in the film, something particularly associated with Pitmilly House, and an insurance investigator is a major character. A psychical researcher, presumably a version of Price, is the most authoritative person present, directing the investigation. Events at 'Hilton Grange' in the film, largely played for laughs (supposedly), go beyond even the most outlandish aspects of Pitmilly, culminating in the sight of Alfred Drayton discharging buckshot at flying vases, of which there seem to be an unfeasibly large number on the premises. (This was not Drayton's only brush with the paranormal, having been a guest at The Halfway House in 1944, an establishment kept by ghosts) There is a poltergeist focus at Hilton Grange, a school-age daughter based on Mary, though despite the uniform she looks as if she probably left her school days behind a good few years earlier.

There has been surprisingly little written about Pitmilly House since the 1940s. Apart from Lambert's mention in JSPR, Alan Gauld and A D Cornell include it in the appendix to their 1979 book Poltergeists, as Case 429, but do not discuss it. Sadly, it seems unlikely that a complete explanation for Pitmilly House will ever emerge at this late stage. Eyewitnesses attested to remarkable events, but are now beyond further interrogation.

Herries was convinced that the poltergeist was genuinely paranormal, with an intelligence behind it. Hope's verdict was much more tentative, and was essentially 'open'. He did not think there was collusion, yet no one person seems to have been present during all of the events. Hope thought the "easiest" solution was that Captain Jeffrey began it, and Vibeke was frightened, then realising he was responsible, when he was away she also faked events to get even, which frightened him in turn. Surprisingly, given that he was supposed to have witnessed paranormal events, Hole told Hope that he thought that Captain Jeffrey had faked some. Presumably Hole would have told Herries and Price the same thing, but neither mentions it as it would not have suited the 'genuine poltergeist' narrative.

However, even this, Hope thought, was not satisfactory, and a scenario to cover all of the phenomena would require at least one more participant, or self-deception by large numbers of people. Hope adds the titbit that Mrs Jeffrey was not positively disposed towards her husband, who drank heavily. Captain Jeffrey had seen ghosts in a previous house and his wife considered him to be psychic.

On the other hand, Hope speculated that Mrs Jeffrey might be a focus, torn between duty to husband and a desire to be away from him. There certainly seem to have been a lot of emotions swirling around, perhaps including Vibeke's for her largely absent husband.

Macintyre wonders if Mary was responsible as the poltergeist focus, and she was an obvious suspect given her age. Price certainly saw a parallel with the Amherst Mystery, which featured fires, though Mary at Pitmilly House was never as obvious a focus as Esther Cox was at Amherst. Price also mentions a maidservant at Pitmilly who seemed to be associated with some of the outbreaks of fires, but this may relate to Vibeke, who was accused by a fireman. Some of the events occurred when Mrs Jeffrey, Vibeke and Mary were living in the Dower House, away from the main building, but Hope states that the poltergeist had followed them, and they were reporting activity there as well. That hints at possible fraud by at least one of them, and Hope had both of the younger women in mind as possible fakers though he also more charitably thought that they might be so "nervy" in the Dower House that they were misinterpreting normal occurrences as "supernormal".

Ivan does not seem to have been regarded suspiciously at all, and was in France when things were particularly bad. Even so, one would expect a bit more precision for such a significant event like coal appearing suddenly on the dinner table than that he was merely "comparatively young", if it had actually happened. He may have been covering for his wife by suggesting that phenomena had occurred before he met her.

Although Price claimed that all of the descriptions of activity in his book were contained in signed witness statements in his possession, Macintyre notes that there appears to be no sign of these in Price's methodically preserved archives. Items have certainly disappeared from the Harry Price Library over the years, but one wonders if the reason for the lack of documentation is that Price eventually came to the conclusion, given the florid nature of the communications from Hole, that despite the numerous signed statements, he had been hoaxed. He did not visit the house himself, though as he died in March 1948 perhaps he simply never had the opportunity. Presumably then all of the statements in his possession were gathered by Hole on his behalf, and perhaps he concluded that his initial trust in his contact's probity was misplaced. His categorising of the house as "Poltergeist Manor" was certainly premature.

The reports gathered by Hope, Herries and Price seem to suggest some paranormal element, but once a narrative gets going, it is easy to misinterpret innocent events as paranormal, and later reports could have been stimulated by the place's reputation, or there could have been opportunistic mischief-making. As far as someone giving the story to the American Weekly is concerned, its article appeared on 12 July 1942, but Price refers to stories in the British press about the insurance pay-out earlier than that – the Daily Telegraph and Daily Mail carried the story on 8 April 1942, and .it appeared in other papers as well, so it is possible that the American Weekly picked up the story from one of those, though that begs the question who leaked the story to the British press. Or, rather than Price giving the story to the American Weekly, as Macintyre suggests, it could have been Hole, who seems to have been willing to tell anybody about it; the story was certainly common knowledge in the area.

There has been a great deal of confusion over the insurance claim, how much damage was done, how much was claimed, how much was paid out, and what it signified. Hope put the cost of damage at some £600 and wondered if the family would make an insurance claim as this might prompt the police to investigate it as arson. Hole it would seem was, ironically, concerned that a lawsuit might involve unwelcome publicity, but considered that a failure to claim might be tantamount to a confession of arson. In the event a claim was made, and Price stated that the insurance claim was settled for £400, reduced from a whopping £800.

However, an article in Psychic News, dated 16 December 1967, was published to coincide with the demolition of the house. It said that Herries had stated in a lecture that £400 of damage had been done (indeed the figure given in the Psychic Science article), and this had generally been assumed to be the amount of the claim. In the event, according to Psychic News, the claim was for only £50, which may have meant that the insurers did not bother to look into the matter too closely.

Price considered payment an acknowledgement by the insurers that poltergeists existed, as it was conceding that the fires were not started accidentally, but were not started by the occupants either. Without seeing the insurance report, though, it is impossible to know what the insurer paid out for, and why, leaving us with hearsay as to the grounds for payment. That the company could not assign a cause, if that is what happened, did not entail endorsement of a paranormal agency. All that the payment signified was that the insurers did not consider the family responsible, because they would have instituted an arson investigation if they had. As so often, Price overstated the situation.

It would be interesting to learn if the insurer's report still exists so that these questions can be settled. As such loose threads suggest, there is still some mileage in this fascinating old case, even if ultimate explanation is elusive. Discussion of the poltergeist activity actually takes up only a very small part of Lorn Macintyre's well-illustrated 26-page booklet, but he brings together some details about the house and its various occupants, and gives a name to Poltergeist Manor for readers of Price's rather ill-titled Poltergeist Over England.

References for the above article:
Archives of the Society for Psychical Research, Poltergeist file P4, 1940/1967.
'Fife's Fiery Ghost', *Psychic News,* 16 December 1967.

Gauld, Alan and Cornell, A D. *Poltergeists,* London: Routledge and Kegan Paul, 1979.

Herries, J W. '*Poltergeist in a Scottish Mansion house*', Psychic Science, Vol. 21, No. 3, October 1942, pp.88-92.

Lambert, G W. '*Scottish Haunts and Poltergeists II*', JSPR Vol. 42, March 1964, pp.223-7.
Price, Harry. *Poltergeist Over England: Three Centuries of Mischievous Ghosts,* London: Country Life, 1945.

Lorn Macintyre's *Pitmilly House, Poltergeist Manor.* (Priormuir Press, October 2011) is available on Kindle. It features rare photos of the house and its occupants and is highly recommended.

***

Pitmilly Cottage
One of the former employee lodges, adjoining the former grounds of Pitmilly on the main road has been witness to its own activity. With several unaccountable noises and brief visitations by the 'Green Lady' of Pitmilly herself, who it seems still roams the area Pitmilly House and Hotel once occupied.

Pittenweem

Priory of Pittenweem
photo by the author

The Priory of Pittenweem

This ancient priory was built more than 600 years ago by monks having inhabited St. Adrian's priory on the Isle of May then moving to here in 1318.[xli]

A narrow stairway runs down the back of the priory, leading down to St. Fillans cave by the sea below. The cave was discovered in 1900 when a hole was exposed in the garden from the weight of a plough falling into it. The cave had been used as a prison for suspected witches in the 17th to 18th centuries and one corner of the grounds by the Gate House is known as "The Witches Corner," an area where those condemned for the crimes of witchcraft were finally reduced to ashes and their remains then buried.

Pittenweem was particularly mob handed when it came to the witch trials. The smaller the place, the greater the paranoia and in turn the greater the hysteria it generated. Unlike today, the later part of the 17th century and early 18th century was not a time for standing out from the crowd and being noticed for being different. This was the age of conformity and adherence to the church; it was not a time to be an individual unless in-keeping with its administration and doctrine.

[xli] Refer to Isle of May, p.162

One account in particular I have included here concerning the period of the witch trials is centred on Pittenweem and typifies the level of hysteria that was generated in a number of locations. The following is quite an example:

In January 1705 Janet Cornfoot of Pittenweem was accused of being a witch. She was imprisoned in St. Fillans Cave and beaten up, but after a time was allowed to escape by some that believed in her innocence. Soon after though she was discovered and grabbed by an angry mob who found out about her release. They dragged her through the town by her heals and finally to the sands where she was tied up by rope and suspended in mid air between a ship and the shore (no man's land), held taught she was stoned and beaten as well as being stretched in a manner most brutal.

St Fillans Cave entrance
photo by the author

Eventually they let her fall onto the sands and continued beating her. The mob by this time were caught in a fury that couldn't even be quashed by the local magistrate and clergy roused by the foray, so they stood helplessly by unable to do anything.

The rabble then got a door and laid it on top of her followed by many stones of great weight, she cried out that she would tell the truth, but when the weights were lifted they found it not to their liking and quickly resumed crushing and pressing her to death. If this wasn't already enough, to make quite certain she was dead they called a man with horse and sledge who proceeded to ride over her corpse a few times.

Ghostly figures have been seen here, flitting around the garden of this priory and strange noises have been heard in the silent hours.

Clair McKim reported the following in Deadline News on the 13th April 2012:

Pittenweem say "no" to Witch memorial

A SCOTTISH village has voted against creating the country's first official memorial to witches tortured and killed by vengeful mobs.

The 1,600 citizens of Pittenweem in Fife, took part in a controversial referendum last month on whether they wanted a memorial and where it should be built.

But after the community delivered a 50-50 split result, the community council has decided they will not be supporting the monument.

A leading supporter of the memorial has called the council's decision "pathetic," and described the vote result as a "complete joke".

At least 26 "witches" were tortured and 18 of them killed in the picturesque fishing village in the early 18th century.

Sandy Guthrie, community council chairman, said: "The opinion in Pittenweem is completely divided half and half and so we are not supporting it.

"If there had been an overwhelming support then we would have gone ahead but as far as the council is concerned it will have to be done privately and without our support.

"I was expecting the vote to be quite divided, but as there was no positive reaction then we have gone down that road," he added.
The local council had written to every adult in the community asking if they agreed in principle with the plan to build memorial.

The campaign to build the country's first witch monument was spear-headed by local historian Leonard Low, author of the Weem Witch.

Low, whose family have lived for generations in Pittenweem, had proposed the memorial be built at the village's West Brae, in memory of 26 local victims who was falsely accused of witchcraft.

During the witch trials at Pittenweem, sixteen of the accused were burnt at the stake, and one died during torture.

The most notorious witch killing was that of Janet Cornfoot.

Sir Sean Connery's ancestors were reportedly among the lynch mob that tortured and killed her in 1705.

After she was accused of witchcraft, Cornfoot was swung from a rope, stoned, and then crushed under a heavy door piled high with boulders.

To make quite certain she was dead, a horse and cart was repeatedly driven over her body and her remains buried in the area called West Braes.

Mr Low today called the community council's decision not to honour the Pittenweem witches "pathetic".

He said: "Even though I knew in my heart that it would fail, I am still very disappointed.

"The Pittenweem community council say they are scared of getting a bad image, but they had the chance to put themselves on the map, as the place with the first official apology to witches in the UK.

"To say there was a 50-50 split is a complete joke. The decision will have come down to the church and they are not budging on it. I actually think it's pathetic.

"In Salem they had the exact same scenario but the church backed a motion to build a memorial, and it has become a massive tourist attraction, bringing in millions of pounds a year.

"I have received a lot of support for the monument and even though it is very disappointing result, I think the fact that it came this far, after 300 years, and has got people talking, is a success," he added.[60]

Refer also to *Lingo House* owned by the Priory of Pittenweem
13th to the 16th centuries, p.187

The Grey Woman of the Church House of Pittenweem

Now living in California Mrs Cawley whom we met earlier concerning the secret room of *Cameron House* also gave me this account of when she and her family stayed in Pittenweem, residing in an old Episcopalian Church House. "The church house in Pittenweem," she said "had a very gentle feel about it. I became aware of it being haunted by a benevolent woman who created a deep feeling of peace; a very gentle presence like that of a caring and concerned motherly figure. Sometimes I caught glimpses of her flitting around the house. She was a kindly old woman with golden hair and wearing a grey dress." The identity of this mysterious woman became clear when a very pleasant elderly gentleman visited them one day. On introducing himself he told them he had lived within the house for many years. After chatting about Pittenweem and the East Neuk she asked him if anyone had died within the place. In answer it was found that his wife had died a few years earlier within the house. The story ran that their son took ill and had seen doctors about his condition, but had been wrongly diagnosed, what he had was Appendicitis and because it hadn't been discovered he died of Peritonitis. They were both very upset on his passing but it was his wife that never quite recovered from the experience and died finally herself of grief and despair. This was the kindly old woman that she had seen for brief moments flitting around the house.

Red Slippers

There is told a tale of red slippers haunting a house in Pittenweem. I have not been able to find any further reference to this, but with Kellie Castle being just inland, and being the haunt itself of red slippers we have probably found the origin of this local tradition.

Prior Muir

A959, Anstruther to St. Andrews Road

A couple of miles along this road toward St. Andrews from Dunino the ghostly figure of a woman was seen by a St. Andrews man a few years ago near Prior Muir. He was travelling one night from Anstruther to St. Andrews by motorbike with another riding pillion. The bike developed engine problems after leaving Anstruther, so their progress along the road became a reasonably slow one.

On reaching Prior Muir about three miles from St. Andrews he noticed a woman standing by the road-side wearing a headscarf and a dark coat. They were about to pass when she suddenly stepped out in front of the bike as if to cross the road. Although no impact was felt he was sure they must have struck her. Horrified he stopped the bike and fearing the worst turned to look, but to his surprise the woman was nowhere to be seen, only the dark deserted road stretched out before them into the distance.

After answering a query from his passenger who thought they had stopped because of engine problems, on speaking of the woman and he not seeing anything they searched the area for her. Finding no sign they continued to St. Andrews and went to the police station. With the aid of police and dogs the area was thoroughly searched and the neighbouring houses visited, but no trace was to be found of this mysterious woman.

"We must have driven straight through her," he said, "as she couldn't have stepped out of the way in time. The whole thing was very strange; it was as if we were connected in some way with the woman as the bike ran fine after the encounter."

It was as though the woman had purposefully slowed them down to save an accident.

Rathillet

The Phantom Rider

A couple were driving along the A914 Dundee to Kirkcaldy Road one clear morning. When just past Rathillet the passenger saw in a clearing to the right of the road a hill with a rider wearing dark clothing on horseback. The rider travelled down towards them at great speed then stopping by the side of the road at the edge of a clearing. There was a great deal of morning mist around this area, settling and swirling through the trees and hovering a few feet thick above the ground.

A few miles further along the road the passenger mentioned the mysterious rider to her companion but he never saw anything, after that she never concerned herself any more with the encounter and went to work as usual. That evening, on travelling once again along this road, the woman when nearing the area and looking to make conversation pointed out where she had seen the horse and rider that morning. She discovered to her bewilderment there was no clearing in the trees at all where the horse and rider had been seen, and because of the trees it was not possible to view the hill beyond where the horse had so clearly come from.

Her description was brief but the horse was very large and jet black, the rider bearing some stature wore clothing of many years ago.

One suggestion is the rider was that of Hackston of Rathillet who lived in this area and was riding along a track long gone to meet with the others at Magus Moor as part of a conspiracy to scare one William Charmichael. But when Charmichael got word of their ambush and didn't show, circumstance delivered Archbishop Sharpe to them who was travelling back to St. Andrews from Edinburgh. During the frenzied bloodshed that was to follow Hackston of Rathillet remained mounted on his horse some distance away. He was like a mysterious highwayman, watching the maddening slaughter with cloak covering the lower half of his face. He had taken no part in the actual murder but that didn't stop him and the others present from being hunted down and tried for Sharpe's murder, along with the attempted murder of his daughter.

Refer to *Magus Muir*, p.195

Rosyth

Ferry Toll Road

On the 20th Aug 2009 the Dunfermline Press reported: 'The *ghostly* apparition of a soldier was spotted at dusk last month on Rosyth's *Ferry Toll Road* "trudging" towards the Dockyard by a west fife woman on her daily commute. The female driver reported passing a young man dressed in military uniform walking towards the dockyard. She looked into her rear view mirror to have another look at him, but he had vanished. The witness said there would not have been time for him to turn off.'

Springfield

Crawford Priory and an early Goth!

Visiting restrictions/fees

Private land and what is left of the building is very ruinous and dangerous. It is mainly the front castle like portion on the left of this wonderful old picture of the building that remains intact.

Directions

Situated in wooded grounds three miles south-west of Cupar, just south and into the woods of Springfield train station.

The immensely impressive ruin of this grand Gothic mansion is a breath to behold. It was Lady Mary Lindsay Crawford who commissioned the Gothic styling of this building in 1813. She added to the façade of the original Scottish lodge and turned it into a celebrated Gothic mansion. It was described as being "perhaps the most important Gothic Priory house in Scotland," and looking at the picture it is easy to see why this statement would be made.

The house was originally built in 1758 for the 1st Earl of Crawford and was occupied up until as recently as 1968, when the upkeep became so expensive parts of the building had to be closed off, then following the death of the 2nd Baron of Cults a house sale eventually took place in 1971. Following the sale the Gothic mansion was then abandoned. With this it wasn't long before it fell into decay and became the ruins we now see today. A somewhat eccentric figure in her day, Lady Crawford who had the ceiling of one of the rooms painted a dark blue colour and studded it with stars. There were many features such as this, her taste excelling as a minority of the time, shared in today's terms primarily by those in the 'underground' Gothic scene who appreciate such imaginative beauty. When she died she had a funeral befitting of her styling and taste in 1833. A lover of animal's; in-keeping with the genre of such ways of being, her ghostly figure wanders the grounds of her beloved Gothic estate to this day. Playing with the animals she cared for and generally appearing to be enjoying the grounds she loved so much in life.

In the early 1990s when I was initially putting together the material I had amassed for this book, I spent a number of months staying opposite Highgate Cemetery in London. One Sunday morning I opened the curtains and there across the road in the eastern cemetery near the railings, a Victorian Gothic funeral was taking place. Complete with glass hearse pulled by two large jet black horses, each supporting large black plums. The smattering of mourners was all attired in black Victorian garb with veils of black stretching all the way to the ground. This was a most impressive, unusual and rare sight to behold indeed and one shared with my partner at the time. On enquiring some years later whilst visiting, I was informed by the Highgate Trust that no funerals take place in the cemetery on a Sunday. With this I began to wonder, and to this day I can't be certain that what we saw that morning was of our own time at all.

St. Andrews

Over 75 haunted locations in the town with well over 100 separate occurrences.

Refer to the GOF Castle Trail, St. Andrews Castle, p.15, Kinburn Castle, p.33
Refer also to Ghosts of St. Andrews by the present author (2013)

St. Michaels

The Ghost of St. Michaels Wood

Just out of Guardbridge on the A914 Dundee Road towards Newport stands the 200 year old former coaching inn of St. Michaels Inn on the corner of a crossroads. Taylor in 1875 writes of this place. It is 'frequently called Saint Michaels, named after Michael Irvine, who, in the balmy days of stage-coaching, had a public-house here and kept good grog. Doubtless, he was as worthy of the title as many who have been more formally canonised. He was familiarly spoken of, by the old people who knew him, as Michel Eurn.'[61]

Just across from this Inn is St. Michaels Wood in which the body of a tramp was found one winter not far from the road. The woods and the crossroads are said to be haunted by this stranger, who, on passing through and not having the money to stay at the Inn, had slept for the night in the woods and due to the cold had died where he lay.

St. Michaels Inn

Paranormal Discovery investigated this Inn and this is what they found.

'St Michaels Inn was built in 1799 and served as a coaching in and drop-off point for the Dundee Penny Post. It is situated at a crossroads called Carrick Junction which is nowadays known as St Mike's. This crossroads is where the roads from St Andrews, Cupar, Tayport and Newport all meet. The surrounding area used to be forest but, of course, as with other areas of the British countryside, this has changed over time.

Paranormal activity at the inn has been reported by guests and staff and is still ongoing. The staff feel that there is nothing malevolent at the inn and feel that the guest bedrooms are welcoming and homely.

Reports include:
A guest telling staff that he had been speaking to a little girl on the stairs one morning only to be told that no children were staying at or visiting the inn.

Several guests reporting at different times that someone was trying to open the bedroom door during the night (no other guests staying at the time).

A female figure has been seen from outside standing at the window of room 6.

Feeling of someone rushing past felt by staff when in the back cellar.

Cold spots and cobweb sensation felt in the function room by staff.

A baby has been heard crying throughout the night on several occasions and reported by guests but no babies had been staying in the inn. This has been heard while guests were in room 2 and was thought to come from room 3.

The window of room 6 seems to open by itself and the bedclothes on the middle bed are disturbed frequently as if someone has been sitting on the bed This has been reported by domestic staff.

Lights mysteriously turning on and off in the function room – these lights had not worked for several years!'

St. Monans
Historic Kirk – The Ghost of General Leslie

photo by the author

St. Monans Kirk stands at a remote spot on the rugged sea battered cliffs a few fields from the Castle on the western edge of St. Monans. Many artists are drawn here to paint this picturesque church and its surrounding seafront landscape. Along with Crail harbour St. Monans is one of the most artistically portrayed fishing villages in Scotland. It is also said to be the closest church to the sea in Scotland with waves battering the cliffs only a short distance away.

David Leslie was an elder of this church up until his death and was buried in its north transept. In 1828 during restoration of the building his bones were removed and given burial elsewhere. The ghostly figure of General Leslie is reputed to have been seen haunting the church and the surrounding burial grounds.

The following is a report of the story from Fife News in 2007:

'A pale face in the gloom of the kirk...
One dark, winter night a lad was cleaning the ashes from the furnace in St Monans Kirk.

1803 engraving of the interior. This is how David Leslie would have known it.[62]

He was just locking up when he looked back and saw a light flash from the gloom of the tower and, to his horror he noticed a pale face which shone.

He ran to the minister's home and he was rooted to the spot – to his amazement there was a portrait of the apparition he saw moments earlier.

It was a painting of Sir David Leslie of Newark who had long since been dead.'[63]

Another story about this is as follows: 'There was a young man who had to rise early in the morning in order to light the boilers in the old church and well in advance of the congregation due to arrive later in the morning so they would be warm. On one particular day, however, and having performed his duties, he ventured into the main area of the church and saw a bright light descending from the roof. As he approached, facial features appeared within the light!

The man was so scared that he ran towards the Laird's house located at Abercrombie; a distance of nearly two miles, and where, upon admittance and seeing a painting upon the wall, swore that the image in the picture was the face he had seen in the light! Variants of the story say that he died from fright and exertion and that the picture was that of the Laird's late wife!'

Refer also to *The GOF Castle Trail, Newark Castle*, p.46

Strathkinness

Apparition and Premonition
In 1989 I journeyed to Strathkinness from St. Andrews to meet a couple having responded to my call for accounts in the local newspaper. I found them to be a lovely relaxed and very hospitable couple, who lived in a charming character

filled dwelling in Strathkinness. On the night of 17th November 1980, Richard Batchelor, a scientist and spiritual healer in St. Andrews told me he had a dream that he was working in the garden of a two storied house, the windows of which were square with green painted frames. Feeling an evil presence he was afraid to go near this place. He then found himself on the other side of this house in another, looking out of the window he saw a grotesque face peering out of the window in the house with the green frames. He told me the experience was most vivid and more akin to a nightmare than a dream.

On the night of Christmas eve in 1980 he and his wife moved from St. Andrews into a house in Strathkinness, at the end of this house is a window looking on to another. The windows of the neighbouring house, somewhat dilapidated were the same as in the dream he had. Complete with green window frames. When he looked at the window of a ruined part of the house facing his, he saw an "evil face," menacingly staring at him, also like that in the dream. After that he didn't like going near that part of the house, feeling a strange atmosphere was attached to it. Unnerved at what had happened he eventually performed a cleansing of the house as a kind of exorcism, with the result of sending good vibrations through that part of the house. The effect whether psychological or otherwise succeeded in dissipating any of the negative feelings.

The house where the face appeared was built by the Younger family and had at some point been used as an old man's club. The part of the building where he had seen the face had been the caretaker's quarters. He later learned that a ghost, maybe of the caretaker himself, was indeed said to haunt the club. In the mid 1980s the building was renovated, while the caretakers quarters were left to ruin until April 1989 when it was demolished to make way for a garage and perhaps laying to rest the ghost it housed.

Strathmiglo Castle & the Knights Templar
Poltergeist Activity

So far as castles go, this one had a short lived in history. Maybe it was down to the disturbances reputedly to have taken place within its walls. Built in the 16th century it was taken down in 1734 to provide stone for other buildings in the area including the steeple in front of the town-house, now the Town Hall, built in the same year.

The castle was frequented by bouts of poltergeist activity, which translated into the world of folklore as the work of fairies and brownies steeling food from the castles pantry. Perhaps the real answer was kept quiet by the hungry servants of their day who found fairies an obvious scapegoat, but maybe I am being too cynical.

This area was known as Templelands. The Parochial Directory for Fife and Kinross of 1861 says: The area 'anciently belonged to the Knights Templar, and appears, after the suppression of that order, to have come into the possession of the Knights of St John of Jerusalem, as the proprietor of the eastmost feu is bound by his title to maintain the cross of St John on a conspicuous part of his house, to mark the boundary between Templeland and burgage property.'[64]

Strathmiglo area

The White Lady and the Ghost of Jenny Nettles
The ghost of a White Lady on the B936 Auchtermuchty to Falkland Road by Dunshalt. *Fife Today* in 1994 reported:

STRANGE STORY OF THE GHOSTLY 'WHITE LADY'

'A GHOSTLY encounter on the road from Falkland to Auchtermuchty has uncovered a centuries-old tale which has aroused the collective memory of local people.

The supernatural sighting was made by 19-year-old Thomas Armstrong when he was driving back to his home in Auchtermuchty with two friends.

At the side of the road just past Falkland wood, the friends saw a blanket of mist which took on the appearance of a ghost as they drove by.

When Thomas returned home, he told his mother Wilma, who immediately remembered what she thought was an April Fools' Day joke played by her brother 20 years previously.

Wilma explained: "My brother saw a ghost on the same stretch of road. He was walking along the road with it right by his side and it wouldn't leave him until he neared Dunshalt.

"He was in a state of shock when he came home that night, but nobody would believe him because it was April Fools' Day.

"When I phoned to tell him that Thomas had seen the ghost he laughed and said 'I told you so'.

"Nothing was ever done after my brother saw it, but when Thomas told me that he had seen a ghost in the same area I thought I would try to find out a little bit more about it."

Wilma's appeal for information prompted a number of responses from local people familiar with the history of the area. Now she thinks that the ghostly apparition may have been that of the 'White Lady', a well known local legend who many believe is the ghost of Jenny Nettles, a Strathmiglo lass who was buried on the Nuthill estate in 1716.

According to local historian Helen Cook, whose book 'A Haunting of Ghosts' deals with the area's supernatural folklore, Jenny committed suicide after she was deserted by her lover. The mystery man was known to be a member of the Macgregor clan who had occupied Falkland Castle during the Jacobite Uprising of 1715, but he disappeared from the area along with the rest of his clansmen when they were forced to leave the castle.

According to legend, Jenny's ghost now wanders the countryside between Strathmiglo and Falkland, where she used to meet her lover.

Wilma said that while she never knew of the story before, the tale has now aroused her curiosity.

"In a way I would like to see the ghost for myself, but on the other hand that is maybe not such a good idea!" she added.'[65]

The connection between Jenny Nettles and the haunting by this White Lady is possible, but a very tenuous one. It is spurred more by the widespread familiarity of Jenny Nettles in the folklore of the area, then attributing sightings to her by association. The above account by Thomas Armstrong occurred on the Muchty to Falkland B road, the B936, but as Helen Cook suggests 'according to legend, Jenny's ghost now wanders the countryside between Strathmiglo and Falkland, where she used to meet her lover.' Now this is also where she hung herself, from a tree by the A road, the A912, midway between Strathmiglo and Falkland. This is around half a mile to the west as the crow flies from where the other apparitions were sighted. What we are looking for then with the ghost of the white lady of the B road is an identity, because she is a different ghost.

The Ghost of Jenny Nettles

A more detailed account of Jenny Nettles follows from the words of John M, Leighton writing in his *History of the County of Fife* in 1840:

'In the middle of a muir[xlii] at the north part of the Lomond's, south of Barrington, and about half a mile west of Kilgour[xliii], the well-known Jenny Nettles, (who has given name to a lively and very fine Scottish air, and forms the subject of an old song published by Herd, beginning, "Saw ye Jenny Nettles

---

[xlii] Barrington Muir.
[xliii] The Royal Burgh of Falkland was formerly known as the parish of Kilgour.

coming through the market,") was buried. This unfortunate heroine was a native of the neighbouring parish of Falkland, and was famed through all the surrounding country for her great beauty. When Rob Roy took possession of Falkland Palace, after the battle of Sheriffmuir, one of his Highlanders paid too successful attention to the rustic beauty; and she, on being deserted by her faithless lover, in a fit of despair put a period to her existence, by hanging herself on a tree at the roadside, about halfway between Falkland and Strathmiglo. Her body was, of course, in those days, denied the use of a coffin, and refused to be allowed to be interred in a churchyard. It was conveyed on two rough sticks to the muir already mentioned, and there consigned to the earth. Two other females, who had committed suicide, were subsequently interred in the same place.'[66]

The old song published above by Herd refers to a piece written by Robert Burns about an unwed mother and goes as follows:

> *Saw ye Jenny Nettles,*
> *Jenny Nettles, Jenny Nettles;*
> *Saw ye Jenny Nettles,*
> *Coming from the market?*
> *Bag and baggage on her back,*
> *Her fee and bountish in her lap;*
> *Bag and baggage on her back,*
> *And a babie in her oxter?*

Leighton continues; 'It is the area of Barrington Muir that is haunted by Jenny Nettles. She was a resident of Strathmiglo and her final resting place is at a crossroads here of two forest paths, a few minutes' walk out of Strathmiglo. Local lore has it that Jennie's ghost wanders the muir on bright moonlit nights, looking for her lost Highland love.'

A mention in Robert Burns' song attributed to her is not included in the local folklore surrounding her *And a babie in her oxter?* but it would be in-keeping with one of the reasons for her suicide. When her lover, together with Rob Roy and the other highlanders fled back to the safety of the highlands she might also have been made pregnant by him. Knowing she wouldn't be able to cope she committed suicide with her baby still in her womb.

A legend from the nearby Lomond Hills also speaks of Jenny Nettles. Interestingly this particular legend would be wholly in-keeping with her being pregnant:

On the lonely beautiful Lomond Hills wanders the fair-haired ghost of Jenny Nettles who died on these hills with her child after being betrayed by a soldier at Falkirk Palace.

In this legend it is just the ghost of Jenny that haunts the hills, again her child died with her because she was not yet born. So given the legends it would make sense for her to have been still pregnant with the Highland Officers child when she hung herself and the betrayal in the Lomond legend could be her lover reneging on any promise for them to raise their child together and adding to her heartbroken state. This area is also the location of gallows which stood in the days of King James V by the roadside some half a mile to the west of the Palace. James V was notorious for hanging people without trial and on the surface for that matter without a thought. Oddly it would seem, with this he considered himself to be a fair man and it was not without warrant that he disposed of people in this way. These were harsh times and the penalties exacted were both swift and ultimate.

photo of the Lomond Hills by the author

Concerning this the Reverend Andrew Small in 1823 wrote: 'Being one day up on the Lomond Hill, the King [James V] met a chapman or pedlar, and bought his whole pack from him; but left it in a hollow till he got time to convey it away, or perhaps rather with a view to try the pedlar's honesty. But it appears he was not able to resist the temptation; for, immediately after the King was out of sight, the pedlar returned and took away his pack again, not thinking that the King would find him out; but this he soon did, and hanged him for his pains. It was by such methods as these that he attempted to reform the morals of his subjects, or correct abuses prevailing in his kingdom; but these were too widely spread, and to deeply rooted, for him to be able to eradicate, all the time he lived amongst them. The pedlar was hanged on the side of the public road, about half a mile west from the palace, at a place still known by the name of the Gallows by the old people. A little to the westward of this, also, a famous heroine of the name of Jenny Nettles, in a fit of remorse hanged herself on a low crooked tree on the road side, which ever after retained the name of Jenny Nettles' Gallows, and only gone a few years ago. She lies buried at the foot of the hill, at a place called Jenny Nettles' Grave.'[67]

Facing north towards the Strahmiglo surfaced path

photo by the author

A bench now sits at the crossroads, seen on the photo on the left. Concerning the grave Leighton says: 'On a recent occasion [pre-1840], two earrings and twenty-four beads were found in her grave; one of each of which are now in the possession of Mr Fraser, Edinburgh, lapidary[xliv] to her majesty' [Queen Victoria].'[68]

The crossroads of the two forest paths Leighton mentions in Barrington Muir is georeference: 321259 708039.

This is the most likely location of Jenny Nettles Grave. It is the crossing of the paths in the middle of the Muir; a forest called Drumdreel Wood at the foot of the Lomond Hills. It has Barrington to the north and Kilgour to the east.

These two pathways converging from the east and the north are also ancient byways so they cover the same route they did many years ago. The eastern path comes from the A912 turning off for Kilgour (the road beginning at the lively organic farm the Pillars of Hercules). The forest path then commences at the end of this road into the forest just by Wester Kilgour itself. From the north the

Facing south – the Falkland woodland path

Photo by the author

---

xliv A lapidary is a gem smith.

path comes down Cottown Road from California in Strathmiglo and is a four mile cross country pathway to Falkland. Skirting the Lomond Hills it converges with the eastern path en-route to Falkland around a mile south of Strathmiglo. The flatter routes now have tarmac. A directional signpost mark only the tarmacked cycle paths rather than the woodland path continuing from the crossroads in a straight line from Strathmiglo to Falkland. Instead the tarmacked pathway turns to the left at the crossroads eventually meeting with the A912,

Jenny was born in Falkland but she lived in Strathmiglo and her lover was in Falkland. In all likelihood it would have been this Strathmiglo to Falkland path they would have taken. This would not have been far from the spot where they would have met up. It is direct between the two and would have been more discreet than using the highway now forming the A912.

Crossroads in the woods looking south towards Falkland
photo by the author

Suicides were buried at crossroads so their spirits on becoming confused would be trapped at that location with not knowing which direction to go in. If this was the intention for Jenny it didn't work. However Leighton does say there were two other female suicides buried at the same spot. Keep a watchful eye out the next time you take a wander through these woods to see what you will see.

Tayport

The Auld Hoose
The distinctive long white building of the Auld Hoose with its black painted window surrounds at 1-3 Whitenhill is located on the east side of the town. Like many pubs it has had a number of unexplainable disturbances over the years, with incidents being witnessed by staff and clientele alike. The following

is a synopsis of the report by Paranormal Discovery of Dundee when they investigated this premises:

A presence has been felt, especially in the lounge area. Doors have been opened by unseen hands, beer glasses have leapt off the bar shelves and the pumps for the bar taps have been turned off. All in all the sporadic display here is of classic poltergeist type activity – but without the age group producing PK as you might expect in a private dwelling. The strangest episode and the one typifying the mischievous conduct of the ghost was a pack of cards which had moved from the bar and was now lying some distance away on the ground spread out in an arc. Nobody had been in the bar at the time and only the back of the cards were displayed – apart from the 2 jokers which were lying there face up!

There have also been plenty of noises mainly from the sounds of someone playing pool when the room has been empty. A gust of wind has also frequently been felt through the bar area when the doors and windows have been shut.

Unfortunately also like so many public houses this family run pub has suffered with the recession and is currently up for sale.

Tentsmuir

The Ghost of Tentsmuir Forest

Spanning the coastline along North East Fife from the River Eden to Tayport is the area known as Tentsmuir, a large woodland area with beautiful expansive beaches. The area encompasses a nature reserve for the wealth of birds that rest here on their migratory trek. By day this very beautiful picnic area of northeast Fife is visited by many for its natural picnic areas, sandy beaches, blue sea and bird watching, but as night falls it becomes easy for the unwary to become disorientated and lose direction. At night it rapidly transforms into the dark forest of Sleeping Beauty, with the dense woodland quick to hide the familiar landmarks of the day.   James Wilkie writes:

'At Tentsmuir under cloud of night, he who is brave enough, or has the misfortune to be belated on the bent and heather, may catch sight, now and then, of a lantern's glimmer. It flits to and fro, and in the dim light of the stars, it is sometimes possible to discern its shadowy bearer. Centuries ago, a bonnet laird, afraid for the safety of his hard-earned gold, the idol of his miser heart, hid it somewhere on the waste. The times were troubled; might was too often right; no banks existed; places of security were hard to find. There it would lie in safety till he looked on it again.

To his consternation, when next he found himself able to add to the hoard, the place where he had laid it underground eluded him. All was alike on the wide expanse. Frantically he sought and dug; nothing but sand and the tough roots of heather met his efforts. Night after night, winter after winter, when darkness and loneliness favoured his search, he returned to his task. Death did not end it, though it has long turned for him into withered leaves the gold he loved. The ruling passion outlived his mortal years, and he yet wanders there on his vain quest, unstartled by the night-birds' cry, or the wail of the homeless winds.'[69]

Wemyss

Wemyss Castle
The Ghost of 'Green Jean'

Refer to Wemyss Castle, p.62

Wormit
The Tay Bridge Disaster & the Ghost Train

Photo of the original Tay Rail Bridge

The Tay Bridge Disaster of December 28th 1879
On the 28th December 1979 I managed to drag my parents and a couple of their friends to the foot of the Tay Rail Bridge on the shores of the River Tay in Wormit. I felt sure a large crowd would have gathered for the 7pm train due to cross the bridge from Edinburgh to Dundee, as this was the 100th Anniversary

of a terrible disaster. With a tremendous storm the bridge had collapsed with a passenger train and had killed approximately 75 people. It was believed on the anniversary of the disaster the ghost train that drove the poor unknowing occupants to their watery grave would to once again appear and recreate its fateful journey. By all accounts it trundles across the air along the former bridge then amid screams and crashing sounds as carriages and girders smash to pieces the train once more plunges into the icy cold River Tay below.

The publicity for the 100th anniversary was rife in the area. The Dundee *Courier and Advertiser* had a four page facsimile paper as part of a 100th anniversary edition of the disaster.

W. T. Linksill the noted ghost writer was on this very train in 1879 from Edinburgh. He got off at Leuchars to get a taxi to his eventual destination but it hadn't arrived. It was caught up somewhere in the same storm that was raging about the area. So he decided to stay on the train and just go to Dundee for the night. As the train was pulling out of the station the stationmaster called out to him that his taxi had just arrived. Linskill and a boy in his care had just enough time to jump out of the train before it sped off to its impending doom. The following day they were struck as the whole country was with shock and horror at the news of what had happened to that train that evening. More so for Linskill, with memories so recent of those poor travelling souls they left behind to suffer the fate he and the boy in his charge had come so close to meeting with themselves.

The previous train to go over to Dundee that evening had a rough time of it by all accounts, and by the time this train began to cross, a force 8 to 9 gale had struck up across the River Tay. The train should never have been allowed to go over the bridge with winds so high. As it started its way across the bridge from Wormit it was soon in trouble.

A progression of panic!

There was a great deal of speculation about how the disaster happened. Popular belief attributes it to the raging storm that caused the disaster, but Mr William M. Dow head of the science department at the Dundee College of Education in 1979 wrote the main article of the 4 page 100th anniversary edition of the *Courier and Advertiser* with a new understanding of what may have happened that night, which makes for some rather gruesome reading.

Mr Dow in his article proposed the following:
In picking up the story…

'My own view is that the train reached the high girders without derailment and without damage.

But in the first of the high girders, the one nearest Wormit, at least one carriage was derailed – at the kink in the rails not mentioned at the court of inquiry. The vehicle most likely to be derailed was the second class carriage, the second last in the train.

In my opinion, it was then pulled along the level, wooden floor, sandwiched between the big third class coach just ahead of it and the guard's van just behind it.

The original rail bridge showing the rails and wooden floor.
A locomotive similar to that which went over can also be seen in the picture.

It ran in this state through three girders but collided at speed with the angle plate between the fourth and fifth girders.

This would have several effects –

1 – The guard's van would telescope into the second class carriage and the bodywork of both vehicles would disintegrate. That this is actually what happened is borne out by the fact that only the chassis, telescoped together, were found.

2 – All the vehicles forward of this would have their couplings burst. This was the way in which they were found, several feet apart.

3 – The coal in the tender would shoot forward as the jolt came from the burst couplings.

The stoker's body showed that his face was badly burned as he'd been pressed against the hot boiler.

4 – The vehicles in the front portion of the train would suffer little damage. This is exactly what was found when the girder, still with the train inside, was raised from the river.

5 – Because the bodies of the carriage in the front part of the train remained intact, they would be buoyant at the point at which they hit the water. The heavy wheels would then turn the train upright and an instant later the heavy girders would come crashing down on their roofs.

It is not that easy to see, but sitting on top of this rolling stock in Dundee is one of the chassis brought up from the depths Dow is talking about.

The roofs were found to be slashed at the angles of the lattice girders.

Most people's impression of the disaster is that it happened in an instant with the passengers not knowing anything was amiss until the moment the train fell.

I don't think that was the case.

The passengers in the rear of the train would be the first to realise that something was wrong as their carriages bumped along the wooden floor.

But at the front of the train, the driver and stoker were probably unaware that anything was wrong.

They probably put down the extra drag they must have felt to the force of the gale.

This theory goes some way to explain why the engine's brakes were never applied.

Imagine the scenes on the train. There must have been a progression of panic as the passengers in succeeding carriages became aware they were in trouble.

Those in the rear carriage probably realised as early as the first high girder.

If the train was travelling at 30 m.p.h., they had half a minute of that realisation before the train began to fall.

Mr David Mitchell, the engine driver

The fall itself was probably much slower than is commonly imagined. I estimate that the girder, with the train trapped inside, took some 30 seconds to fall the 98 feet to the river. The lack of damage to the engine and tender indicates that the fall was a slow and terrifying one.'

The jinxed girder

The fatal girder which had caused the all-important kink in the rail had an eventful history as Mr Dow continues:

'It had been blown down river on August 23, 1876, when it was on its way by barge to be lifted into place by the tide.

One of the tugs towing it failed. The other tug could barely hold the 190-ton girder against the gale.

A boat was hurriedly sent to Dundee harbour to summon another tug and, with minutes to spare, the girder was brought back on site in time to be put into place.

Then, on February 2, 1877, the girder, along with two others, was blown down.

It was recovered from the river, straightened and put back in place.

There was a big argument about whether this particular girder should be straightened and re-used or simply replaced with a new girder.

The final decision was to reuse the girder.

From the moment that decision was taken the Tay Bridge Disaster was almost inevitable.'[70]

In another part of this article he writes: 'That girder had been at the bottom of the Tay following a fall during the construction of the bridge. It, and the one next to it, fell down. One, seriously damaged, was left on the river bed. The other was lifted out, straightened and put back in place.'[71]

The gales and storm was not enough to cause the disaster – although it was a contributing factor. In all 6 people had spoken of their concerns about the kink in the rail which was to eventually derail the second last carriage of the train. The derailment then caused the others to be thrown about before the second last carriage hit the high girders. As we have heard the chasse of the last carriage went straight into and over the one in front, immediately killing all who were in both and on impacting the high girder, this great iron structure complete with train broke up and all fell crashing into the unforgiving stormy waters of the River Tay below.

The evening I was there in 1979 was very similar to that of 1879. High winds blowing a winter's gale, with icy cold rain pouring down and the lapping of waves battering against the shore. The only comfort if there were any to be found on this bleak evening, came from the lights of Dundee twinkling in the distance across the Tay.

This was a time of great sadness, a time for reflection and a time of commemoration for the loss of so many souls that night. The new rail bridge was opened in 1887 close to the original bridge. It ran across the Tay parallel to the original and 14 construction workers had drowned in its making.

Some of the original supports of the original bridge are still visible jutting out of the Tay. We saw no such ghost train trundling over its long forgotten rails on this night. With the rain and the building gales the Edinburgh train on the 100th anniversary of the disaster passed slightly later than 7:15pm and moved relatively slowly over the bridge, with carriage lights blazingly brightly in contrast to the blackened stormy sky and the darkness of the bridge we had been looking at.

Apart from the driver looking forward to pulling into the station of Dundee, I could only see one person on board that train that night, a man in dark clothing, seated oddly enough in the middle of the second last carriage, and appearing to look out of the window – I waved but I wouldn't have been seen. A curious part to this was a comment I made at the time to the others present; "with only one passenger on the train perhaps it was Death himself paying his respects."

This was before I read Mr Dow's article and his suggestion that the second last carriage was the first to be derailed from the buckled girder that began the fatal process. So might this occupant have been a ghost?

While updating this book I read an article written in the 'Kirkcaldy Book'[72] (original source not listed) that given my experience above sent a shiver up my spine:

'Reports came in about strange happenings on trains travelling to Dundee on the anniversaries of the tragedy. One such story involved a young man who joined the train at Kirkcaldy station. The thought never occurred to him that he was travelling on the same day as the tragedy, 28th Dec or that the train was running the same timetable as the doomed train followed years ago. He entered one of the compartments which was empty except for an elderly gentleman dressed in old fashioned clothes. Out of courtesy he asked the gentleman if he could join him in the compartment. The elderly man did not reply but just sat staring out of the window. He looked very ill. His complexion was a grey white colour. The young man sat down and passed the time with a book. The journey was uneventful until the train began its crossing over the new Tay Bridge. The old man turned and faced the young man. His features were contorted with fear and pain and his eyes were filled with tears and sorrow. Without a word being exchanged between the travellers, the elderly gentleman faded away and the young man was left alone in the compartment.'

It is always possible for a ghost train to career across the former bridge, but it is far more plausible for former passengers of the train that went down with it, to be seated on the train that crosses on the anniversary of the when they lost their lives. These are known as 'Anniversary Ghosts' and without realising, maybe it was one such occupant that I saw on the 100th Anniversary of the disaster as the train began its journey across the new Tay Rail Bridge. It is believed up to 30 bodies have never been recovered from that tragic disaster.

To see one of these poor victims maybe it is better to be on the anniversary train than waiting for the ghost train to pass across the site of the original bridge, as the following may put pay to any thoughts of a ghost train per se.

The Original Ghost Train
Another article in the same supplement of the Courier explains the origins of the Tay Bridge Ghost Train, which would then suggest the actual ghost train from the disaster to be an urban myth built round this following story:

'Original estimates of the death toll reached 300 at one stage. The reason for this was that all the tickets collected at St Fort on the whole day were counted – not just those for the last train.

Passengers with season tickets or heading for destinations beyond Dundee were not accounted for. Similarly, children were not included in the tally.

Because the total number of passengers was unknown, several local criminals, mostly wanted men, tried to take advantage of the situation.

Witnesses were hired to state that these men had been seen boarding the train at various stations.

The point was that, as they were officially dead, the police were no longer looking for them and they were free to continue their criminal careers without interruption.

This gave rise to the term "the ghost train" being used when referring to the train lost in the disaster.

But many of the "ghosts" were alive many years after the disaster!

The final death toll was estimated at 75, but fewer than fifty bodies were recovered from the Tay.'[73]

It is easy to think the train is still at the bottom of the Tay, or that it was smashed to pieces, but another qualification perhaps for the ghost train being an urban myth is that the train that went down was actually brought back up again. Because it went down with the high girder structure in the middle of the bridge it remained in relative good repair. So remarkably the train that went down was overhauled and put back into service in 1880. It then ran for another 39 years until 1919 – the train was nicknamed 'The Diver'!

Here is the very train herself, No.224 – 'The Diver'! After being salvaged
This photo was taken in 1880 and was originally a postcard with the caption
"Old Tay Bridge Disaster, 1879 The Engine"

We will never know the actual death toll of that tragic night, or the names of some of those poor souls who were never recovered. Nor the incalculable heartache suffered by their loved ones who in not knowing their fate, believed them to have simply disappeared. Perhaps blaming themselves, never realising they had actually been involved in this awful tragedy. Those lost with no name, they are the real ghosts that may be encountered here. The Tay Bridge Disaster remains today one of the worst we have ever known.

The above photos are from the National Library of Scotland in Edinburgh.

Appendix
The Ghost Criteria

Do you believe in ghosts?
Walking through walls or locked doors, becoming transparent, gliding above ground or moving silently are all familiar aspects of hauntings that may be accompanied by dramatic drops in temperature, strong winds, unusual sounds, and the movement of objects. Ghosts usually appear solid in form and can cast shadows, the reflection of a ghost can be seen in mirrors and telepathic communication can occur with spirits of the departed, but not with impressionistic ghosts mentioned later.

Alongside the stereotypical and more obvious experiences we are unable to explain away, there are additional experiences we don't realise are attributable to the paranormal. Ghosts can appear to be so real in every detail we might see them all the time in the street and not realise they are not living beings of our own time.

In many cases they have only given themselves away when the usual sensory information that should accompany the presence of the living is either distorted or absent; making no sound when passing, not being seen by others, obnoxious smells, drops in temperature or they are wearing unusual clothing.

Without the sensory interaction it is only when they display something out of the ordinary that we are alerted to their unusual nature. Typically we only realise their supernatural origin after the event, when we start thinking of the impossibility of what has just occurred. Despite our tendency to look for even the most tenuous of physical or indeed psychological explanations to account for our experiences, it is this impossibility that alerts us to the unusual nature of what we have just experienced. In *Ghosts of St. Andrews* Greta Boyd relays an account of her encounter with the monk at St. Rules Tower. The apparition manoeuvred past her on the stairway, then in retrospect she realised this would have proved impossible without the figure squeezing past.[xlv]

Ghosts within themselves can only cause slight physical harm, on brushing past they have caused rashes to appear and among the feign hearted a mild psychological disturbance but nothing matching the malign potential created by their counterpart – the Poltergeist.

To be psychic or to be a medium is to be aware of a deeper reality not picked up by those with a mind fully absorbed in the everyday aspects of life.

[xlv] Refer to *Ghosts of St. Andrews*, p.128

We can get so caught up with life it is easy to forget what life is all about. Also, if we were more educated in what constitutes paranormal phenomenon out with the stereotypical concepts we are accustomed to, we would be more open to the realisation of what has always been waiting in the sidelines for us to recognise.

It is believed 1 in 10 people will have an experience they are unable to account for. The figure is actually quite a bit higher than this.

In the main it is only our conformity, prejudice and our lacking in understanding that prevents us from receiving this greater influx of potential to the unseen than we are currently aware of.

As unusual as supernatural phenomenon appears to be, it is still natural phenomenon. With this in mind we are all gifted with so termed 'psychic' tendencies or abilities that enable us at times to perceive, and sometimes interact a little more with the generally hidden elements of reality. In our expression we can say paranormal activity stems from a different realm or realms. In this we would be correct but we would also be correct in saying all realms are aspects of a greater or deeper reality we are all part of. Everything fits squarely in the same reality we exist within. This may be thought of as being a greater reality existing alongside and through the familiarity of our own. With this there is a potential hidden from our physical nature. Our conscious mind has been conditioned to suppress this deeper awareness to such things, and all is reinforced by those sciences which primarily fall short of acknowledging this greater existence. There is more than meets the eye to our reality and to perceive a little more of it, we just need to be a little more open within ourselves.

Some seem to be more prone to attracting phenomenon more readily than others in this respect. Often I am asked why this might be. Well the answer is held within the nature of this attraction itself, which by degrees is directly linked to how open and receptive we are. Without realising it we are all constantly exposed to phenomenon all the time – because our existence coincides with this greater reality. The more receptive or in-tune our awareness is, i.e.; the more open we are, the more we will then perceive. So we don't attract phenomenon so much as we have the ability to perceive what many miss. We can acknowledge it, and we are able to observe it. We are often unaware of the conditions or requirements for this to happen because our level and depth of awareness is just simply part of the natural level of who we are. None of us are more special in this regard. As I say, we all have the ability to develop our receptivity to this constant exposure.

Greta in this respect is certainly one gifted with this particular receptivity for the unseen.

Over the years a tremendous amount of case data has been collected from all areas of the world, compiled and researched by such eminent bodies as the Society for Psychical Research established in 1882. The subject is finally gaining respect not only with the layman but within particular scientific circles, with the study of this subject being developed by parapsychology. In many ways paranormal research is still a new subject of study, hampered in many ways by the constraints of a physical quantification than by its illusive nature. As more ground is covered however so too are the barriers of separation becoming that little bit less daunting. Research is not so confined as it was in its early days to the laboratory. More research graduates are conducting field work alongside psychical researchers, but investigations can – and should be very time consuming. This often presents the additions of cost, coupled with no guarantees of immediate or long term success in witnessing any such phenomenon, let alone then being able to quantify it in some way.

A concrete foundation of validity has been laid by a mass of accumulated data from all over the globe. The independent correlations far outweigh the theories of speculation or mass fabrication – be it knowingly or tricked in some psychological fashion. This vast subject area has been dismissed out of hand for far too long as superstitious nonsense. A dismissive that should now be unworthy of any intelligent enquirer in our present age. There are and will always be those who will seek to deceive or trick for whatever reason, but no longer can the question be asked "does phenomenon exist?" It must surely be one of enquiring how and why it exists.

As the Society for Psychical Research developed and data was amassed, it became apparent that patterns were emerging that could be quantified into more specific relationships or category types of phenomenon. Mr G. N. M. Tyrell, President of the Society for Psychical Research from 1945-6 divided apparitions into four categories as follows:

Experimental Ghosts: Astral Projection

Crisis Ghosts: Appearing around the time of great crisis such as severe illness or death.

Post-Mortem Ghosts: Appearing after death to somebody known.

Ghosts: Habitual hauntings.

What follows in brief are categories for the phenomenon incorporating Mr Tyrell's formula, although his 'Ghosts' category is too much of a generalisation, as it amalgamates all habitual hauntings. I have therefore found it necessary to break it down and substitute it with further classifications.

Experimental Apparitions

Appearances of people still alive, caused by astral projection and crisis phenomenon.

Experiments have been conducted through astral projection with the aim of one person appearing in front of another who may or may not be miles away. The 'agent' concentrates the mind on appearing in front of the 'recipient' for which results have shown marked degrees of success.

Crisis Apparitions

Seen, heard or felt by somebody known to the apparition. The appearances are triggered by very powerful emotions projected as associative energies to the recipient in a time of extreme crisis. Occurring some twelve hours before or after death or a severe illness, but appearing sometimes up to four days after.

Accounts are on record that during the First World War, soldiers appeared to their loved ones when they were many hundreds of miles away, suffering the primitive and barbaric carnage taking place on the battle fields. The timing of their appearances being around the same time they either died or were seriously wounded in action.

Post-Mortem Apparitions

The apparition of someone close that has passed away may appear in times of great stress or to warn of some impending danger that may still befall them. One of the most common post-mortem sightings is when a close member of the family having passed away comes back to comfort the loved ones and deliver a message of reassurance that they are ok. These are similar to Crisis Apparitions but rather than just appearing they tend to warn or impart something and can appear long after they have died.

Impressionistic/Recurrent Apparitions

Ghosts of these two types are the most durable, lasting for many centuries.

Impressionistic Ghosts

As far as ghostly phenomenon goes this is the most common type witnessed.

Everything comprises of energy, everything generates energy and everything at every moment – every action and every expression including thought, emotion etc., is permanently recorded on the atmosphere. This is a continual infusing of impressions on the energy make-up comprising the 'space' of the locality, as a continual record of unfolding of events. It is possible for these to be picked up. We do it all the time. We are continually walking into an 'atmosphere'. It could be at work or socially where we just sense or feel something. It could be elation, or foreboding, it could be sorrow or feelings of joy. Places do affect our emotions and so our moods, our happiness, and our thoughts can be directed by them. Consequently they are very powerful forces.

We pick up the residues of past and present events all the time. The general air of a church or the collective feeling experienced at a concert, or just walking into a room, or an old building. A hospital or police station can be dramatic, even if we are not ill ourselves or have done nothing wrong. Everything is impacting upon us in a great many obvious and subtle ways. The obvious gives us our immediate evaluation and the subtle may change our mood.

When we are in a space of apparent neutrality – emotionally speaking, and there is no obvious suggestive psychological emotion that we might gather from a police station or a hospital, it is only the very powerful emotional impressions of events past such as at times of great stress, illness or death – especially violent death that will generally impact with enough energetic force to then attract our awareness. This attraction is through our acknowledgment of them. This is then translated to our level of susceptibility to phenomenon, which is through a determination of how it then affects us psychologically etc. Extreme emotional or traumatic events such as a gruesome murder or an intense sense of fear can impact the area of the locality with a very intense energy.

It is also possible for an event repeated many times over to also gradually build up this same intensity; perhaps a person with a great love for a certain place or area visiting it many times. Or the repartition of a particular act such as prayer – which is one of the reasons the inordinate amount of peace can be felt when entering into a church. Coupled with this is often that deep sense of sorrow as we empathise with the 'space' acutely and so more deeply.

The force; be it sudden or repetitive carries with it such an outburst of energy that it can be perceived. The recipient acts as a trigger, unlocking the impression held within the energy makeup, like unlocking an embedded period in time, a capsule locked in the reality fabric of the locality.

The imbedded sequence or impression is a 'none participatory' re-enactment of prior events. The phenomenon perceived is not aware. There is no intelligence, so there can be no interaction. In the same way characters in a film are not aware of you when you watch them. So it is much in the same way as walking into a room and starting a projector in motion, then watching a certain sequence of events unfold. This is what we call ghosts.

Recurrent Ghosts

These appear at the same place and time at certain times of the years, perhaps on the anniversary of their death.

Because these two types are impressions left on the energetic atmosphere it explains why a ghost may haunt various places at the same time. Especially those of the famous who either haunt many places around the country, or at least have been attributed to do so. Before moving on to the next category it is worth noting how the attribution of a haunting is usually to that of the most famous patronage that fits the description. While some certainly are those of the Kings and Queens etc, that haunt the many locations, those attributions stemming from a one off visit of an afternoon are highly unlikely to be of those they are purported to be. The impression they leave is simply not dramatic enough to leave its mark, especially after a few hundred years. On the opposite side of the coin to this, it is wholly possible for the most famous person to be haunting a locality even with a very brief visit. The residue is initiated by them, and reinforced by those who were there at the time, followed by a reinforcing and strengthening over time by others aware of their associations with the. We have all heard of charisma. Mary Queen of Scots had it in abundance. Within charisma is an intensity of energy, almost magical in the way it draws and attracts. There are many other aspects to this but space must dictate it be given on another occasion.

Ghosts of the Living

The living persons double is also known as a doppelganger. There are many cases of people observing, sometimes even speaking with somebody they know or are familiar with that were elsewhere at the time, although they appear real in every detail to them. Unlike Experimental Ghosts, no explanation is ever forthcoming as to why they are appearing, other than historical associations correlating an appearance as being portents of death or as a sign of longevity.

Wandering Spirits

These are of people who don't realise they have died or they cannot rest and move on until unfinished business has been completed, a grave injustice, or a murderer for example and wander the earth or rather the locality of where they died in a kind of limbo between this world and the next. These kinds of spirits are intelligent and communicate with mediums. They can be the cause of the most frightful occurrences to be witnessed in order for their presence to be made known. This has resulted in either mediums or more dramatically in exorcists being called to put the unhappy spirits at rest. The medium is always more preferable than the exorcist. The medium is a lot gentler with the spirits, far more in-tune, receptive and responsive to their requests. They can find out what ails them and maybe see about rectifying an injustice. If the spirit doesn't realise they have passed on, they can diplomatically and sensitively inform them of their situation and guide them gently rather forcefully (in the case of the exorcist) to the light of the energy realm where they need to be.

Poltergeist Activity

As with other aspects of the unknown it has always been easy to place the odd occurrence within the category of the paranormal rather than looking for the rational explanation for say – the mislaid object or the odd bang. Within buildings a whole host of natural occurrences have been mistaken for being supernatural in origin; windows rattling, strange noises, groans, creaks, bangs, doors closing etc can all be caused by a dwelling expanding and contracting, by hot water pipes, by vibrations from heavy traffic, by the wind, by changes in air pressure, by underground streams, and a surprising amount by rodents knocking objects off shelves etc. While these count for many reported disturbances and need to be eliminated before a metaphysical explanation is sought they don't account for all disturbances.

Along with this and often adding to the physical possibilities there is the more delicate matter of the many psychological aspects of an involvement requiring its own consideration. This may include any potential motivation afoot for anything untoward such as attention seeking or fraud. An example of this would be claims of poltergeist activity masking a family looking to be re-housed by the council because of bad neighbours. These are an all too common feature of many reports having been collated and studied over the years. With researchers of the Society for Psychical Research (SPR) and its Scottish arm the Scottish Society for Psychical Research (SSPR) along with Parapsychology units across the country finding the same. Recipients of supposed disturbances are often – if not always surprised when the line of questioning is initially directed toward them before being directed to any of their reported disturbances.

The word 'poltergeist' is an old German word meaning 'noisy ghost' or spirit. A term still used by investigators to describe such phenomenon, although not all phenomena can be placed within this category.

Not always destructive but always mischievous, poltergeist activity has been thought of as an external invisible force notorious for all manner of trouble. Characteristics of which include the moving or throwing of furniture and objects and a dangerous reputation for pyromania. Unlike other forms of ghostly phenomenon poltergeist activity has also caused physical injuries to occur both directly and indirectly. Indirectly by way of flying objects etc and although uncommon, directly, causing wheal marks, scratches, rashes and human teeth marks to appear on its victims body and arms. There does seem to be an unwritten rule where any serious harm is attributed to the psychological rather than to the physical. Cases are on record of kitchen objects such as knives, cutlery, plates and pots being hurtled across the kitchen but they seem to aim to miss. There has never to my knowledge ever been any deaths directly caused by such activity.

This mischievous behaviour of manifestation coupled with incidences such as human teeth marks may lend a brief insight to their nature. When the possibilities of natural causes and the elements of deception or psychological intrusions have been eliminated, there are two main categories: Psychokinesis and External Paranormal Phenomenon or EPP I call it, with the latter fitting the term Poltergeist more accurately.

Psychokinesis is a form of energy building in the soul or spirit of the individual and streaming from the subconscious mind of an individual to physical manifestation. When it is consciously applied it has positive and beneficial attributes as it is controlled by the host. When the host is unaware of its generation and especially manifestation it is a chaotic, negative and often destructive force. The destructive aspects more often stem from an individual experiencing a very traumatic period in their life, one filled with great emotional tension and stress. Instead of physically releasing the spent up emotional energies, psychokinetic energy or PK is generated from within the individual that is added to by the natural energies in the locality – more on that in a moment.

Through this great build up of emotional pressure a very powerful force can gather, and when it finds its release, the psychokinetic energy can cause all manner of phenomenon. Simple objects can disappear – often generally important objects such as door or car keys, objects moving or flying across the room akin to the spontaneity of physically throwing an object as a way of releasing built up emotion and anger. The release of psychokinetic energy is often just as spontaneous and just as uncontrollable as a fit of anger. The only difference being the host is rarely (if ever) aware of how the outbursts are caused. When not aware they may be the cause of the phenomenon themselves it is not controllable so the somewhat violent manifestations can be a very frightening ordeal for any involved, and understandably the phenomenon leads to the conclusion of the location being haunted.

As will have been noted, the behaviour of the poltergeist appears in many circumstances to mimic that of a young mischievous child, it may not be surprising then to find the age of individuals concerned range from around ten years to their early twenties. The latter is uncommon, with activity tending to cease altogether when maturity is reached, due in part to the extreme pressures and stresses of youth becoming more balanced and easier to cope with in adulthood, growing out of puberty and all the difficulties the teen years can bring – especially when physical or psychological abuse is involved and unfortunately as is so often the case, these forms of abuse tend to be coupled with a threat if silence isn't maintained. With this silence comes pain, confusion and can build into a tremendous force that causes great personal damage to the psyche and can manifest itself through psychological problems in later life. So PK is one way of releasing this spent up anger and frustration.

Usually outbreaks are confined to the home where most stress is generated, and in the main it all only lasts a few months. If the host moves to another address the change in both surroundings and circumstance have often been sufficient to alter the emotional stance, thus laying to rest any of the former activity; whether aware or not of causing the disturbances (albeit indirectly) themselves. When the disturbances do still continue, it has sometimes led to the first intimation that the cause may lay with a particular individual as opposed to the previous place being haunted per se. In these circumstances psychologists, parapsychologists, mediums and priests have often been sought. Only around one percent of known poltergeist outbreaks have resulted in an exorcism by a priest. In the main the phenomenon does not respond to exorcism because it is being generated by the host rather than by an external agency. Equally, if there is abuse issues a priest is likely to exacerbate them through attributing the wrong diagnosis as it were to the cause of the phenomenon. Exorcisms have never succeeded in ridding a house from the abuse by others. An exorcism is an extreme form of trying to deal with such manifestations, not least because the priests are going in blind as to the causes they are looking to dispel. It is possible for the dramatic nature to change the temperament of both an individual and others who suffer the phenomenon, but I have to say when it is poltergeist activity stemming from an individual and not an external agency, an exorcism is rarely enough to allay any proceedings. At best they give a temporary abeyance brought about by the dramatic and surreal nature of the situation at hand. Queen Mary's House in St. Andrews was such a case; "'the Bishop was brought, with bell, book, and candle; now, it appears, Queen Mary's and the adjacent house are undisturbed.'[xlvi] In reality however, the exorcism succeeded it seems in allaying for a time more the fears of the occupants than the disturbances."

External paranormal phenomenon can display the same characteristics as Psychokinesis but the phenomenon has its cause from an external energetic agency, force or spirit – this is the classic poltergeist activity that is often associated with the 'classic haunting' where ghosts and spirits are also in accompaniment. The energies causing a disturbance can remain external or in the case of the former where it feeds off a host, it latches onto, and works through an individual by taking possession of the individuals raw energies to strengthen its own ends. The outbursts are then released in like manner to Psychokinesis, but they can last for much longer and become much more violent and disturbed, and indeed then result in possession. These are the situations where exorcisms have worked in riding the individuals of the entities having latched onto them. Being of the nature of energy they feed off the charged energies of a host and the energies imbued in the atmosphere of the locality, then collectively the concentration of energy is focused on causing the manifestations to occur, which brings us to the following:

External phenomenon associated with the 'Classic Haunting'
When the cause is purely external and the energies are operating without using the energies of an individual, they may last for many years utilising the energies of the locality. For an agency to affect physical objects it often needs to utilise physical energy to produce the manifestations concurrent with paranormal phenomenon. So it needs to collect physical energy to then be able to utilise it. A great deal of energy is required. The agency is able to couple physical energy with its own to affect the physical by energetic means. The process it uses to do this is similar to the initial process of a dehumidifier. With a dehumidifier the air is attracted into the fans, the water condenses on the cold surface of the refrigeration unit and the moisture is collected, the dry cold air is then warmed up and returns to the air of the location. In the case of how an agency gathers additional energy to cause manifestations, it utilises the energy in the heat of the location. Rather than dissipating the warm energy by cooling the air down, the agency extracts the warm energy out of the atmosphere – or rather it collects the electromagnetic energy, focuses it and along with its own form of psychokinetic energy it creates what we would call paranormal phenomenon. All that is left in

---

[xlvi] Refer to my book *Ghosts of St. Andrews (2013)* and the section *The Ghosts of Queen Mary's House*, p.140

the atmosphere is the moisture as a residue which then forms the puddles of water on the ground we see so often in accompaniment to a great deal of disturbances. Unlike a dehumidifier the air is not then warmed up again, so the air becomes cold but also dry and produces the customary cold spots that are also common aspects of phenomenon. With the energy being extracted as a concentration it is often why these cold spots can just be localised to the space of a foot or a few feet. The more humidity in the air, the more energy there is available to create 'physical' phenomenon. In a haunted location the dampest area is often where a lot of the phenomenon will stem from, even though the phenomenon may manifest elsewhere – when in the field researching phenomenon, it is the dampest area associated with a disturbance that the humidity meter needs to be placed in. The inherent energies of an agency have similar characteristics to those we associate with physical energy, but they are not the same and should not be confused as being such. They are not dependent on any physical energetic constraint for their own existence, but when they affect physical objects, they have to use a physical means to affect them. We call their displays 'super' natural though with them using physical energy, what they produce is natural phenomenon, science just don't know enough about it yet to switch categories to encompass it all under the umbrella term 'natural'. When we eventually do, we might just keep the 'super' bit to highlight how extraordinary it really is – extraordinary because of its rarity but natural all the same.

Phenomenon and Energy Centres

Phenomenon is more prevalent at particular energy centres which attract these raw and often destructive energies. These are known as energy lines or ley lines which cover the earth like a web of energy. The crossing of ley lines accentuates the energy and a building on these sites will often have the familiar aspects of the 'classic haunting' in residence. With unexplained noises, footsteps, doors locking and unlocking, banging, heavy knocks and faint music etc all being characteristic of its display. Essentially the veils between worlds at these points are more tenuous. Stone circles often mark the crossing of leys, standing stones have also been used for this purpose but they are far less common, singular standing stones are usually placed as markers along ley lines rather than at the crossing points. Importantly the configuration of stones have all been placed in these locations marking this web of energy that it can then be accentuated and put to service in positive ways – always positive ways, never negative.

If a house is built on the crossing of a number of leys chances are it will suffer disturbances. The phenomenon at these centres may be accompanied by, or be associated with spectral visitations or intelligent spirits having departed this earth generally under violent or sudden circumstances. Other types of intelligent phenomenon are also attracted to these centres of energy as they are natural conduits between realms of existence. The opening in the veil can be almost like a seepage of sorts, where they can move more freely between this realm and their own. In these latter cases it is possible for mediums to communicate with the departed, allowing them to then continue their journey and bring an end to at least their involvement in whatever is taking place.

Iron stakes have been placed around such locations where it has been possible to do so. The energies are then diverted around the house instead of through it. This technique has had marked degrees of success in allaying disturbances – so long as the stakes are not then removed! It must be remembered the line of energy doesn't disappear, it is just re-routed.

These energies are not exclusive to ley lines, electricity pylons also convey degrees of electromagnetism and again exposure to phenomenon is increased accordingly when underneath them – especially when living underneath them, but unlike the energetic properties of ley lines, the residue from electricity pylons can cause damage to the physical health.

The Residual Impact of Energy

Interestingly a number of the places displaying poltergeist activity I have mentioned in *Ghosts of St. Andrews* are former hotels. The Star Hotel (now shops and flats), the Britannia Hotel (now The West Port Bar and Kitchen – although still with rooms to let), the Grand Hotel (now Hamilton Grand), Chattan Hotel (now McIntosh Hall) and the St Leonards – St Katherine's Junior School for girls in North Street (now the Crawford Arts Centre). The activity displayed is all part of the 'classic haunting' phenomenon and while they have *not* been caused by a 'living and breathing' adolescent they often bear testimony to all the same hallmarks.

It is not exclusive to hotels by any means, but why hotels? With such a high turnover of occupants and the diversity they bring, there is an equally high turnover of energy. This energy is increased when the occupants suffer physical and mental difficulties, the resulting turmoil can – and often does attract its own phenomenon. It is also more than possible for the occasional person to die while in residence and however imperceptible, everything leaves its impacting residue of energy on the locality. This is impressed on the atmosphere of the location to then be picked up at a later. Given the right conditions it can and does manifest into poltergeist type phenomenon, as well as apparitional.

References

[1] Chalmers, Alexander, *The General Biographical Dictionary* Vol. IV, Nichols, Son & Bentley; London,1812, pp.240-241

[2] Ibid, p.242

[3] *The Topographical, Statistical and Historical Gazetteer of Scotland*, Vol.2, A Fullarton and Co, 1856, pp.523-524

[4] Lesley, John, *History of Scotland*, book 10, Cody ed., (1895) p.296: Thomson ed., (1830), Edinburgh, p.195

[5] Knox, John, *History of the Reformation*, vol.1, Blackie, Fullarton & Co; Edinburgh, 1831, p.61

[6] Chambers, Robert, *The Scottish Songs collected and Illustrated*, Ballantyne & Co for William Tait; Edinburgh, 1829, pp.19-20

[7] Kirkton, Rev. James, *The Secret and True History of the Church of Scotland*. Edited from the MS By Charles Kirkpatrick Sharpe; Edinburgh 1817, p.407

[8] *National Observer, St. Andrews Ghosts*: 7th Jan 1893.

[9] Wilkie, James, *Bygone Fife, From Culross to St. Andrews,* Blackwood; Edinburgh, 1931, pp.366-367

[10] Lyon, Rev. C. J, *History of St. Andrews*, Vol.1, William Tait; Edinburgh, 1838, p.202

[11] Ibid

[12] Grierson, James, *Delineations of St. Andrews;* Cupar, 1807, p.147

[13] Ibid

[14] http://thehistorylady.wordpress.com/2012/05/15/historic-st-andrews-queen-marys-great-escape-from-loch-leven/

[15] http://www.visit-standrews.com/standrewsmuseum.html

[16] Bord, Janet and Colin, *Modern Mysteries of the World,* Harper Collins, 1990, p.349

[17] Sibbald, Robert, *History of Fife and Kinross*, 1710, R. Tullis, London (1803), pp.348-349

[18] *St. Andrews Citizen*: 5th January 1929

[19] Wilkie, James, *Bygone Fife, From Culross to St. Andrews,* Blackwood; Edinburgh, 1931, p.202

[20] *The Weekly Scotsman, Christmas,* December 1899

[21] http://www.castlesandmanorhouses.com/ghosts.php

[22] http://canmore.rcahms.gov.uk/en/site/70949/details/crail+castle/

[23] Wilkie, James, *Bygone Fife, From Culross to St. Andrews,* Blackwood; Edinburgh, 1931. p.294

[24] Ibid. pp.282-283

References Continued

[25] Ibid. p.294

[26] McKenzie, Richard: *They Still Serve – A Complete Guide to the Military Ghosts of Britain,* Lulu, 2008. p.81

[27] Fleming, David Hay, *Guide to the East Neuk of Fife,* John Innes, Fife Herald Office, 1886

[28] Ibid

[29] Ibid

[30] http://www.kilconquharcastle.co.uk/about-kilconquhar.html

[31] Fleming, David Hay, *Guide to the East Neuk of Fife,* John Innes, Fife Herald Office, 1886

[32] Leighton, John, M, *History of the County of Fife,* Vol. 3, J. Swan, Glasgow, 1840, p.120

[33] Fletcher, William Younger, *English Book Collectors,* Kegan Paul, Trench, Trubner and Co Ltd, London, 1902, p.400

[34] Ibid, p.401

[35] Fleming, David Hay, *Guide to the East Neuk of Fife,* John Innes, Fife Herald Office, 1886

[36] Fletcher, William Younger, *English Book Collectors,* Kegan Paul, Trench, Trubner and Co Ltd, London, 1902, p.399

[37] Leighton, John, M, *History of the County of Fife,* Vol. 3, J. Swan, Glasgow, 1840, p.120

[38] Fletcher, William Younger, *English Book Collectors,* Kegan Paul, Trench, Trubner and Co Ltd, London, 1902, p.401

[39] Chambers, Robert, *The Book of Days: A Miscellany of Popular Antiquities,* W and R Chambers, London, 1869

[40] Fleming, David Hay, *Guide to the East Neuk of Fife,* John Innes, Fife Herald Office, 1886

[41] Wilkie, James, *Bygone Fife, From Culross to St. Andrews.* Blackwood; Edinburgh, 1931, p.190

[42] Campbell, David Graham, *Portrait of Perth, Angus and Fife,* Robert Hale Ltd, London, 1979, pp.218-219

[43] Wilkie, James, *Bygone Fife, From Culross to St. Andrews.* Blackwood; Edinburgh, 1931

[44] Countess of Munster, *My Memories and Miscellanies,* London 1904, pp.159-165

[45] *London Magazine, The Duke of Argyll, Real Ghost Stories.* November, 1901 (Fife Herald, 8th February, 1905)

References Continued

[46] Countess of Munster, *My Memories and Miscellanies*, London 1904, pp.159-165

[47] http://balgoniecastle.co.uk/history.htm

[48] Ibid

[49] Ibid

[50] Beveridge, David, *Between the Ochils and Forth*. William Blackwood & Sons, London and Edinburgh, 1888, pp.242-243

[51] BBC's Doomsday project - 1986

[52] McKenzie, Richard, *They Still Serve – A Complete Guide to the Military Ghosts of Britain*, Lulu, 2008, p.81

[53] Morison, David, *Memorabilia of Perth*, William Morison, Edinburgh, 1806. pp.169-170

[54] *The Peoples Journal*, 29th August 1970

[55] http://www.historic-scotland.gov.uk/index/places/propertyresults/propertyoverview.htm?PropID=PL_202

[56] Ibid

[57] http://www.nts.org.uk/Property/Falkland-Palace-Garden/News/1548/

[58] Leighton, John, M, *History of the County of Fife*, Vol. 2, J. Swan, Glasgow, 1840, Footnote , p.153

[59] Laing, Alexander, *Lindores Abbey and its Burgh of Newburgh, Their History and Annals*. Edmonson and Douglas, Edinburgh, 1876, p.382

[60] Martine, Roddy, *The Scotland Magazine*, entitled, *Visiting those old Haunts*, Issue 14, May 2004, p.22

[61] Burke's Peerage, 1912

[62] Boucher, Robert, *The Kingdom of Fife: Its Ballads and Legend*, J. Leng & Co, Dundee, 1899, pp.38-49.

[63] *Fife Herald and Journal*, 20th July 1904

[64] http://www.smithsgore.co.uk/

[65] Kirk, Russell, *St. Andrews*, B. T. Batsford Ltd, 1954, p.139

[66] Smellie, A, *Men Of The Covenant*, London. 1908, p.340

Part Two
The A-Z Collection
of Fife's Paranormal Haunts

[1] Linskill, W. T, *St. Andrews Citizen, St. Andrews Haunted Tower*, 1925 (refer to Falconer, Richard, *A St. Andrews Mystery*, Obsidian Publishing, Nottingham, 2014)

[2] Psychic News, 13th December 1966

[3] *Strange Tales of the Kingdom of Fife*, Langsyne Press. 1986

[4] Stevenson, Rev. William M.A., F.S.A.Scot, *Minister of Auchtertool, The Kirk and Parish of Auchtertool*. With a Memoir by the Rev. J. Campbell, B.D. Kirkcaldy: James Burt, 1908. pp.99-100

[5] Skinner, J. S, *Autobiography of a Metaphysician, being the life of Reverend James Skinner*, Sidgewick and Jackson, London, 1893, p.25

[6] Taylor, James, W, *Historical Antiquities of Fife, connected with some of its districts*, Johnstone, Hunter & Co, Edinburgh, 1875, p.155

[7] Ibid, p.157

[8] *The Weekly Scotsman*, Contributed by Harris, J. E. 26th December 1896

[9] Wilkie, James, *Bygone Fife, From Culross to St. Andrews*, Blackwood; Edinburgh, 1931. pp.312-313. Also Geddie, John, *The Fringes of Fife*, David Douglas; Edinburgh, 1894, pp.164-165

[10] Beveridge, Erskine, *The Churchyard Memorials of Crail*. T & A Constable, Edinburgh, 1885. p.61

[11] Geddie, J, *The Fringes of Fife*. David Douglas; Edinburgh, 1894, p.169

[12] Beveridge, David, *Culross and Tulliallan or Perthshire on Forth. It's History and Antiquities*, William Blackwood; Edinburgh, 1885, Vol. II, p.160

[13] Wodrow, Rev Robert, *Analecta. Or Materials for a History of Remarkable Providences Mostly relating to Scotch Ministers and Christians*, Edinburgh 1721-1722. Vol. III, p.519. Published 1842 by the Maitland Club

[14] Playfair, G. L, *The Haunted Pub Guide*, Harrap, London, 1985

[15] Green, Andrew, Website - Mystical World Wide Web – Article: *The unexplained explained.*

[16] Beveridge, David, *Between the Ochils and Forth*, William Blackwood & Sons, London and Edinburgh, 1888, pp.242-243.

References Continued

[17] Martin, Roddy, *Scotland Magazine, Visiting those old Haunts*, May 2004, Issue 14, p.22

[18] BBC's Doomsday project - 1986.

[19] Sibbald, Robert, *History of Fife and Kinross*, R. Tullis, London (1803), 1710, p.360

[20] Wilkie, James, *Bygone Fife, From Culross to St. Andrews*, Blackwood; Edinburgh, 1931. pp.325-326

[21] Ibid

[22] Ibid, p.55

[23] Buckner, J. C. R, *Rambles In and Around Aberdour and Burntisland*. 1881. p.53

[24] Jack, J. W, P. 106, taken from: *County Folklore*; Simpkin, John Ewart. Vol. VII, 1914, p.40

[25] Sibbald, Robert, *History of Fife and Kinross*, 1710, p.100, taken from the *New Statistical Accounts*, 1791-1799. Vol. IX, p.612

[26] *The Independent*, Thursday 4th August 1994.

[27] *The People's Journal*, 5th October, 1907

[28] Ibid

[29] *Fife Herald. & Journal*, 20th July, 1904

[30] *The Parochial Directory for Fife and Kinross*, 1861

[31] *New Statistical Account of Scotland*, 1791-1799, Vol.1 IX, p.971

[32] Mackay, J. G, *The County Histories of Scotland, Fife and Kinross*, W. Blackwood & Sons, 1896

[33] Skene, William F, *The Historians of Scotland*, Vol. XX. John of Fordun's *Chronicle of the Scottish Nation*. (Translated and edited) 1871, p.177

[34] From an online book called *The Kirkcaldy book*: http://www.kirkcaldybook.com/modules/sections/index.php?op=viewarticle&artid=7

[35] Farnie, Henry, *Handy book of the Fife Coast from Queensferry to Fife Ness*, 1860, (Sidgwick and Jackson Ltd, London, 1914)

[36] Rorie, Dr, *The Fifeshire Advertiser*, 1903.

[37] Gardiner: *Gardiner's Miscellany of Literature, Science, History and Antiquities. Original and Selected.* Cupar 1842, p.67, also Farnie, Henry: *Handy book of the Fife Coast from Queensferry to Fife Ness*, 1860, p.63

[38] *The Scotsman*, Wednesday 4th May 1994

[39] *Dundee Courier*. 2nd November 1972, *Edinburgh Evening News*, 2nd November 1972

References Continued

[40] *Journal of the Society for Psychical Research*, Vol. 40, pp.116-117

[41] *Chambers*: 1826 Edition, p.62

[42] Wilkie, James, *Bygone Fife, From Culross to St. Andrews*. Blackwood; Edinburgh, 1931, p.202

[43] Simpkins, John, Ewart, *Folklore of Fife*, Sidgwick; London, 1914, p.47

[44] JACK, J. W: *Glenfarg and District Past and Present*, 2nd Edition 1893. p.54

[45] Simpkins, John, Ewart, *Folklore of Fife*, Sidgwick; London, 1914, p.50

[46] Smellie, Alexander, *Men of the Covenant*, London, 1908. p.226

[47] Wodrow, Robert, *The History of the Sufferings of the Church of Scotland*. Vol. III. 1721-1722. Reproduced by Blackie Fullerton & co, Glasgow, 1829. p.45

[48] Ibid, p.463

[49] Ibid, p.462

[50] Ibid, p.219

[51] Smellie, A, *Men Of The Covenant*, London, 1908, p.340

[52] Robertson, James K, *About St. Andrews and About*, J & G Innes Ltd, Cupar, 1973, p.73

[53] *National Observer, St. Andrews Ghosts*: 7th Jan 1893.

[54] *The Topographical, Statistical and Historical Gazetteer of Scotland*. Vol.2, A Fullarton and Co, 1856, p.437

[55] Chambers: p. 261; Mackay, E. J. G: *A History of Fife and Kinross*. 1896. p.287

[56] Geddie, John, *The Fringes of Fife*. 1894, p.173

[57] *St. Andrews Citizen*, 16th December 1967

[58] *St. Andrews Citizen*, 8th June 1929

[59] http://www.spr.ac.uk/main/publication/pitmilly-house-poltergeist-manor

[60] http://www.deadlinenews.co.uk/2012/04/13/pittenweem-say-no-to-witch-memorial/

[61] Taylor, James, W, *Historical Antiquities of Fife, connected with some of its districts*. 1875, p.112

[62] Engraving of St. Monans Kirk from the Frontispiece of Sibbald, Robert, *History of Fife and Kinross*, 1710, R. Tullis, London (1803), Engraved for the R. Tullis edition

[63] *Fife News*, Titled *'Beware the Witching Hour'*, 30th October 2007

[64] *Parochial Directory for Fife and Kinross*, 1861

[65] *Fife Today*, 29th of April 2004

[66] Leighton, John, M, *History of the County of Fife*, Vol. 2, J. Swan, Glasgow, 1840, p.189

References Continued

[67] Small, Rev. Andrew, *Interesting Roman antiquities recently discovered in Fife,*
John Anderson and Co, Royal Exchange, Edinburgh, 1823, pp.286-287
[68] Ibid
[69] Wilkie, James, *Bygone Fife: From Culross to St. Andrews,* Blackwood;
Edinburgh, 1931. p.164
[70] *Dundee Courier and Advertiser: The Tay Bridge Disaster – 100th Anniversary
Four Page Special,* from an article written within by Mr William M. Dow.
December 1979
[71] Ibid
[72] Kirkcaldybook.com
[73] *Dundee Courier and Advertiser: The Tay Bridge Disaster – 100th Anniversary
Four Page Special,* from an article written within by Mr William M. Dow.
December 1979

Appendix
The Ghost Criteria

[1] Kirk, Russell: *St. Andrews.* 1954, p.88

Lightning Source UK Ltd.
Milton Keynes UK
UKHW010737031221
394904UK00001B/33